Beginning VFX with Autodesk Maya

Create Industry-Standard Visual Effects from Scratch

Abhishek Kumar

Apress®

Beginning VFX with Autodesk Maya: Create Industry-Standard Visual Effects from Scratch

Abhishek Kumar
Varanasi, Uttar Pradesh, India

ISBN-13 (pbk): 978-1-4842-7856-7   ISBN-13 (electronic): 978-1-4842-7857-4
https://doi.org/10.1007/978-1-4842-7857-4

Managing Director, Apress Media LLC: Welmoed Spahr
Acquisitions Editor: Spandana Chatterjee
Development Editor: Laura Berendson
Coordinating Editor: Divya Modi
Copyeditor: Kezia Endsley

Cover designed by eStudioCalamar

Cover image designed by Freepik (www.freepik.com)

Distributed to the book trade worldwide by Springer Science+Business Media New York, 1 New York Plaza, Suite 4600, New York, NY 10004-1562, USA. Phone 1-800-SPRINGER, fax (201) 348-4505, e-mail orders-ny@springer-sbm.com, or visit www.springeronline.com. Apress Media, LLC is a California LLC and the sole member (owner) is Springer Science + Business Media Finance Inc (SSBM Finance Inc). SSBM Finance Inc is a **Delaware** corporation.

For information on translations, please e-mail booktranslations@springernature.com; for reprint, paperback, or audio rights, please e-mail bookpermissions@springernature.com.

Apress titles may be purchased in bulk for academic, corporate, or promotional use. eBook versions and licenses are also available for most titles. For more information, reference our Print and eBook Bulk Sales web page at http://www.apress.com/bulk-sales.

Any source code or other supplementary material referenced by the author in this book is available to readers on GitHub via the book's product page, located at www.apress.com/978-1-4842-7856-7. For more detailed information, please visit http://www.apress.com/source-code.

Printed on acid-free paper

To Mom, Usha Sinha and Dad, Prof. B. K. Prasad and my beloved wife, Alka, for 12 fantastic years of marriage and many more to come. To my daughter, Rishika Ryan, and my son, Shivay Singh Ryan. I love you all.

Table of Contents

About the Author

Dr. Abhishek Kumar is an Apple Certified Associate, an Adobe Education Trainer, and is certified by Autodesk. He has a PhD in computer applications and a master's degree in animation and computer science. He finished his post-doctoral fellowship at Imam Mohammad Ibn Saud Islamic University, Saudi Arabia.

He is actively involved in course development in animation and design engineering at various institutions and universities. He has published a number of research papers and covered a wide range of topics in various digital scientific areas (including image analysis, visual identity, graphics, digital photography, motion graphics, 3D animation, visual effects, editing, and composition). He holds ten patents in the fields of AI, design, and IoT.

Dr. Kumar has completed professional studies related to animation, computer graphics, VR, stereoscopy, filmmaking, visual effects, and photography from Norwich University of Arts, University of Edinburg, and Wizcraft MIME & FXPHD, Australia. He is passionate about media and the entertainment industry and has directed two short animated films. Dr. Kumar has trained more than 1,00,000 students across the globe from 153 countries (including from India, Germany, United States, Spain, and Australia). His alumni have worked on national and international movies.

Dr. Kumar has delivered more than 100 workshops and seminars as a subject matter expert/resource person at Delhi University, GGU Central University, Savitribai Phule University, Anna University, Rajiv Gandhi Central University, Allahabad University, Banaras Hindu University, MANNU Hyderabad, Gujrat Technological University, TMU, GIET University, NITs, IITs, and several international institutes/universities. His goal is to bring awareness to the future of e-learning, MOOCs, virtual reality, animation design, and VFX as a career opportunity and as an immersive technology for educators.

About the Technical Reviewer

 **Yupeng Zhang** is a senior software developer for Autodesk Maya Animation, which developed the Cached Playback workflow for the Nucleus and Bullet FX system. Before working at Autodesk, he received his master's degree in computer graphics from the University of Toronto, building multiple modeling and animation tools for VR. Besides coding, he may have a video game addiction!

Acknowledgments

It gives me immense pleasure to express my deep gratitude to my mentors, Prof. Saket Kushwaha and Prof. Alok Kumar Rai, and my PhD supervisor, Dr. Achintya Singhal, Associate Professor, Banaras Hindu University.

Prof. Kushwaha and Prof. A. K. Rai are my inspiration for this endeavor; without their encouragement, support, and guidance, this book would not have been possible.

I would also like to thank Yupeng Zhang (TR), Spandana Chatterjee (AE), Divya Modi (CE), and Laura Berendson (DE) for the initiation to publish this book. Their comments and suggestions resulted in numerous refinements and corrections that improved its quality.

A special thanks to Mrs. Rini Dey, PhD research scholar at JAIN; Dr. Vijayakumar Varadarajan, Professor at The University of New South Wales, Australia; and Thinagaran Perumal, Associate Professor at Universiti Putra Malaysia, Malaysia for providing unconditional support.

CHAPTER 1

Introduction to Visual Effects (VFX)

Visual effects play a vital role in every aspect of the entertainment industry. They have extended their purview into e-learning and are an emerging technology in the field of digital education. Creative visual effects design saves designers, manufacturers, and customers time, money, and effort. This book dives into the nuances of visual effects design, from planning to execution. Visual effects give viewers an immersive experience by creating realistic CGI (Computer-Generated Imagery) effects.

This chapter discusses the significance of visual effects, as well as the many sectors in which visual effects, also called VFX, operate. The chapter covers the present scope of visual effects and its growing popularity in visual media.

The Importance of Visual Effects

Visual storytelling is no longer an alien concept. What makes the visual medium so amazing to watch are the mind-boggling computer-generated special effects, as shown in Figure 1-1. Films, television series, games, and now even the educational tech industry is overflowing with bewildering visual effects. Moreover, with the emergence of OTT (over the top) platforms, there has been increasing demand for content, which has led to a demand for all kinds of visual effects. As Jim Morris, VES general manager and president of Pixar Animation Studios, stated, "We are in the golden age of visual effects and we should take time to recognize that and celebrate it."

© Abhishek Kumar 2022
A. Kumar, *Beginning VFX with Autodesk Maya*, https://doi.org/10.1007/978-1-4842-7857-4_1

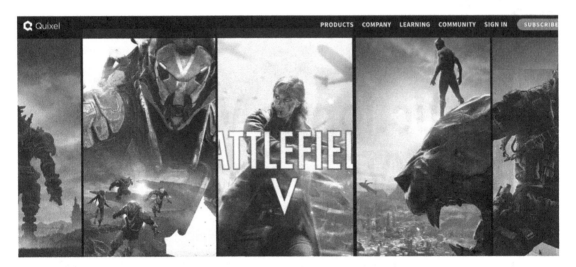

Figure 1-1. *Visual effects in games (Source: https://quixel.com/)*

This has resulted in an enormous demand for well-trained animation and visual effects artists. From educational content to games to virtual reality (VR) to artificial intelligence to advertisements, all areas of digital content use or intend to use VFX. While it was once thought that remote working would never work in this industry, the COVID-19 pandemic forced companies to engage in remote working, virtual productions, and unexpected outputs in certain areas. In fact, the lockdown prompted collaboration and knowledge-sharing among rival companies, working together to solve a problem. As a result, companies broke down the processes and pipelines in a way that drove the pace of production. This showed business leaders that talented creative teams will continue to be vital players in the future of VFX.

The constant advancement of new technology and new techniques has broadened the scope of the visual effects industry, making it critical to keep the creative team up to date on what's trending, as shown in Figure 1-2. As a result, the domains of animation, VFX, and gaming have become the fastest growing segments of the global media and entertainment (M&E) industry.

Figure 1-2. *VFX before and after*

Almost every sector of the global M&E market is emphasizing content with CGI integration.

To meet this rising demand, businesses are employing a variety of strategies to make production more globally competitive. Subsidiaries, tax breaks, financial assistance, regional low labor costs, the establishment of facilities in low-cost countries, and so on, are some of the paths taken by businesses to produce outputs from the global market of visual artist creatives.

Global audiences are demonstrating an increasing appetite for high-definition visual experiences, necessitating the need to produce content. The rise of cloud computing has greatly aided in meeting this demand. Cloud computing is being used in character rendering and modeling processes for animation films, which is proving to be more effective and efficient because it saves time and money over traditional techniques.

However, regardless of the technology used and of the duration or quantity of the finished output, animation and VFX are both time-consuming professions that necessitate extensive hours of planning, pre-production, and post-production work. As a result, experienced and skilled creative minds are required. A VFX artist's or animator's role can be varied and extensive. They are virtually responsible for everything from conception to planning, execution, and delivery of the final product because they are domain experts. Furthermore, with the growing popularity of immersive technology, computer-generated imagery is becoming increasingly important. There is no denying that animation and VFX have now become a part of our daily lives. Especially with COVID-19, immersive digital content has infiltrated every aspect of human life.

The importance and necessity of visual effects is largely determined by the content of the visual medium. The complexity, treatment, and style of the special effects that are used will have a different impact depending on the message they convey to the target audience. Visual effects used in feature films, for example, will differ from those used in educational video content. The budget for these will vary greatly as well. The primary purpose of using special effects in content is to complement the visual medium with the primary goal of engaging the audience. As a result, the extent to which it should be used must be justified in terms of the content and purpose it is intended to serve. A film with no special effects may become boring, whereas too many special effects used to explain an educational concept may cause students to become disoriented. It goes without saying that the salt must be measured.

The ever-changing face of visual effects in terms of quality and quantity can be seen in Spielberg's 1989 blockbuster *Indiana Jones and the Last Crusade,* which involved 80 VFX shots, to the 1997 blockbuster *Titanic*, which involved 500 visual effects shots, to the 2009 blockbuster *Avatar*, which involved over 3,000 VFX shots. Visual effects are more than just a matter of pushing buttons; they are the result of talented minds equipped with exponentially increasing computing power that master the artistry. Consider how *Gravity* could have been made without the use of special effects. Similarly, films like *Life of Pi* would not have been possible without the magic of visual effects.

To be a successful visual effects artist, you must first understand the story in terms of mood, tone, style, and context in order to make it visually more powerful and compelling. Every project is constrained by time and money. Examining every detail and planning to precision is critical to completing the project on time and within budget. The entire team of visual effects artists involved in the project must agree on what needs to be done, why, when, and how. This communication alone has the potential to make or break the VFX workflow. As a result, the VFX supervisor must be present on the set and fully aware of what is going on and how things need to be worked out during the post-production stage. It is critical to remember at this point that visual effects are not done alone, so clarity in visualization is critical for the team to deliver the final visual as perceived by the director. Furthermore, you must consider the time and money involved in the process. Visual effects take time and money to create. Without proper planning, the entire show could fall apart.

The Need to Create Visual Magic

Visual effects, as we see them today, have become as essential to us as salt is to our food. Who could imagine *Dr. Strange* without his abilities or *Avengers* without its vengeful superpowers? Wouldn't these characters appear dull and glamourless if they lacked their powers? And would these comic book characters ever come to life as a result of this? Without the use of visual effects, stories once imprinted on the pages of books could not leave such vivid impressions on our minds.

We have entered an era in which we can visualize anything and everything using a medium known as CGI. Creativity and imagination, combined with computing technology, have given the visual medium wings. Visualization has become more convenient and cost effective thanks to CGI. Directors can see their stories before they are shot. This saves a significant amount of time and money during the final shoot and also allows the entire team of artists to visualize with the director. 3D *previz* (pre-visualization) is now a proven reality, whether for a small project or a feature film. Visualizing the project before investing in the actual production allows the director to understand and adjust to the possibilities within the constraints of time and budget.

Aside from the entertainment industry, visual effects have made inroads into the education sector, with the emergence of the ED tech industry flourishing, particularly in the midst of the COVID-19 pandemic. The introduction of CGI-integrated visual effects into the education sector has made learning more convenient, simple, and enjoyable. The visual medium has helped to simplify complex concepts, theories, and formulas. Who would consider dissecting a human body in the absence of the physical body? However, with the advent of AR and VR, medical science students can now dissect a human body without having to use their hands. With the help of virtual reality, a mother was able to communicate with her deceased daughter. For the first time, virtual reality was used for emotional comfort in a South Korean documentary that went viral on YouTube on February 14th, 2020. The project used real-time rendering to allow interactions between a mother and a daughter.

Visual effects can transform visually unappealing content into visually appealing content. Visuals have a lasting impact on the mind, as seen and explained by psychologists around the world in various learning theories. One behavioral study found that visual aids boost learning by 400%. The human brain processes visuals 60,000 times faster than text. The average human brain only retains about one-fifth of what it hears. Thus, it has been demonstrated that visual effects not only add a magical wow factor to entertainment but they also improve retention.

What's in this Book?

This book aims to introduce you to the methods and techniques required for 3D FX generation from scratch. This includes the fundamentals of visual effects production, tools and techniques for creating believable rigid body collisions in CG space, and knowledge to generate effects using particles like dust, fire, water spray, and many more. This book also formulates strategies for creating vortexes, rain, and other soft body simulations. It also demonstrates nature simulations for CGI production. There is a capstone project that enables you to make your own visual effects scene in a practical way.

After going through this book, you will be able to start building your computer-generated visual effects from your imagination to production. 3D visual effects, from idea to production, are covered in the following 13 chapters in this book.

Chapter 1: Introduction to Visual Effects

This current chapter covers a brief description of the visual effects industry. It includes the following subtopics:

- The importance of visual effects

- The need to create visual magic

Chapter 2: History of Visual Effect

In this chapter, you learn how visual effects came to be used in games with the rise of the digital era. It covers how the enthralling world of computer-generated imagery triggered the visual effects industry. This chapter covers the following eras:

- The early years (1829–1959)

- The optical years (1960–1976)

- The glorious years (1977-1982)

- The digital realm (1983-1988)

- The fall of optical (1989-1993)

- Going mainstream (1994-1996)

- Every man and his dog (1997-1999)

- Coming of age (2000-2003)

- No going back (2004-2009)

- Beyond the impossible (2010-2013)

- Oscar for best VFX movies (2014-2020)

- VFX in games

Chapter 3: Industrial Application for VFX

This chapter covers the software used for visual effects design. It covers the various applications used in the rendition of visual effects, industry-acclaimed software, and practices. You learn how to plan a visual effects shot and the software applications that are used as standard industry practice. This chapter covers the following subtopics:

- Planning for visual effects shots

- Industry practices for VFX software

- Tools and techniques used onscreen

- Visual effects plugins

Chapter 4: Introduction to FX in Maya

You learn about the FX tools in Autodesk Maya and how the Maya FX system contributes to creating visual effects for CGI. This chapter covers the following subtopics:

- Understanding Maya's user interface (UI)

- Viewing the Maya viewport configuration

- Getting Started with visual effects simulation with Maya

- Using Maya Nucleus

Chapter 5: Working with nParticle FX

In this chapter, you will work with particle systems and simulate motion graphics and other CGI productions. You learn about soft body, nParticle systems and their collision systems. This chapter covers the following subtopics:

- Having fun with emitter
- Using the nParticles tool and Instancer

Chapter 6: Creating Effects with Particle Emissions and Fields/Solvers

In this chapter, you start creating galaxy effects using nParticle. The chapter discusses the real-life physics implementations in Maya in-depth using Air, Drag, Gravity, Newton, and many more. This chapter covers the following subtopics:

- Running real-life FX simulations with solvers and fields
- Creating galaxy and particle based effects

Chapter 7: Maya's Rigid and Soft Body Systems

This chapter unveils the power of realistic animation using Maya's rigid body and soft body dynamics. You will explore the rigid body dynamics mode with a domino example. This chapter covers the following subtopics:

- Understanding rigid bodies
- Running the dominos rigid body simulation using Bullet Solver
- Constraints on the Bullet rigid body
- FX simulation with soft bodies

Chapter 8: Working with Maya Fluids

This chapter explores simulation for liquids and gaseous media. At the end of the chapter, you will produce a real-world fire simulation effect. This chapter covers the following subtopics:

- Understanding the concept of fluids

- Creating fluid FX

- Working with containers in Maya

- Working with emitters in Maya

Chapter 9: Magical FX Using Maya

In this chapter, you explore the predefined effects available in Maya, including their purposes and effective usage. You also focus on using attribute editors. This chapter covers the following subtopics:

- Creating fire, fireworks, lightening, shatter, and smoke effects

- Getting the Effect Asset library

- Colliding with effects

Chapter 10: Playing with Maya nCloth

This chapter explains various methods for simulating cloth. You will go through all the necessary steps using the nCloth tool to create realistic rigid body and soft body animations. At the end of the chapter, you learn how to simulate a realistic flag using nCloth. This chapter covers the following subtopics:

- Using nCloth

- Working with a passive collider

- Playing with nCloth attributes

- Using nConstraints for effective and efficient simulations

Chapter 11: Maya Hair FX Simulation

In this chapter you dive into the functions of hair and fur simulation in Maya and learn how to create realistic hair . This chapter covers the manual techniques for creating hair and fur and discusses the issues and challenges of simulating hair. This chapter covers the following subtopics:

- Creating hair

- Grooming hair

- Simulating long hair

- Using the Maya Hair library

Chapter 12: Technical Fluid Simulation with Bifrost

In this chapter you learn about the recently introduced Bifrost system for Maya, which helps animators create realistic water simulations. You learn how to simulate a large volume of water efficiently. You will use effective simulation techniques to generate a complete ocean simulation shot in Maya. This chapter covers the following subtopics:

- Understanding the importance of Bifrost fluids

- Computing and executing a water simulation shot

- Working with Bifrost library

Chapter 13: Procedural Animation FX and Live Action Integration

In this chapter, you learn how to work on a complete scene in Maya using the FX system that you learned about in previous chapters. You will create a seamless integration of live action footage within a 3D virtual world. This chapter covers the following subtopics:

- Integrating 2D and 3D worlds

- Creating a 3D visual effects with MASH

In Chapter 2, you learn about the evolution of science in visual design, the state of art technology in the digital era, and the history of visual effects.

CHAPTER 2

History of Visual Effects

This chapter describes how visual effects have evolved over time and have influenced computer graphics in the media and entertainment industries.

VFX is a term for visual effects that's used in film and video games, as well as in higher education, scientific research and study, and other forms of entertainment. Any onscreen fantasy that does not exist in the real world is referred to as a visual effect. VFX can be used by filmmakers to combine live action video with other live action material and to create realistic images by incorporating CGI elements. The modern era of the M&E (media and entertainment) sector would be unimaginable without the use of special effects. Cutting-edge visual effects technology is the forerunner of future reality. Understanding its history can assist you in understanding how things worked in the past and how they work now. Examining historical visual effects techniques and comparing them to current trends provides a more in-depth understanding of the medium. Figure 2-1 shows a timeline of the history of visual effects.

© Abhishek Kumar 2022
A. Kumar, *Beginning VFX with Autodesk Maya*, https://doi.org/10.1007/978-1-4842-7857-4_2

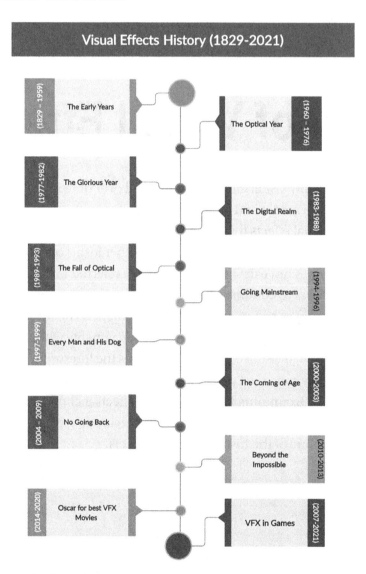

Figure 2-1. *Visual effects history*

Before delving into the history of visual effects, the concept of *persistence of vision* must be addressed. What exactly does vision persistence mean? It is the phenomenon that occurs when your eyes and brain see two or more images at the same time, one after the other. Your eyes can blend these images together so that the brain perceives them as smooth movement. When you watch a movie, an iPhone video, or a flipbook, your eyes and brain are doing exactly that. They combine individual images to create the illusion of real movement. Remember that this works best when each image is similar to the one before it.

Now that you are familiar with the concept of persistence of vision, you can look visual effects throughout history.

The Early Years (1829–1959)

One of the earliest examples of animation can be traced back to a Belgian named Joseph Plateau and his *phenakistiscope*, which was an animated device that used the principle of persistence of vision to create the illusion of movement. This was a device with an outside disc with pictures painted on it, where the slits were placed. The disc spun to create an illusion of movement that appeared through the series of painted pictures. This structure was constructed in 1829. In the phenakistoscope, a spinning disc attached vertically to a handle was used. In practice, this device could be used by only one person at a time. It was the very first optical toy.

In 1833, William George Horner invented the *zoetrope*. The concept of the zoetrope, on the other hand, can be traced back 200 years to Ting Huan's invention in China in 180 AD. A zoetrope is a cylinder with vertical cuts on its sides. A band with images from a series of sequenced photographs adorns the cylinder's inner surface. As the cylinder spins, the user looks through the cuts. Scanning the slits prevents the images from simply blurring together, creating the illusion of motion. The zoetrope works on the same principle as its forerunner, the phenakistiscope, but it was more portable and allowed multiple people to watch the animation at the same time.

The *kineograph*, which translates to "moving picture," was patented by John Barnes Linnet. Every image in a "flipbook" is fixed. Each image on each page is motionless on paper—it does not move at all. It could be a drawing of a house, a photograph of a butterfly, or a picture of a dinosaur. When you quickly flip through the pages, however, the images appear to move. Every movie in a theatre, every TV show you watch, every YouTube video, every iPhone video, every video game, and even every IMAX movie works on the same fundamental principle as a flipbook. The illusion of moving images is created by rapidly displaying still images. His kineograph animation technique was the first to use a linear sequence of images, similar to a booklet, rather than circular drums.

The oldest surviving film is Louis Le Prince's 1888 film titled *Roundhay Garden Scene.* It was shot at 12 frames per second in Leeds, UK. William Dickson's film, *Dickson's Greetings*, was one of the first public showings of motion pictures in the United States, in

1891. In 1892, George Eastman invented motion picture film and founded the Eastman Kodak company. The same year saw the release of the Lumiere Brothers' first film, titled *La Sortie des usines Lumière à Lyon,* which was most likely the first real motion picture ever made. Alfred Clark directed the first special shot in film history, *The Execution of Mary, Queen of Scots,* that same year. When watching this film, it is clear that the cut edit technique was employed. This type of technique, which involved cutting from one thing to another to create an illusion, was popular at the time.

Several pioneers of moving images made incredible discoveries and inventions between 1875 and 1900. Eadweard Muybridge is one of the most well-known figures in the history of photography. He had been a very successful landscape photographer for many years before inventing a method of rigging many cameras so that they would take similar photos in rapid succession in the early 1870s. Moving images were created when the photos were arranged in such a way that they could be viewed quickly one after the other. Animators still use his photographs of the Animal in Motion and Human Figure in Motion as references today. Muybridge continued to develop better cameras and eventually collaborated with Thomas Edison to create the first movie camera and the kinetoscope, an early viewing device. At the same time, the Lumière brothers in France were inventing movie cameras and projectors, and it was they who first showed a movie to a public audience.

Remember that in the early days of moving images, any movie was incredible to see, whether it was just 15 seconds of a man walking down the street or a train pulling into a station. When an ordinary event was shown as the illusion of a movie, it became extraordinary. However, the audience quickly became enthralled and demanded more. At this point, a nod should be given to George Melies, a pioneer in the use of special effects.

In December 1861, Marie-Geroges-Jean Melies, a French illusionist and film director, was born in Paris. He invented the *stop trick* effect, which he accidentally discovered in 1896. The stop trick technique involved stopping the camera, doing something, and then continuing, similar to what we saw in *The Execution of Mary, Queen of Scots*. He was among the first to use multiple exposure, time-lapse photography, dissolves, and color hand-painting in his films. Many of the techniques we use today were discovered by him at the time. Melies' career began primarily as a stage performer. He bought the Theatre Robert-Houdin and spent the next nine years creating new stage illusions. Later, he worked as a director, producer, writer, set designer, costume designer, and illusionist behind the scenes. Melies saw the Lumiere brothers' film for the first time in public at the Grand Cafe Paris in 1895. Melies traveled to London to purchase films and an Animatograph Film projector, which he used in his own theatre. Between 1896 and 1913, Melies directed 531 films. The subjects of the films were frequently similar to those of his magic theatre shows. Melies founded the Star film studio in 1896. The same year, Melies began work on a film studio just outside of Paris. To allow sunlight in for film exposure, the main stage structure was entirely made of glass. *A Trip to the Moon,* Melies' most famous film, was released in May 1902.

Jules Verne's *From the Earth to the Moon* and H.G. Wells' *The First Men in the Moon* inspired the story. Melies' longest film was 14 minutes long and cost 10,000 francs. Melies went on to make another major film, *The Impossible Voyage*, in 1904, and two years later, in 1906, he made two more, *The Merry Deeds of Satan* and *The Witch*. Melies made *Humanity Through the Ages,* one of his most ambitious films, in 1908, based on the history of humans from Cain and Abel to the 1907 Hague Peace Conference, but the film was a failure. Melies' career was ruined and he went bankrupt after a string of unsuccessful films between 1910 and 1913.

During WWI, the French army turned Melies' studio into a hospital for wounded soldiers, melting over 400 films for their celluloid and silver content. Melies' film raw materials were used by the army to make boot heels for soldiers' shoes. His theatre was demolished in 1923, and his studio was burned down, resulting in the destruction of many of his films. Melies passed away from cancer in 1938. Melies was later featured in both the book *The Invention of Hugo Cabret* and the film adaptation *Hugo,* in which he was played by Ben Kinsley.

The film *The Great Train Robbery,* directed by Edwin S. Porter for the Edison Manufacturing Company in 1903, rose to prominence and is a must-see for anyone interested in visual effects. For the bank robbery scene, Porter used the same matte techniques as Melies in *The Man with the Rubber Head.* The film's commercial success was unprecedented, thanks in part to its popular and approachable subject matter, as well as its dynamic action and violence.

In 1908, George Albert Smith invented *Kinemacolor*. It was the first successful color film process, and it consisted essentially of two additive color processes: photographing and projecting a black-and-white film behind alternating red and green filters.

Moving on to 1914, the year that saw the release of *Gertie*, which, while not the first animated film, was certainly the first to feature a personality-driven character, created by Winsor McCay.

The first stereo movie ever shown to a paying film audience was shown in 1922. The film's title was *The Power of Love*. As a result, stereo is not a new technology. It has been in existence since 1922. Unfortunately, the film was not a success in 3D, and it was only shown twice. Later, it was released in 2D as *Forbidden Lover* (1923-1924).

In 1923, Walt Disney established The Walt Disney Animation Studio. Cecil B. DeMille directed the film *The Ten Commandments* the same year, which was later remade in 1956. To create the visual effect of keeping the sea parted, a slab of jelly was used. Unlike the effect simulation done today with Houdini, this type of effect was absolutely amazing at the time because no one had ever seen anything like it.

Another film, titled *Dorothy Vernon of Haddon Hall,* and directed by Marshall Neilan, was released a year later, in 1924. For this film, only the lower section of the castle was built in full size; the upper section was a miniature that was positioned closer to the camera and aligned with the main set. As a result, it appears to be a full fort when filmed. This is referred to as *forced perspective*, and is a photography technique that is widely used today.

Willis O'Brien's groundbreaking stop motion visual effects work in Harry O. Hoyt's 1925 film *The Lost World*. To create the movement, each model with an armature inside would have been painstakingly moved frame by frame.

In 1927, motion picture film was standardized to 24 frames per second. In the same year, Fritz Lang's groundbreaking film *Metropolis*, with visual effects by Eugen Schufftan, was released. This film used special effects such as miniatures, unique camera moves, and, most notably, the *schufftan process,* which is a process in which you have a miniature and a mirror that reflects the miniature, and behind the mirror, which had frosty glass, you have an object, so that as you film through the mirror, you see the reflection and then the object. This effect was frequently used in *Metropolis*.

Steamboat Willie, released in 1928, was one of Walt Disney's major productions at the time. Mikey, a well-known character from the *Steamboat Willie* film, was introduced to the audience for the first time. The 1.33:1 film ratio, also known as 35mm, was introduced in 1929 by the Academy of Motion Picture Arts and Sciences. Four years later, Merian Cooper and Ernest Schoedsack introduced the film ratio to the film *King Kong*. It was created using the stop motion special effect and the miniature rear projection base technique. Willis O'Brien was also in charge of the visual effects in the film.

In 1933, James Whale directed *The Invisible Man*. In this film, another novel visual effects technique, double exposure, and it created the illusion of invisibility in this film.

In 1935, *Audioscopiks* was nominated for an Academy Award for fast stereo film. It was MGM's first 3D production. The 3D effect was created using a red and green anaglyph process.

In 1937, Disney's technical department invented the first multiple camera setup. The short film *The Old Mill* was shot quickly with multiple cameras. After experimenting with various camera setup techniques in *The Old Mill,* Walt Disney went on to create the first animated full-length film, *Snow White and the Seven Dwarfs,* in 1937.

In 1939, Victor Fleming directed *Gone with the Wind.* The grand house in the middle of the story was created using a large scale matte painting. The same year, Clarence Brown directed *The Rains Came,* which became the first film to win an Academy Award for best special effects.

In 1940, Ludwig Berger, Michale Powell, and Tim Whelan directed *The Thief of Bagdad.* This film pioneered the use of blue screen and the traveling matte technique. This film was nominated for an Academy Award for Best Picture.

In 1941, Orson Welles directed *Citizen Kane.* It was a hybrid film that employed a variety of techniques such as matte painting, stop motion animation, optical composition, and so on. Ernest B. Schoedsack directed the *Mighty Joe Young* films in 1949. Willis O'Brien and Ray Harryhaussen created it with live action, stop motion, and rear projection.

In 1950, Irving Pichel directed the film *Destination Moon.* Rudolph Mate also directed *When Worlds Collide* in 1951. Both films are extremely detailed and visually appealing. Two years later, in 1953, Byron Laskin directed *War of the Worlds.* It was entirely a VFX-driven film. 144 separate matte paintings were used to create the effects of the Martian war machines.

Richard Fleischer directed *20,000 Leagues Under the Sea* in 1954. It was the most expensive film production at the time. Ishiro Honda directed the 1954 film *Godzilla.* It was a Japanese production. Also this year, another technological breakthrough contributed significantly to the growth of the film industry—Alex Poniatoff's introduction of the two-inch VR100 video tape recorder.

Cecil B. DeMille's remake of *The Ten Commandments* is also notable in the history of visual effects. To achieve the miniature effect, a large scale of traveling matte painting, pyrotechnics, rear projection technique, and green screen were used.

Fred M. Wilcox directed *Forbidden Planet* in 1956. Veteran animator Joshua Meador had a significant role in this film. The film was filled with hand-drawn animated sequences, such as the attack of the Id Monster.

The Optical Years (1960–1976)

At MIT, Ivan Sutherland invented the *sketchpad* in 1960. The sketchpad was widely regarded as the forefather of modern CAD, as well as a significant step forward in the evolution of computer graphics. In the same year, MIT released *Spacewar*, Steve Russell's first computer game. The first version of the *Spacewar* game required 200 man hours to develop. It was built on a DEC PDP-1 minicomputer.

Fluid Dynamics was quickly invented in 1963, making it a watershed moment in visual effects history. The Los Alamos National Laboratory was responsible for its development. Fluid Dynamics has recently become popular for creating visual effects. The first computer-generated film was created that same year. It was invented at IBM's Bell Labs by Edward E. Zajac. It was just a cube moving around a space at random.

Ray Harryhausen created *Jason and the Argonauts* in 1963. It was, in essence, a stop-motion animation film. This was a detailed rendition of a live action/stop motion hybrid.

Walt Disney produced *Mary Poppins* in 1964. It was directed by Robert Stevenson. This film was made with a mix of live action photography and 2D animation techniques.

In 1966, Richard Fleischer directed the film *The Fantastic Voyage*. Large models were used to create body parts in this highly detailed VFX film. Ray Harryhausen created the creature stop motion effect the same year that Don Chaffey directed *One Million Years B.C.*

In 1968, Aristid Lindenmayer invented the L-System. The L-System is a method of creating an organic structure that is now easily created in Houdini, Maya, or any other 3D software. *2001: A Space Odyssey* was directed by Stanley Kubrick. It was almost certainly the first front projection with retroreflective matting film.

Thompson and Ritchie invented the UNIX computer in 1969. In 1970, Ivan Sutherland of the University of Utah created the first 3D digesting device. This device is still used to digest objects today.

In the same year, the IMAX film format was introduced. Robert Wise directed *The Andromeda Strain* in 1971, which was another landmark year in the history of visual effects. Douglas Trumbull created the first computer-generated science fiction film. In 1971, Henri Gouraud created Gouraud shading at the University of Utah. This Gouraud shading technique was developed primarily to achieve continuous lighting on triangular surfaces.

In the same year, the first floppy disc became commercially available. When IBM announced Type 1 Diskette, its first media, in 1970, the term "floppy disc" first appeared in print.

Ed Catmull created the first 3D computer animated hand in 1972. Stan Winston Studios was founded in 1972 by Stan Winston. It was primarily a visual effects company. The majority of the well-known visual effect films were created by this studio. Stan Winston died in 2008, and the Stan Winston studio was renamed Legacy Effect in his honor.

In 1973, Michael Crichton directed *Westworld*. This was the first feature film to use 2D computer graphics and digital image processing. Ed CatMulla of the University of Utah invented the textured mapping technique in 1974, along with the Z-Buffer. Bui Tuong created Phong at the University of Utah the same year. Richard Heffron's 1974 film *Future World* was directed by him. It was the first film to use 3D computer graphics and digital image processing. Superpaint was founded by Alvy Ray Smith and Richard Shoup. It was the first paint program, similar to Photoshop today.

In 1975, Benoit Mandelbrot began his research into Fractal geometry. The term "fractal" comes from the Latin word *fractus*, which means "broken or shattered glass." In 1976, Ed Catmull developed the first animated tween software at the University of Utah. Microsoft was founded in 1976 by Bill Gates, and the first Apple computer was released in 1976 by Steve Jobs and Steve Wozniak.

The Glorious Years (1977–1982)

R/Greenberg Associates and Industrial Light and Magic were both founded in 1977. These are excellent companies for producing visual effects. John Dykstra invented the first motion control device, the Dykstraflex, the same year. In 1977, Nelson Max created the first scientific visualization. The first computer-generated title sequence was created for the film *Superman* in the same year, followed by *Star Wars*. The same year, the film *Close Encounters of the Third Kind* featured a fiber-glass model of the main ship. The Blinn-phong Shader was created by James Blinn the same year. James Blinn also invented bump mapping.

Rotoscoping was used extensively in the 1978 animated film *The Lord of the Rings*. This film was made entirely with live action footage and 2D animation. This year also saw the release of James Blinn's *The Mechanical Universe*. It was a 52-part series that introduced concepts from university-level physics such as quantum mechanics. In 1978, Turner Whitted of Bell Labs created *The Compleat Angler*, a famous raytracing scene.

In 1978, George Lucas also hired Ed Catmull to lead Lucasfilm's computer division. Many technical aspects of filmmaking were influenced by this division, including digital nonlinear film editing systems, digital sound editing systems, digital film printers, and future computer graphic exploration.

Dream Quest Images was founded in 1979 by Hoyt Yeatman and Scott Squires, along with Robert Abel and Associates and Jim Henson's Creature Shop. Both had significant contributions to the history of visual effects.

In addition, the 1979 invention of the Reyes render engine aided greatly in hastening its growth. Robert Cook and Loren Carpenter were working on Reyes' software at Lucasfilm's computer graphics research group. Reyes is an acronym for the phrase "Renders Everything You've Ever Seen." It was quickly used in *Star Trek 2: The Wrath of Khan*'s genesis effect sequence. For NASA, Jim Blinn created the well-known Voyager animation fly. It was a significant achievement for computer graphics. Paint3, created by Alvy Ray Smith, was the first 24-bit (RGB) paint system. Alvy Ray Smith, Ed Emshwiller, Lance William, and Garland Stern created the Sunstone animation. Ridley Scott redirected *Alien* in 1979. The wireframe rendering process was extensively used in this film to depict Nostromo's navigation charts. That year, this film won the Academy Award for Best Picture.

In 1980, Pacific Data Image and the Kleiser-Walczak Construction Company were both founded with the goal of developing visual effects. That same year, Michael Crichton directed *Looker*. It was a film in which a computer-generated human was featured. *Pac-Man* debuted in 1980 as well. Namco was the one who came up with the idea. It was a simple and enjoyable computer game. It had a very simple graphical user interface.

In 1981, Adam Powers created the famous animation *The Juggler*. James Blinn, Frank Crow, Craig Reynolds, and Larry Malone created the software. The same year, Nelson Max created the first CG clouds and water for the film *Carla's Island*. That same year, ILM used optical and particle effects in *Raiders of the Lost Ark*. In his 1981 film *Dragonslayer*, Phil Tippett also used Go-Motion to achieve the desired effect. Go-Motion was a stop motion variation.

In 1982, Adobe and Autodesk were founded. Adobe and Autodesk's design and visual effects software is now the industry standard. That same year, Rebecca Allen of the New York Institute of Technology's computer graphics lab invented the first motion capture system device. In 1982, the Mandrill was used for texture mapping or background image processing for the first time. Texture mapping is the process of warping the top surface of a 3D model. At CGRG, Dave Zeltzer developed a skeleton animation system the same year. In 1982, Douglas Trumbull created the *Blade Runner* effects, which included a combination of optical and miniature effects. The Genesis effect sequence in *Star Trek 2: The Wrath of Khan* was created using a particle system the same year.

The Digital Realm (1983–1988)

In 1983, Walt Disney collaborated with Magi Liaison to create *Where the Wild Things Are*. This project featured 2D hand-drawn animation over a 3D CGI background. Disney worked on the animation for this project, while Magi worked on the CGI background. In 1983, NAB introduced the Bosch FGS computer graphic system. It was the first 3D animation system that was completely automated. Simutrek Inc. also founded Cube Quest that year. It was a very early version of a computer game. Richard Marquand also directed *Star Wars Episode 4: Return of the Jedi* that year. For that film, the Lucasfilm Computer Graphics Group created an indoor moon sequence. Bill Reeves and Tom Duff created it with vector graphics.

Another large company, Wavefront, was founded in 1984, and their first product was PreView. That year, Greg Turk and Marc Levoy also built The Stanford Bunny. It was created by scanning a CGI model of a real bunny. Tippett studio, Boss Film studios, and the BUF animation studio and visual effects were all founded in 1984 and are all very good at visual effects work. That same year, Apple released the first Macintosh computer. It was the very first computer to have a graphical user interface. The Cornell illumination box was also invented by Cohen the same year. It restricts the RGB plot to 49 patches per side, each with a consistent coloration. Don Greenberg created Radiosity, a new global illumination technique that he presented at Cornell University's Siggraph in 1984. Alvy Ray Smith created *The Adventure of Andre and Wally B* in 1984, and it was most likely one of the first fully 3D animated films. Furthermore, Robert Abel and colleagues created the first computer-generated 30 second commercial, *Brilliance*, in 1984.

Deluxe paint was a digital drawing software created by Dan Silva in 1985 for the electronic arts. In 1985, Max Headroom was the first computer-enhanced live action figure. In addition, in 1985, Barry Levinson directed *Young Sherlock Holmes*. It was the first film to feature a computer-generated character mixed in with a live-action plate. Ted Berman and Richard Rich directed *The Black Cauldron* in 1985. It was the first full-length 3D computer-animated film.

Softimage was founded in 1986, and its first product was a creative environment application. It was a program for creating 3D assets. In 1986, Lucas sold The Graphic

Group to Steve Jobs, and the new company was known as Pixar, with Dr. Edwin Catmull as President and Dr. Alvy Ray Smith as Executive Vice President. Randal Kleiser directed *Flight of the Navigator* in 1986. It was the first feature film to employ the technique of reflection mapping. *Howard the Duck* was directed by Willard Huyck. It was also the first feature film to use digital wire removal. Adobe Illustrator 1.0 was released in 1987. Prisms was also released by Side Effect Software in 1987. Prisms are now known as Houdini. In 1987, John Wallace created the Dutch Interior at Cornell University.

In 1988, the animation and visual effects studios Rez.n8 production, Matte World Digital, and Froyer Films were founded. Michael Wahrman and Brad deGraf of deGraf/Wahrman created Mike the Talking Head, the first live performance of a virtual character, in 1988. Computer Animation Production System (CAPS) was another collaboration between Disney and Pixar that year. That collaboration had a significant impact on visual effects history. They also won the Academic Award for their work on *Tin Toy*.

The Fall of Optical (1989–1993)

Thomas and John Knoll of ILM created Adobe Photoshop in 1989 for the Macintosh computer. The same year, Electric Image released the Electric Image Animation System (EIAS). Animator, the first cell-based animation application for the DOS operating system, was released by Autodesk the same year. In addition, in 1989, Apollo Computer released AVID/1. It was the first nonlinear editing software that was made available. Mental ray was released as a render engine in 1989. In 1989, James Cameron directed *The Abyss*. It was a love story with CGI flourishes. It included a base shot with a complicated animated visual effect.

In 1990, The Mill, Metrolight Studios, and VIFX were founded. Those studios had a significant impact on the history of visual effects. This year, the Yost Group released 3DStudio software for the DOS operating system. In addition, NewTek released Electric Lightwave in 1990 as part of the video Toaster suite. 3Ds Max was released the following year. In 1990, films with VFX shots such as *Die Hard 2: Die Harder, Back to the Future Part III, Total Recall, Dick Tracy,* and others were released. In 1991, two outstanding visual effects companies, Hybride and Animal Logic, were founded.

In 1991, Scott Squires released Commotion Pro. It was a fantastic piece of software at the time, especially when compared to Adobe After Effects. Another 3D software, initially known as FastRay and later renamed Cinema 4D, was released in 1991, but it was only available for the Amiga. That same year, Alias released Power Animator 1.0, a

3D computer graphics program. In 1991, Michael Jackson released a black-and-white music video. That was the time of the most fluid morphing. Morphing is the process of seamlessly transitioning from one image or shape to another.

James Cameron directed *Terminator 2: Judgment Day* in 1991. It was a fantastic live-action visual effects film. In that film, there was a nuclear war scene that was shot in a very complicated way. The first human-detailed character was also created for this film. *Beauty and the Beast,* directed by Gary Trousdale and Kirk Wise, was released by Walt Disney in 1991. In this film, Disney included the first 3D animated sequence in one of their animated feature films. In 1991, Ron Howard directed the film *Backdraft*, which featured the first use of photorealistic computer-generated fire.

Hydraulx and Sony Picture Imageworks, which is now known as Sony Picture Animation, were both founded in 1992. In 1992, the film *Death Becomes Her* was released. In this feature film, the first computer-generated skin was used. *Doom* is a computer action game released in 1993. CoSA released After Effects in 1993. It was later purchased by Adobe. This year, Digital Domain released NUKE, a very useful full compositing software. In 1993, many visual effects-heavy films were released, including *The Nightmare Before Christmas, Cliffhanger, Babylon 5, RoboCop 3,* and the Academy Award-winning *Jurassic Park.*

Going Mainstream (1994–1996)

Bryce was released in 1994 by Eric Wenger and Kai Krause. It was 3D software used primarily to create landscapes and backgrounds for CGI-enhanced films. TrueSpace was also released by Caligari Corporation the same year. It was also a 3D show. In 1994, Larry Gritz also created the Blue Moon render engine, the first open source renderMan or Reyes-compliant renderer system. Silicon Graphic acquired Alias, which had developed Wavefront Technologies, the same year. In 1994, Cinesite and C.O.R.E Digital Picture were founded. That same year, Mainframe Entertainment created the first computer-generated television series, *ReBoot. The Lion King*, Disney's first crowd-simulated feature film, was released this year. Also that year, *The Flintstones* featured the first digital fur, and many great visual effects-heavy films were released, including *Forrest Gump, The Mask, The Hudsucker Proxy,* and many others.

Many great visual effect studios—such as Manex Visual Effects, Blur Studio, Banned from the Ranch Entertainment, Pacific Ocean Post Studio, and Rising Sun Picture—were founded in 1995, changing the course of visual effects history. Matador software was first made available in 1995. The same year, Adobe purchased After Effects, and Parallax Software released Advanced, which was later renamed Illusion. Kaydara also released Filmbox, which later evolved into MotionBuilder and is now part of the Autodesk family. ADSG also released Elastic Reality this year. Christ Noonan directed *Babe* in 1995, and it is most likely in this film that the first computer-generated talking animals were created. The films *The City of Lost Children, Johnny Mnemonic,* and *Judge Dredd* were released this year. In 1955, Pixar Animation Studios released the first full-length computer-generated feature film, *Toy Story*.

In 1996, Dream Quest Images was renamed The Secret Lab, and several studios were established, including Digital Dimension and The Foundry. Eyeon Software also released Fusion this year, which later added many features such as a paint tool, text tool, color correction tool, 3D environment and 3D particles, and so on. GIMP, a paint system for Mac and Linux, was created by Spencer Kimball and Peter Mattis. Light was also created by DreamWorks Animation in 1996. In 1996, many great visual effect films were released, including Chris Landreth's *The End, T2 3-D Battle Across Time, Broken Arrow, Twister, Event Horizon,* and others.

Every Man and His Dog (1997–1999)

It was in 1997 that three major visual effects companies—Prime Focus, Frantic Films, and Blue Sky—were established.

Shake software was developed by Sony Picture Imageworks and released in 1997. ColorEngine, also known as Rotoshop, was developed by Bob Sabiston in the same year. E-on introduced Vue in 1997, which was developed by Marcos Fajardo of Solid Angle. Arnold was also developed by Marcos Fajardo of Solid Angle. Dan Ritchie was also the founder of Project Dogwaffle, which was established in 1997. The first 3D morph was created in 1997 for the film *Spawn,* directed by Mark A. Z. Dipple. In addition, many excellent films were released in that year, including James Cameron's *Titanic,* Robert Zemeckis' *Contact,* and Luc Besson's *Fifth Element*. James Cameron's *Titanic* was the most notable.

Method Studios and Double Negative Studios were established in 1998, but a number of other studios, including Colossal Pictures, POP, and Metrolight Studios, went out of business that same year. In 1998, Microsoft sold the Softimage 3D 3.8 version to Avid, and 3D software progressed to the next generation of technology. A similar piece of software, Maya, an excellent 3D computer-generated content creation tool, was released by Alias or Wavefront in 1998. A number of excellent 3D programs were released in 1998, including Rhinoceros 3D by Robert McNeel and Associates, Next Limit Technologies' RealFlow, NeoGeo's Blender, and Not a Number Technology's Not a Number Technology. (NaN).

In 1998, Paul Debevec developed High Dynamic Range Radiance (HDRI) maps, which are now widely used. The Visual Effects Society was founded in 1998 as an organization dedicated to the advancement of visual effects technology. Chris Landreth was also responsible for the well-known film *Bingo* in the same year. Aside from *Tightrope*, Digital Domain also produced Stephen Hopkins' *Lost in Space,* which was the first feature film produced in collaboration with a large number of UK production companies. Also released that year were numerous excellent films, including *Mighty Joe Young, What Dream May Come, Godzilla, Deep Impact, Small Soldiers,* and *Armageddon.*

Gentle Giant Studios first opened its doors in 1999. VIFX was sold to Rhythm and Hues Studios in the same year it was founded. Boujou was developed by Vicon, a 2D3 company. The year 1999 saw the release of several excellent visual effects-heavy films, including *The Matrix* by Lilly and Lana Wachowski, *Star Wars Episode 1: The Phantom Menace* by George Lucas, *The Mummy* by Stephen Sommers, *Stuart Little* by Rob Minkoff, and *Fight Club* by David Fincher, among many others.

The Coming of Age (2000–2003)

Fuel VFX was established in the year 2000, and Pixologic released Z Brush 1.0 at the same time that Maxon released BodyPaint 3D. It was the first software to paint a texture directly on top of a 3D model, making it a historical milestone. Furthermore, in the same year, Silicon Grail released Chalice, an excellent node-based compositing software that is similar to Nuke. DNA Research developed 3Delight, a fantastic render engine.

During the same year, a pose space deformer was developed. The short film *Work in Progress* was released by Industrial Light and Magic in 2000, and it was a fantastic 3D animated film. This year, Bruce Branit and Jeremy Hunt also produced 405 short films, according to the Hollywood Reporter. Many great feature films were made in 2000 by many great directors, including Ridley Scott's *Gladiator, The Perfect Storm,* and *O Brother, Where Art Thou?*. It was the first film to be produced using a digital intermediated suite, and it was followed by *Dinosaur*, a Disney production in which 3D elements were added to live-action footage, as well as *Hollow Man, Red Planet*, and a slew of other projects.

Endorphin was the first to invent natural motion in 2001. It was the first skeleton to have adaptive behavior. That same year, Maya 4.0 was also released. A number of films were released in 2001, including *Vidocq, Pearl Harbor, Final Fantasy – The Spirits Within, The Lord of the Rings: The Fellowship of the Ring, Driven, The Mummy Returns,* and *Moulin Rouge.*

Pixomondo and Luma Pictures were founded in 2002. Curious Software released the gFx Pro software in 2002, and RealViz released the Matchmover software in 2003. Chaos released V-Ray the same year, and SplutterFish created Brazil the following year. In 2002, Sony Pictures Imageworks also produced the animated films *BIRPS* and *BONSAI*. Mental Ray was tightly integrated with Maya 4.5 during that year. The Scientific and Technical Academy also recognized Maya's achievements. Paul Debevec also composed a live action piece for the stage in 2002. The year 2002 also saw the release of many excellent films, including *Star Wars Episode 2: Attack of the Clones, The Time Machine, Reign of Fire, The Lord of the Rings: The Two Towers, Men in Black 2, Star Trek: Nemesis, Star Trek: Nemesis,* and *XXX.*

Founded in 2003, both Zoic Studio and Intelligent Creatures are independent game development studios. Animanium software, developed by Common Lisp and released by SEGA in the same year as PFTrack, was created by Pixel Farm. In 2003, Sony Picture Imageworks also released OpenColoriO, a powerful visual effects tool that was compatible with a wide range of software, including After Effects, Blender, Houdini, Photoshop, Nuke, and others. OpenColoriO was developed by Sony Picture Imageworks and distributed by Sony Picture Imageworks.

Daredevil, The Core, and *The Lord of the Rings: The Return of the King* are just a few of the movies that fall into this category. 2003 saw the release of numerous visually stunning and computer-generated, imagery-infused films, including the blockbusters *X2, Hulk,* and *Peter Pan.*

No Going Back (2004–2009)

Gelato was released by Nvidia in 2004 and was the world's first commercial GPU-accelerated render engine. Additionally, that year saw the introduction of silhouette, which was initially used for Rotoscopy but has since been adopted for other applications. *Ryan*, a 2004 film directed by Chris Landreth, was nominated for an Academy Award. *Van Helsing, The Day After Tomorrow, Spider Man 2, I, Robot,* and a slew of other films were released that year.

Macromedia was purchased by Adobe in 2005. Following that, the visual effects industry was graced with a slew of fantastic applications, including Dreamweaver, Flash, and Fireworks, to name a few of the most notable. Teggagen software, a fantastic landscape generator developed by Planetside Software, was also released in 2005. Toxik was released by Autodesk in the same year. Luxology also released a new product in that same year, called Modo. The year 2005 saw a slew of excellent visual effects films come to the big screen, including *King Kong, The Island, Batman Begins, Stealth, War of the World,* and *Corpse Bride.*

The acquisition of the Pixar animation studio by Disney in 2006 was one of the most significant achievements in the history of visual effects technology. Another acquisition that occurred that year was Autodesk's acquisition of Alias Software. In addition, ILM developed a fluid dynamic system in 2006. Great films from 2006 include *Superman Returns, Poseidon, Night at the Museum, Eragon,* and *Children of Men.*

Similarly, Prime Focus Group acquired Fantastic Films in 2007, and The Foundry acquired Nuke from Digital Domain the following year. Mudbox, another Autodesk product that was released the same year as Skymatter, was also a success. Paul Debevec also pioneered the development of the first Specular and Diffuse normal maps in 2007. *Zodiac, The Simpsons, Pirates of the Caribbean: At World's End, Spider-Man 3, The Golden Compass, Transformers, Beowulf,* and *I Am Legend* are among the notable films of 2007.

In 2008, Paul Debevec established the digital Emily Project. Sony Picture Imageworks created Flix in 2008, and The Foundry released the Ocula virtual reality program in 2009. The Weta Digital team also created Tissue, which is a system for creating realistic muscle, skin, and fat on characters. *The Spirit, Inkheart, Quantum of Solace, The Dark Knight, Hancock,* and *Iron Ma,* were among the best of the year.

2009 marked the first anniversary of the creation and release of Field3D by Sony Picture Imageworks. Kantana was acquired by The Foundry from Sony Picture Imageworks during the same calendar year. The best films released in 2009 included *Watchmen, Avatar, Terminator Salvation, Star Trek, District 9, G-force,* and *The Road.*

Beyond the Impossible (2010–2013)

The Open Shading Language (OSL) was developed by Sony Picture Imageworks and released in 2010. A year later, The Foundry acquired Mari from Weta Digital for an undisclosed sum. In 2010, films such as *Alice in Wonderland, Inception, Iron Man 2,*

Tron: Legacy, Clash of the Titans, The A-Team, The Wolfman, Hereafter, Black Swan, and many more were released.

In 2011, the Alembic file format was also made available by Sony Picture Imageworks and ILM. *Storm,* another game from The Foundry, was released in the same year. *Rango, Thor, Cowboys and Aliens, Hugo, Real Steel,* and *The Adventures of Tintin* were among the best computer-generated, visual-integrated films released of 2011.

Luxology joined The Foundry in 2013, following the acquisition of Fuel VFX by Animal Logic the previous year. Exotic Matter was purchased by Autodesk in the same year. Pixar released RenderMan on Demand. Hiero was released by The Foundry in 2012. PFDepth was also released by The Pixel Frame, and Clarisse iFX was released by Isotropix. Among the best films of 2012 were J*ohn Carter, Snow White and the Huntsman, Battleship, The Avengers, Life of Pi,* and *The Amazing Spider-Man,* among many others.

In 2013, Prana Studio acquired the Rhythm and Hues label. ILM and Weta Digital also released openEXR 2.0, which is an open source rendering engine. Pixar's OpenSubdiv was released the following year. The following year, The Foundry acquired Flix from Sony Picture Imageworks for an undisclosed sum. The Bifrost was developed by Autodesk in that year. In addition to *Star Trek Into Darkness, White House Down, Oblivion, Iron Man 3, Man of Steel, Iron Man 2, Pacific Rim, Now You See Me, World War Z,* and many others, *Star Trek Into Darkness* was named one of the best films of 2013.

Oscars for Best VFX Movies (2014–2020)

The film *Interstellar,* directed by Christopher Nolan, featured some of the best visual effects shots of the year (2014). It is a science fiction film in the traditional sense. In 2015, the film *Ex Machina* was released and was nominated for an Academy Award. Alex Garland was in charge of directing that fantastic film.

In 2016, Jon Favreau directed the film adaptation of *The Jungle Book.* It was nominated for an Academy Award that year for its outstanding visual effects. Director Denis Villeneuve was in charge of the production of *Blade Runner 2049.* With a strong emphasis on visual effects, it was a fantastic film that earned the Academy Award for Best Visual Effects in 2017. The visual effects work on the film *First Man* was complex, which helped it win the Academy Award for Best Visual Effects in 2018. Damien Chazelle was in charge of the direction of the film. The visual effects in the film *1917,* directed by Sam Mendes, were recognized with an Academy Award for Best Visual Effects in 2019. It was a war drama film set during WWI. *Tenet* won the Academy Award for Best Visual Effects in

2021. Christopher Nolan was in charge of the direction. It is a science fiction action film with a unique twist.

VFX in Games

Visual effects (VFX) are now widely used in the game entertainment industry and have a significant impact. This section discusses some of the most impressive visual effects games available.

Ubisoft Montreal developed and published *Assassin's Creed,* an open world action-adventure stealth genre-based game that uses the Anvil Game Engine. The game was developed by Ubisoft Montreal and published by Ubisoft. Patrice Desilets, Jade Raymond, and Corey May collaborated on the development of this game. *Tom Clancy's The Division 2* is an online action role-playing video game developed by Tom Clancy and published by Electronic Arts. The game was developed by Massive Entertainment, and it was published by Ubisoft. Julian Gerighty and Mathias Karlson were in charge of the direction for this game. This game set was created to mimic Washington, D.C. It is a very detailed game, with elements such as trash on the road, wildlife, reflections in building glass, weather effects, day and night effects, and so on. It is also very challenging.

Metro Exodus is a first-person shooter video game developed by 4A Games and published by Deep Silver. Andrew Prokhorov was in charge of the direction of this game. The survival horror and stealth elements that were used in the creation of this game are outstanding. *Forza Horizon 4,* a racing video game published by Microsoft Studio, is a game about cars. This title was created by Playground Games. Ralph Fulton was in charge of the direction for this game. This game includes over 750 licensed automobiles that players can either purchase or unlock through gameplay. Its set was created to look like a very realistic and open-world English countryside.

Control is an action-adventure video game developed by Remedy Entertainment that was released in 2008. Michael Kasurinen directed the project, which was published by 505 Games. The supernatural stories that inspired this game were used as inspiration. With paper flying, reflections of the floor and artistic light, and even reflections of the character's eyes, it was a highly detailed piece. *Battlefield V* is a first-person shooter video game. It was developed by DICE and published by Electronic Arts. The piece was written by Steven Hall. *The Witcher 3: Wild Hunt,* an action role-playing game developed by Polish developers and published by CD Projekt Red, is set in the world of the witcher. The directors of this game were Konrad Tomaszkiewicz, Mateusz Kanik, and Sebastian

Stepien. It includes a variety of weapons, including bombs and crossbows. It also includes two-sided shields, with one side that is steel and the other side that is silver, among other things.

Call of Duty is a first-person shooter video game. It was created by Infinity War, and it was published by Activision. The best part of this game is that players can compete in ladders or tournaments that are divided into several sub-ladders, such as single ladders, double ladders, team ladders, and herd core team ladders, depending on their level of experience. The character in this game is more like a real man than a cartoon, which is a nice touch.

Doom Eternal is a first-person shooter game released in 2011. This video game was developed by ID Software and published by Bethesda Softworks. This game was directed by Hugo Martine. *Red Dead Redemption 2* is an action-adventure video game. It was published and developed by Rockstar Games. Depending on your preference, you can play this game in first or third person, and you can play it as a single player or in online multiplayer mode. With this game set, the designers wanted to create an open world environment that was reminiscent of the Western Midwestern and southern United States. With textures and 3D models, the graphics in this game are extremely detailed, and the setting is designed to appear as realistically as possible, even at night, with light interacting with fog. When the character walks through the maze, their feet are printed on the walls.

This chapter discussed how visual effects evolved over time and how they influenced people's minds, from computer graphics illusion to the media and entertainment industry. The next chapter covers computer graphics imagery techniques and the applications for visual effects generation in depth.

CHAPTER 3

Industrial Applications of VFX

In the previous chapter, you learned about the history and background of visual effects, their significance, and how they emerged as an essential component of the media and entertainment industries. This chapter focuses on how visual effects have become practically ubiquitous in all digital mediums, including games, films, advertising, education, and OTT (over the top) platforms.

Visual Effects and Special Effects

Visual effects, or VFX, are often known as special effects, or SFX, in common language. Movies were never complete without special effects. So, what exactly are effects? They are any changes that occur as a result of any action. SFX are "in-camera" effects, which implies they are physically performed. For example, if an actor drops a lighted matchstick into a can of gasoline and the resulting fire or explosion is filmed on camera, this recorded effect falls under the genre of SFX.

Similarly, if a prosthetic forearm is made and connected to an actor, and then it is pulled off with fake blood spatter, that is SFX. Effects such as gunshot wounds, burn scars on actors that can be achieved with prosthetic makeup, firing blanks, stabbing people, and other artificially manufactured physical effects filmed live, on-camera are common instances of SFX. Such special effects are often used in cinema, television, and even theatre to simulate the imagined events or effects.

The special effects category encompasses any specifically designed/rigged physical device that produces an effect. However, it may be necessary at this point to distinguish between the two, despite the fact that they have many similarities. VFX, on the other hand, are post-production effects that are created using the power of software applications on a computer. For example, creating a computer-generated model of a

© Abhishek Kumar 2022
A. Kumar, *Beginning VFX with Autodesk Maya*, https://doi.org/10.1007/978-1-4842-7857-4_3

spaceship that flies across a matte painted background for a scene in a film is VFX. If you shoot an actor falling from a cliff against a chroma screen (sometimes known as a green screen or blue screen), this is also VFX. VFX is less expensive because computer-generated effects, rather than practical effects, are used for scenes like spurting blood and muzzle flashes. To put it simply, SFX include mechanical effects, optical effects, pyrotechnics, and atmospheric effects. Both SFX and VFX have become increasingly important in recent technological advancements, depending on the needs of the project.

However, it is vital to realize that too much computer-generated action may cause viewers to feel disconnected from reality, whereas some true SFX done effectively and interwoven into the tale is far more powerful on the screen. When shooting against a chroma backdrop, the performers are frequently distanced from the genuine emotions of the action, making it difficult to work. A quick development in computer-generated VFX may result in a slew of poorly created films that are crammed with technology rather than the emotional connection of the performers in the picture. As a result, VFX specialists must carefully and correctly adjust the quantity of VFX and judiciously integrate it for optimal viewer interaction. Filmmakers who use that technology must know when to stop. A good mixture of both will result in outstanding realism on-screen.

Planning for a Visual Effects Shot

Every production is built on the pipeline's backbone. The hitch here is that, while we cannot guarantee that a functioning and adaptable pipeline will indefinitely lead to a successful project, we can ensure that if this is not taken seriously, it will almost certainly lead to project failure. A solid production pipeline not only ensures a high-quality output in the shortest amount of time, but it also ensures content and happy artists whose creativity is not compromised throughout the arduous production schedule.

Production pipeline fundamentals for film and games focus on leading the team to the proper technology efforts with limited resources, allowing them to get the most out of every dollar invested.

The pipeline is the glue that holds the work of every artist from every department participating in the production together. This is analogous to an assembly line, where each worker completes their task before passing it on to the next. The only difference between the two is in the creative process, which involves review rounds during which the final product may be improved and, if necessary, the pipeline itself may be altered. The majority of pipelines are constructed from a network of smaller pipes. At each end, the pipeline links with information from the other end. Films, whether live action VFX or fully animated CG, rely on technology similar to games. CG models, texturing, animation, lighting effects, post-production, and audio are all used in these mediums. However, the manner in which the production pipelines are linked may vary. A film is a non-interactive linear sequence.

Understanding how a production pipeline works boosts your prospects of employment as a student, since no matter how skilled you are at your skill, you must integrate your efforts with the capabilities of others in the studio.

At the very onset of understanding the VFX pipeline, it is helpful to know that it is usually divided into three stages, as shown in Figure 3-1.

- **Pre-production:** It is at this stage that the concept and idea for a film thrives, scripts are finalized, budgets are allocated, timelines are set, financing is sourced, and actors and locations are screened for the final take off.

- **Production:** This is the stage where the actual filming happens on set. This set may be live location or in a studio or against a chroma screen.

- **Post-production:** At this stage, the visual effects that need to be applied to the footage, the sound FX, the editing and DI and color grading take place, and the film is prepared for distribution.

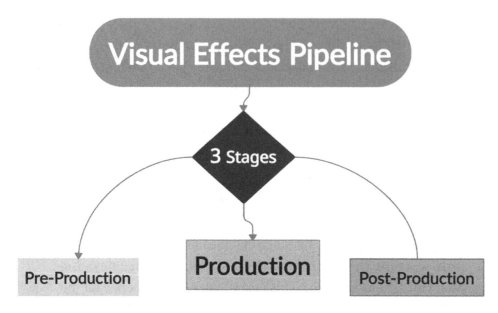

Figure 3-1. *Visual effects production pipeline*

Industry Practices for VFX

Now that you better understand how a pipeline works, let's delve deep into analyzing the industry practices in the various mediums of films and games production, from both an Indian and an international perspective for visual effects.

The Gaming Industry

Let's start with the greatest game that takes advantage of real-time VFX. The effect was developed in the game *Stellar Impact* by artist Florian Dury using Unity FX. Bertram Raahauge Jensen, VFX artist and game designer, was inspired by Riot Games *Shadow Isles* and worked on hand-painted effects. Hyuk Choi, a young VFX artist, rose to prominence for his work on *Hellfire Barbarian* fire simulations of the power splash and whirlwind effect. Antonio Cappiello, a VFX artist at Riot Games, created some incredible real-time effects for his personal project, *Absorption*. The Unreal Engine was utilized by Thomas Francis, VFX Artist at RedHooksStudios, Vancouver Canada, to produce the VFX-Destiny inspired first person caster and VFX-pure nether energy barrier. Fabio Silva,

Senior 3D VFX artist at Blizzard Entertainment, used the Unreal Engine to develop the effects for the stylized FX overwatch style, as shown in Figure 3-2.

Figure 3-2. *Visual effects in games (Source:* `https://www.unrealengine.com`*)*

Moving on to visual effects in films in the Indian context, a famous film *KGF Chapter 1* was released in 2018 with seamless integration of physical on-set effects and additional computer-generated effects for enhancing the appeal of a shot. The film relies heavily on massive sets to capture the vibe of the 1970s and 1980s. The KGF was chosen as the location for the main mine. Despite the fact that filming in this region was risky, the filmmakers thought the landscape to be a wonderful match for the picture. The art direction staff has diligently worked out every element to provide the appearance and feel of that era. Various sets were built across the geography of the area to create the scenes of active mining. The climatic conditions, which can sometimes act as the villain in that perfect take, are a major challenge for physical effects and on-set effects. However, there was a large set, and visual effects were heavily employed for set extensions, particularly in enlarging the city skyline. This film is a perfect example of how physical effects can be seamlessly blended with computer generated effects to create a visual treat, as shown in Figure 3-3. The audience is now anticipating the release of Chapter 2 of the KGF film, which promises to reveal new paradigms of visual effects.

Figure 3-3. *Visual effects used in the KGF movie (Source:* `https://` `hombalefilms.com/`*)*

Moving on to computer-generated 3D animation effects, we may take inspiration from a variety of Hollywood blockbusters. However, for the sake of this research, we will refer to the films produced by the Marvel cinematic universe. As Marvel Studios' visual effects supervisor Dan Deleeuw correctly states, "Visual effects is all about releasing and reaching new heights of technological experimentation with each picture." Major visual effects firms, such as ILM (see Figure 3-4), Weta Digital, Digital Domain, Method Studios, Framestore, DNEG, and Technicolor lead the progression of modern-day movie visual effects.

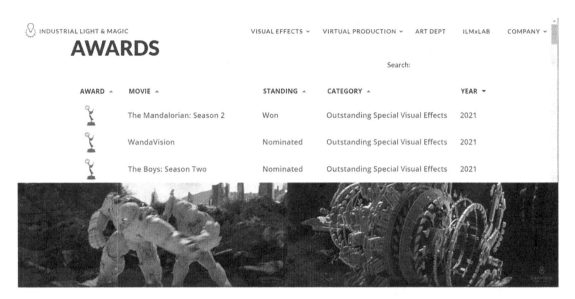

Figure 3-4. *Visual effects projects by ILM (Source:* `https://www.ilm.com/`
`awards-nominations/`*)*

Visual effects were a sizable portion of the $675 million budget for the films *Infinity War* and *Avengers: Endgame.* Nearly 14 VFX studios from across the world worked on the development of 2,623 shots for *Infinity War* and 2,496 shots for *Avengers: Endgame.* This increase in figures can be seen by comparing the number of shots in *Iron Man,* which was 1,000, to the number of shots in *Avengers: Endgame,* which was 2,500.

The influence of VFX, whether modest or large, is felt by the global community of filmmakers. We may cite several illustrious VFX supervisors from prominent VFX studios such as Weta Digital. Matt Aitken's work for Marvel Studios Films includes anything from high-end digital performance work on Thanos, Hulk, Rocket, and Groot to large-scale simulation and demolition work with completely CGI environments. To achieve a realistic style, most films experimented with the seamless integration of motion capture-based digital performance alongside live-action performance, as well as animation-driven physically-based simulation work.

A number of films have covered a wide range of technology-driven effects in terms of—people, settings, devastation, simulation, and vehicles. Marvel Studios has shown the VFX world the huge array of technology assets and narrative that can be combined into a coherent blockbuster. The tremendous quantity of VFX is expertly matched with enthralling plots that keep the spectators spellbound.

Software, Tools, and Techniques Used to Render Visual Splendor Onscreen Effects

After delving deeply into the role of visual effects in the entertainment industry and, by extension, our lives, we've arrived at a vital point: learning and comprehending the many software tools and techniques that contribute to the creation of these visual effects sequences. All of the visual splendor is made with the assistance of these software, which is enhanced with other plugins designed specifically to ease the effort and generate more realistic effects in the shortest period of time. The creative artists that operate behind the computers with their specialized skill sets, on the other hand, have the competence.

The next sections list some essential software/tools needed to do VFX.

Autodesk 3Ds Max

Autodesk 3Ds Max is 3D computer graphics professional software developed and produced by Autodesk Media and Entertainment, previously 3D Studio and 3D Studio Max (see Figure 3-5). It is used to create 3D animations, models, games, and visualizations. Its model-creation skills, along with the architecture of plugin flexibility, make it a favorite among game makers, TV commercial studios, film pre-visualizations, and architectural visualizers. Advanced shaders, dynamic simulations, particle systems, normal map construction and rendering, and global lighting are all included in the current edition of the program. It includes a fully configurable user interface, including new icons, as well as its own programming language.

Figure 3-5. *Autodesk 3Ds Max Graphical User Interface (Source:* `https://www.`
`autodesk.in`*)*

Autodesk Maya

Autodesk Maya, commonly known as Maya, is another commonly used application to
generate 3D assets to be used in films, television series, games, and architecture (see
Figure 3-6). Following a sequence of possessions, Maya was finally acquired by Autodesk
in 2005. The virtual workspace of Maya, commonly referred to as a *scene*, is the three-
dimensional representation of the virtual world where the user builds their models and
edits and textures them along with the lighting integrated rendering system for the final
visual representation. The workflow of Maya follows the node graph architecture, where
each node has its particular properties and customizations.

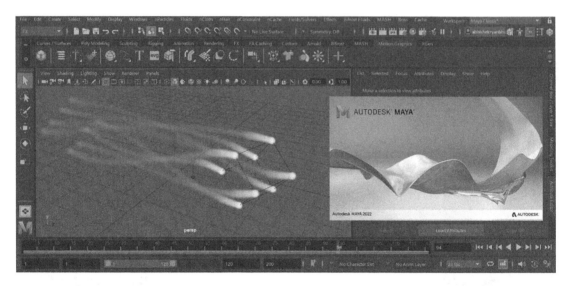

Figure 3-6. *Maya's graphical user interface (Source:* `https://www.autodesk.in`*)*

Maya's widespread use in the M&E sector may be traced back to its creation on the Disney feature *Dinosaur*, which was released in 2000. Maya won an Academy Award for technical accomplishment in 2003, and it has since appeared in prominent films including *The Lord of the Rings: The Two Towers, Spider-Man* (2002), *Ice Age,* and *Star Wars: Episode II Attack of the Clones*. According to *VentureBeat Magazine*, all 10 films nominated for the Best Visual Effects Academy Award in 2015 were developed using Maya, and this has been the norm for every winning picture since 1997. The *Transformers* series is one of the excellent executions of 3D animation work using Maya.

Houdini

Developed by SideFX, Houdini is yet another powerful 3D animation software application (see Figure 3-7). The exclusive ability to handle procedural generation distinguishes Houdini from other 3D applications. Based completely on procedural techniques, Houdini is built from the basic level up to that which empowers artists to easily work, create any number of iterations, and quickly share workflows with others working on the project.

Figure 3-7. *Houdini's graphical user interface (Source:* `https://www.`
`sidefx.com/)`

In recent years, prominent VFX studios such as Walt Disney Animation Studios, Pixar, DreamWorks Animation, Double Negative, ILM, MPC, Framestore, Sony Pictures Imageworks, Method Studios, and The Mill have made substantial use of Houdini. The program has made significant contributions to the animation effects industry, including Disney's feature films *Fantasia 2000, Frozen*, and *Zootopia*, as well as Blue-Sky Studios' *Rio* and DNA Productions' *Ant Bully*.

Unreal Engine (For Real-Time FX)

Unreal Engine has recently emerged as the most open and powerful real-time 3D creative platforms for photoreal visuals and immersive experiences (see Figure 3-8). The artist is armed with the Unreal Engine to bring beautiful real-time experiences to life by utilizing the capabilities of this most powerful real-time 3D production tool. The free and open materials, as well as its inspiring community, enable everyone to achieve their goals.

Figure 3-8. *Epic Game launcher and Unreal Engine graphical user interface (Source: https://www.unrealengine.com/)*

The Unity Game Engine is a major platform for creating interactive, real-time multimedia (see Figure 3-9). It enables the creation of 3D, 2D, VR, and AR experiences for any industry, including games, automotive, architecture, and film. It develops solutions better and iterates them faster. Its multi-platform support and immersive experiences aid in the development of amazing games.

Figure 3-9. *Unity Engine sample work (Source: https://unity.com/)*

RealFlow

RealFlow is an industry standard out-of-the-box program that creates fluid simulation (see Figure 3-10). This multiphysics simulation software is a rapid and versatile program to use, with interoperability on all major 3D platforms. RealFlow is a stand-alone tool that allows you to create fluid and dynamics simulations for use in the 3D and visual effects industries. This application's output may be readily combined with other 3D FX programs for simulation of fluids, water surfaces, fluid-solid interactions, rigid bodies, soft bodies, and meshes.

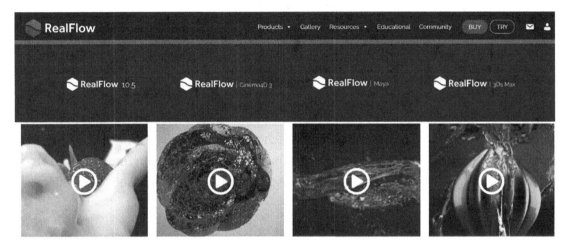

Figure 3-10. *RealFlow sample work (Source: `https://realflow.com/`)*

Blender

Blender is another software program that is gaining popularity in the visual effects industry (see Figure 3-11). Especially since it's a free and open source 3D application with the potential of covering the entire production pipeline under its umbrella. It is emerging as a powerful tool for 2D and 3D, as well as VFX production pipeline.

Figure 3-11. *Blender sample works (Source: https://www.blender.org/)*

Visual Effects Plugins

There are several application development companies dedicatedly working on FX generation software. A few are stand-alone, such as Maya, 3D Max, Houdini, Unity, Unreal, and RealFlow, and a few are add-on applications that you can integrate into key software like Maya. These are called plugins. A few of the commonly used visual effects plugins are discussed next.

Thinking Particles

Thinking Particles (TP) is a productivity cornerstone in the VFX post-production industry (see Figure 3-12). It has been said that 3DS Max has remained a stand-alone product in the Autodesk software collection for so long because of TP. Endless blockbuster films have relied on Thinking Particles' unlimited capacity to re-create complex physics-based particle effects that are completely procedural and rule-based.

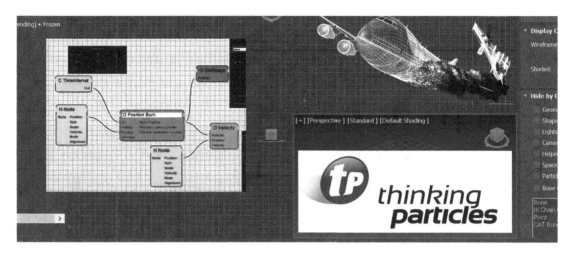

Figure 3-12. *Thinking Particles sample work and interface (Source:* `https://`
`www.cebas.com/`*)*

FumeFX

FumeFX is another industry-leading plugin for creating fluid dynamics in Maya and
3Ds Max (see Figure 3-13). This plugin is specifically developed to produce simulations
and render realistic gaseous effects like as fire, smoke, explosions, and so on. FumeFX's
unrivalled ability to reproduce delicate and minute nuances of fluidity in the behavior of
the gaseous has led to its popularity among visual effects artists, game developers, and
visualizers who are challenged with producing realism in their shots.

Figure 3-13. *FumeFX sample work and Interface (Source:* `https://www.`
`afterworks.com/FumeFX.asp`*)*

Krakatoa

When a large density of particles is required, Krakatoa is the one-stop volumetric particle rendering solution that works nicely with particle flow. It's a customizable version of Autodesk Maya and 3ds Max's built-in event-driven particle system (see Figure 3-14).

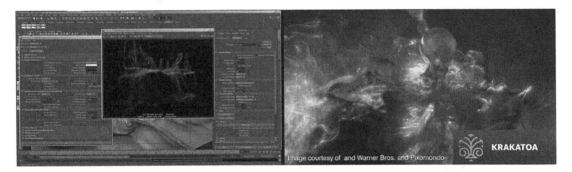

Figure 3-14. *Krakatoa sample work and Interface (Source:* `https://www.awsthinkbox.com/krakatoa`*)*

RayFire

The RayFire tool (see Figure 3-15) is another plugin for Autodesk Maya, 3Ds Max, and Unity that allows you to fragment, destroy, demolish, wreck, break down, wreak havoc on, and blow up objects.

Figure 3-15. *RayFire sample work (Source:* `http://rayfirestudios.com/`*)*

MultiScatter

Designed to be compatible with V-Ray, Mental Ray, Corona, Octane, Maxwell, and other applications, this version of V-Ray uses the Virtual Reality Scatter (VRayScatter) algorithm. MultiScatter (see Figure 3-16) is a 3DS Max plug-in that adds support for FStormRender simulations. This plugin allows you to render engines to emulate enormous numbers of objects in an array. When MultiScatter is enabled with Autodesk, the development of an FX slice shifts from N-System to Bifrost.

Figure 3-16. *MultiScatter sample work (Source: https://rendering.ru/multiscatter.html)*

With 64-bit system support, it may render and build, for example, a forest or even a city with a single blink of the eye.

Pulldownit

Pulldownit is a dynamics plugin that is used by digital artists to simulate numerous kinds and types of shatter effects for 3D models (see Figure 3-17). It is meant to develop demolition effects as well as big rigid body simulations. The Pulldownit solver's capability allows it to compute thousands of objects in dynamics in a stable and realistic manner.

Figure 3-17. *Pulldownit sample work (Source: https://www.pulldownit.com/)*

Fracture FX

Fracture FX is a procedural demolition program that is used in the VFX and gaming industries (see Figure 3-18). Its scalable and event-based design gives artists control over destruction simulations, leading to faster shot finals and fewer work hours per shot.

Figure 3-18. *Fracture FX sample work and interface (Source: https://www. fracture-fx.com/)*

Miarmy

Miarmy (my army) is a Maya plugin that uses the Human Logic based engine for crowd simulation, AI, and behavioral animation (see Figure 3-19). It uses AI and behavioral animation as well as creature physical simulation and rendering. It features such functions as being able to produce Human Fuzzy Logic Networks without any programming or network nodes. It includes support for standard production pipelines,

HumanIK and Motion Builder integration, references, and PhysX: ragdoll, RBD emitters, and force field, cloth, wind, and fluid effects, which are all highly beneficial to an effect artist.

Figure 3-19. *MIARMY sample work and Interface (Source: `http://www.basefount.com/miarmy.html`)*

Golaem Crowd

What would you do if you had the opportunity to create a large crowd scenario using digital characters? To make this happen, you may use a technology called Golaem, which makes it simple and inexpensive to fill environments with directable digital characters ranging from a few to thousands. Artists have used this technique to bring to life advertisements, episodic projects, feature films, and video games. Golaem (see Figure 3-20) enables the rapid populating and variation in animation of 3D scenes with humans, horses, birds, or other unusual species.

Figure 3-20. *Golaem Crowd sample work and interface (Source: `http://golaem.com/`)*

Ziva VFX

The interactive experiences that are brought to life for films and games have been made feasible in large part due to Ziva VFX. The underlying toolset of Ziva VFX (see Figure 3-21) allows artists to easily reproduce physical effects and mimic any soft-tissue substance, including muscles, fat, and skin, in order to generate blockbuster-quality assets. The plugin focuses in character development and human simulation.

Figure 3-21. *Ziva VFX sample work (Source: https://zivadynamics.com)*

Phoenix FD

Phoenix FD is a one-stop fluid dynamics simulation application capable of simulating fire, smoke, liquids, ocean waves, splashes, spray, and mist, among other things. Designed primarily for effects artists who need rapid preset generation, setup, and control, this plugin has it all (see Figure 3-22).

Figure 3-22. *Phoenix FD sample work (Source: https://www.chaosgroup.com/ phoenix-fd/3ds-max#showcase)*

Shave and a Haircut

Shave and a Haircut (see Figure 3-23) is a plugin that is coupled with shaders for offline rendering in Arnold, RenderMan, and V-Ray. It is an interactive grooming and styling tool for hair and fur. Epic Games purchased Shave and a Haircut a few years ago.

Figure 3-23. *Shave and a Haircut sample work and interface (Source: https:// www.joealter.com/)*

In Chapter 4, you learn about FX tools such as Maya Nucleus, Maya's nParticle system, Maya Fluids, nCloth, and nHair and see how the Maya FX system contributes to creating visual effects for CGI.

CHAPTER 4

Introduction to FX in Maya

Engineered with the input of leading research scientists, Maya offers innovative dynamics and simulation features to help you create stunning effects. However, before delving deeper into the technical side of things, let's quickly recap the difference between SFX and VFX. SFX are *in-camera* effects, which means they are physically conducted. For example, when an actor drops a lighted match into a can of fuel and the resultant fire or explosion is recorded on camera, this effect falls under the category of SFX.

VFX, on the other hand, are post-production effects simulated by software programs on a computer. For example, a computer-generated model of a spaceship flying across a matte painted background is VFX.

We are now ready to explore some of these effects in Autodesk Maya. These simulations — created with the help of Maya's particle system, fluid system, and so on — equip artists with the ability to create dynamic simulation renders. These kinds of effects are usually called 3D dynamic simulations, VFX simulations, Maya simulations, or FX simulations.

Maya's User Interface (UI)

Maya's interface groups similar commands together. For example, all the commands for controlling viewports are grouped together in the viewport navigation controls, which are found in the lower-right side of the Maya interface. The Maya interface can be broken into 16 major subelements, as shown in Figure 4-1 and discussed in the following sections.

© Abhishek Kumar 2022
A. Kumar, *Beginning VFX with Autodesk Maya*, https://doi.org/10.1007/978-1-4842-7857-4_4

Figure 4-1. *Maya's graphical user interface*

Menu Sets

Menu sets (number 1 in Figure 4-1) are the menu types. The menu categories are Modeling, Rigging, Animation, FX, and Rendering. The first seven menus are fixed and the rest change depending on the menu set you choose.

Menus

The menus (number 2 in Figure 4-1) contain tools and actions to work in Maya. The main menu is at the top of the Maya window (see Figure 4-2). There are several individual menus for the panels and option windows. You can also access the menus from the main menu or you can use a *hotbox*, which you can activate by holding down the spacebar in a viewport.

Figure 4-2. *A menu command inMaya*

The Status Line

The status line (shown in Figure 4-3) contains icons for common commands, such as object selection, snapping, rendering, and more.

Figure 4-3. *Maya's status line*

The Shelf

The shelf contains tabs that represent each menu set (see Figure 4-4). The real power of shelves is that you can create custom ones and then create a shortcut to quickly access the shelf with a single click.

Figure 4-4. *Maya's shelf*

Sidebar Icons

Sidebar icons are found at the right end of the status line. They open tools for the Attribute Editor, the Tool Settings, and the Channel Box (see Figure 4-5).

Figure 4-5. *Sidebar icons*

The View Panel

The View panel offers different ways of viewing the objects in your scene (see Figure 4-6). You can also display different editors in the View panel.

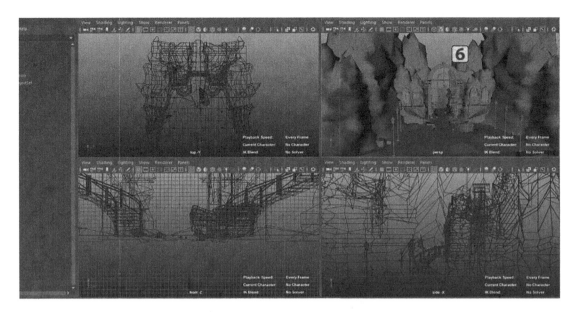

Figure 4-6. *The View panel*

The Channel Box

With the help of the Channel Box (see Figure 4-7), you can edit attributes and animate the values for selected objects.

Figure 4-7. *The Channel Box*

The Layer Editor

There are two types of layers in Maya. The first is the Display layer and the second is the Animation layer.

- Display layers (see Figure 4-8) are used to manage objects, such as to change their visibility and selectability.

- Animation layers are used to blend, lock, or mute multiple levels of animation.

Figure 4-8. *Maya's Display layer*

Tool Box

The Tool Box (see Figure 4-9) can help you select and transform objects in your scene. You can use the QWERTY keys for the Select (Q), Move (W), Rotate (E), Scale (R), and Show Manipulators tools (T). To access the last tool, use (Y).

Figure 4-9.. *Maya's Tool Box*

Quick Layout Buttons

The Quick Layout buttons (see Figure 4-10) allow you to switch between useful layouts with a single click.

Figure 4-10. *The Quick Layout buttons*

The Time Slider

The Time Slider (see Figure 4-11) shows the time range, the current time, and the keys for selected objects. You can also select the key and drag it to a new frame to change the animation frame.

Figure 4-11. *The Time Slider*

The Range Slider

The Range Slider (see Figure 4-12) enables you to zoom in on a playback range so you can more easily modify or correct a specific portion of the whole animation.

Figure 4-12. *The Range Slider*

Playback Controls

The playback controls are found in the bottom-right corner of Maya's interface (see Figure 4-13). You can play and pause the animation, as defined by the Time Slider range.

Figure 4-13. *Maya's playback controls*

The Animation/Character Menus

The Animation/Character menus (see Figure 4-14) help you switch the Animation layer and the current character set.

Figure 4-14. *The Animation/Character menus*

The Command Line

In the command line (see Figure 4-15), you can input MEL (Maya Embedded Language) commands or Python commands. You should be familiar with programming to work with the command line.

Figure 4-15. *Maya's command line*

The Help Line

The Help line (see Figure 4-16) gives you a short description of tools as you scroll over them in the UI. This bar also lists the steps required to complete a specific tool or workflow.

Figure 4-16. *Maya's Help line*

Maya's Viewport Configuration

The viewport in Maya is very handy to use. It has two different navigation viewports—perspective and orthographic.

How to Navigate in the Viewports

If you want to work in the viewport, you press the spacebar to maximize the viewport and restore the four views. Put your mouse pointer inside any of the viewports and gently press the spacebar to maximize or restore that viewport.

For a full extended viewport view, press Ctrl+spacebar. You can also hold the mouse pointer on the viewport and press the spacebar to maximize and restore the particular view, as shown in Figure 4-17.

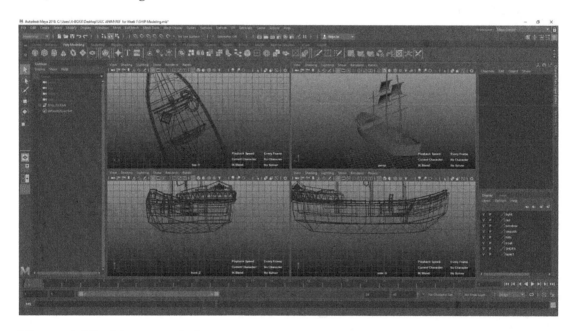

Figure 4-17. *Maya quad view*

Perspective View Navigation

Perspective view navigation (see Figure 4-18), also called 3D view, is your primary view to work in. It is the essential master perspective viewport navigation.

Figure 4-18. *Maya Perspective viewport layout*

Perspective viewport navigation has several shortcut keys:

- Alt+LMB = Rotate

- Alt+RMB = Zoom in/out

- Alt+MMB = Pan left/right/up/down

  - ✓ LMB = Left Mouse Button

  - ✓ RMB = Right Mouse Button

  - ✓ MMB = Middle Mouse Button

Orthographic View Navigation

Orthographic views (see Figure 4-19) are also known as two-dimensional viewports—you can see the top, side, front, and back. In this view, you can move, align, rotate, scale, or model 3D environment objects.

Figure 4-19. *Maya Orthographic viewport layout*

Orthographic navigation has only two shortcut keys:

- Alt+RMB = Zoom in/out

- Alt+MMB = Pan left/right/up/down

To center an object and rotate around its center orbit, press the left mouse button to select an object and press F on the keyboard to center the view. This is a very useful function to access a particular model. It will bring that object inside the scene to your attention. Pressing the F button centers the selected object in the viewport.

Getting Started with Visual Effects Simulation in Autodesk Maya

Great! You are now all set to plunge into the software. Maya's GUI is studded with multiple menus and tools spread out across the interface. On the left you will find a drop-down menu that says Modeling by default. If you click the arrow, the list drops down and you can see the other options, as shown in Figure 4-20.

Figure 4-20. *The default Modeling drop-down in Maya*

To work on FX simulations, you need to click the FX option. (In earlier versions of the software, the same option was called Dynamics.) Once you choose FX here, you will notice that the GUI menus and toolsets change and a whole new set of options are organized in the interface, as shown in Figure 4-21. By the same token, the interface will load the appropriate menus and tools for Animation, Modeling, Rigging, and Rendering when you choose those options from the drop-down.

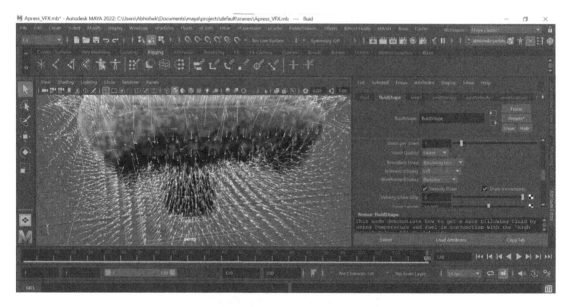

Figure 4-21. *The FX interface in Maya*

In the Maya FX/dynamics system, you are going to work with nParticles, nCloth, nHair, and fluids. Among these options, note that there are some with n mentioned before the effect name, such as nCloth, nParticles, and nHair. This n stands for *nucleus system*. Whenever you are running simulations, there are simulators in Maya that use a nucleus system to run the simulation in a much more efficient and effective manner.

Maya Nucleus is an advanced simulation framework with integrated modules for cloth and particles. With nCloth (see Figure 4-22), you can easily create clothing and other deformable materials from any polygon mesh. Attributes like bend, stretch, shear, and depth can be painted on and topology-independent constraints can be used to attach cloth to other objects and to control its movement. For example, you have the option of changing the clothing or even making the clothing interact with other effects in the scene. Animations that involve simulating a flag or petals of a flower can be comfortably achieved using nCloth, which used to be a tedious affair before the introduction of the nucleus system.

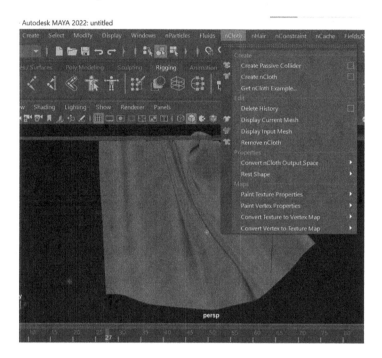

Figure 4-22. *The nCloth drop-down menu in Maya*

nParticles enable you to simulate a wide range of 3D effects, including clouds, smoke, spray, and dust. nParticles can even accumulate volumes and simulate pouring liquids. Additionally, nParticles and nCloth can interact bidirectionally. These features can simulate dust, fire, and explosions (see Figure 4-23).

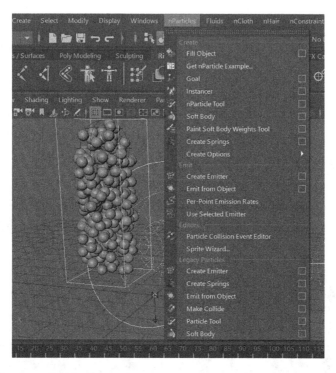

Figure 4-23. *The nParticles drop-down menu in Maya*

Now, moving on to nHair, as shown in Figure 4-24. This is an integrated hair simulation rendering system. It can be used to make any curve dynamic for a wide range of effects. Fur too can be created using nHair; the only difference is that fur has much shorter strands. So, if you need to create hair and fur for creatures, this can be done using Maya's nHair and its varied attributes.

Figure 4-24. *The nHair drop-down menu in Maya*

nConstraints is another very important component you'll use when working with nCloth or nParticles, especially when simulating clothes. Figure 4-25 shows the various command used with nConstraints, including Component to Component, Force Field, Point to Surface, Slide on Surface, Tearable Surface, and so on. In this book, you will learn about all of these and see adequate examples as well.

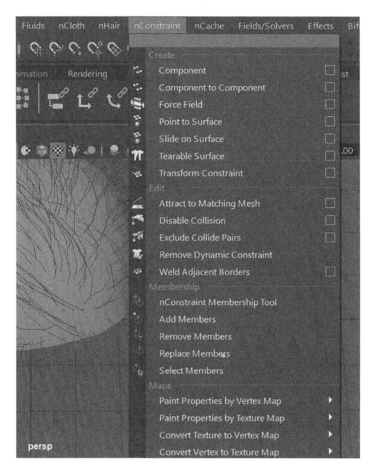

Figure 4-25. *The nConstraint drop-down menu in Maya*

Next to the nConstraint option, you have the nCache menu, as shown in Figure 4-26. Whenever you are dealing with simulations, you will inevitably need the cache memory to store or save simulated data. This data is for previews, which you need while creating simulations. Using nCache, saving simulated data previews is quicker and smoother.

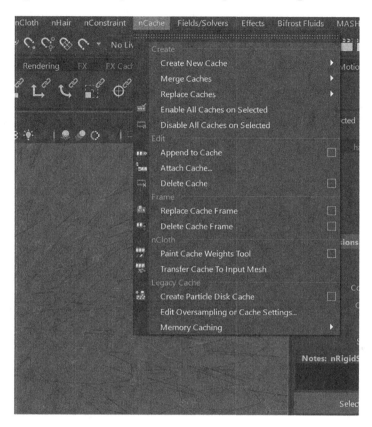

Figure 4-26. *The nCache drop-down menu in Maya*

Moving further, there are the fields and solvers. Within the particles, the attributes of air field, gravity, Newton, radial, and turbulence, as shown in Figure 4-27, play a significant role. In order to mold the particle system to specific directions, or to attract particles at certain times, the tire system and Newton both play an important role. In earlier versions of Maya, the rigid body simulations were individual parts within Maya. With the latest version of Maya 2019, these are integrated as *solvers*.

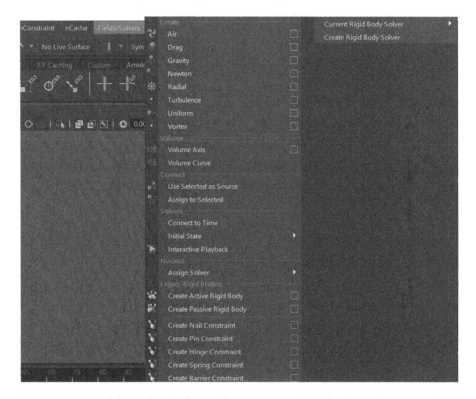

Figure 4-27. *The Fields/Solvers drop-down menu in Maya*

The Effects menu is shown in Figure 4-28. The Bifrost Fluids menu has commands specifically related to liquid simulations and water bodies. Maya's fluid system (see Figure 4-29) enables you to create oceans and open water effects and 2D and 3D fluid simulations, all of which can be integrated into other objects in the scene.

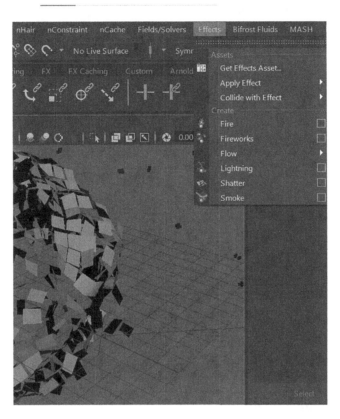

Figure 4-28. *Predefined effects menu in Maya*

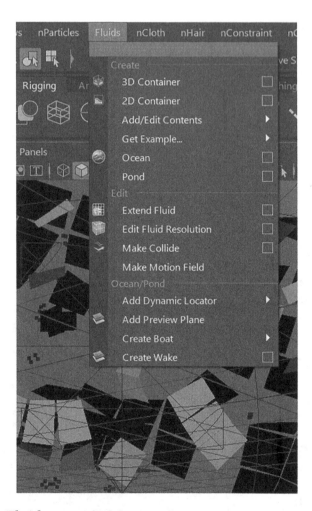

Figure 4-29. *The Fluids menu in Maya*

The chapter has so far covered a quick review of Maya's GUI and discussed the fundamental options in the FX system. The next section explains each of these one by one in detail with relevant examples that will help you create your own VFX simulations.

The Maya Nucleus System

Time to start unfolding the options available in the Maya Nucleus system and to explore them with examples. In the FX GUI of Maya, you choose nParticles to see its options. Figure 4-30 shows the Create Emitter command selected.

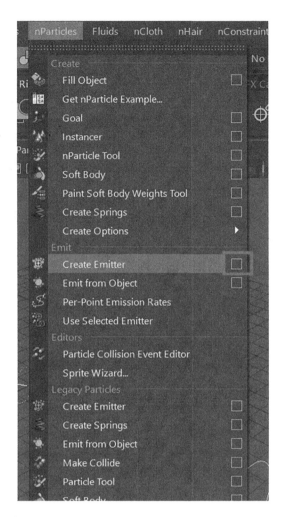

Figure 4-30. *nParticles: Create Emitter*

This command will enable you to create particles from a source. When you click this option, a window will pop up with a range of options, as shown in Figure 4-31.

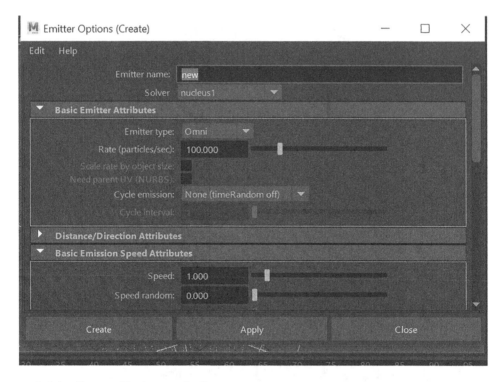

Figure 4-31. *Create Emitter window*

Starting from the top of this window, you need to provide an emitter name. This example uses source for the name. Below this is a solver option and the default is set to Create New Solver.

You can leave the rest of the attributes set to the default values and click Create, as indicated in Figure 4-32.

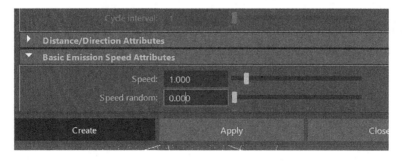

Figure 4-32. *Click Create in the Create Emitter window*

You can now see new nodes being added to the outliner window:

On the viewport, you can see the particle system that looks like an N with a gravity sign pointer on the viewport, as shown in Figure 4-33.

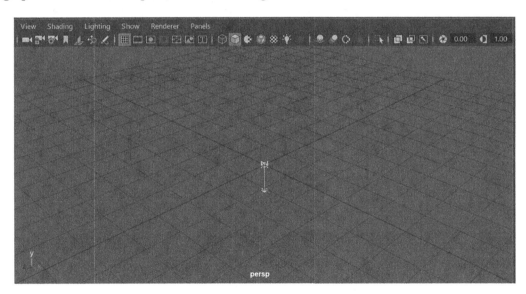

Figure 4-33. *nParticles created on the viewport*

You can select the object and use the Move tool to move it up on the y-axis (see Figure 4-34).

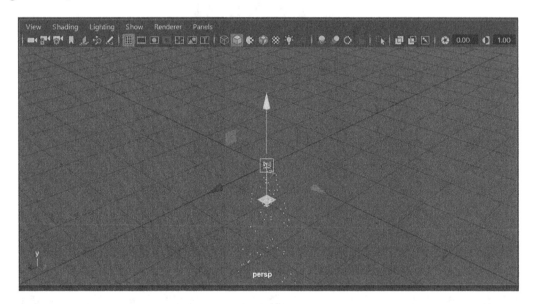

Figure 4-34. *nParticles transform tool for movement*

Click the Play button using the playback controls to see the simulation, as shown in Figure 4-35.

Figure 4-35. *nParticles default simulation*

Let's now check out the Nucleus system. The Nucleus system in dynamics helps simulate realistic animations in a faster and more efficient manner, which would be extremely tedious using the traditional animation technique. To enable the Nucleus attributes of the existing nParticles emitter you just created, you need to select the object on the viewport and then click the Nucleus tab in the Attribute Editor (see Figure 4-36). Or you can press Ctrl+A to open the option.

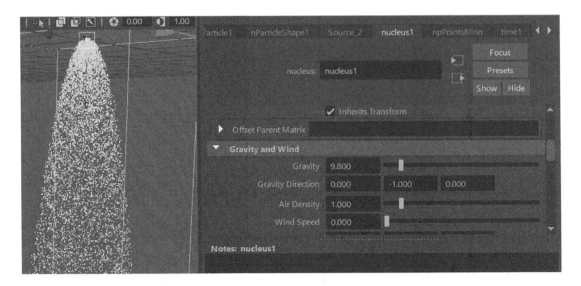

Figure 4-36. *nParticles nucleus system*

Using the dynamics system, you create primary motion, secondary motion, and hyper-realistic animations in a moment. However, for dynamics to function effectively, the system configuration plays a vital role. The Nucleus system within Maya was introduced in version 8.5 and is now available in all the latest versions of the software.

The Maya Nucleus system works like an independent solver that enables you to simulate your animations with more speed and efficiency. For example, if you are working out a cloth simulation, and you set the rigidity of the cloth to 100%, it will automatically react like a hard surface body, showing more rigidity.

I hope by now the foundations, the importance of nParticles, and the Maya Nucleus system are clear to you and I also hope it is clear why the Nucleus solver is such a powerful tool.

We are now going to explore in detail the Maya Nucleus system. Select the Nucleus from the outliner and press Ctrl+A to access the Attribute Editor, as shown in Figure 4-37. In the Focus section, you can see Nucleus 1 in the drop-down list.

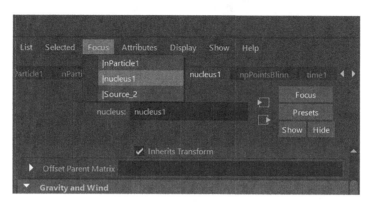

Figure 4-37. *The Nucleus system*

Upon clicking the nucleus node, the entire nucleus system along with the time, nParticles, and the nParticles shape tabs are loaded in the Attribute Editor. There are some default parameters, including Gravity, Gravity Directions, Air Density, Wind Speed, and Wind Direction. However, using the Fields/Solvers menu in Maya, you can add and manipulate dynamic properties like air, drag, and gravity. See Figure 4-38.

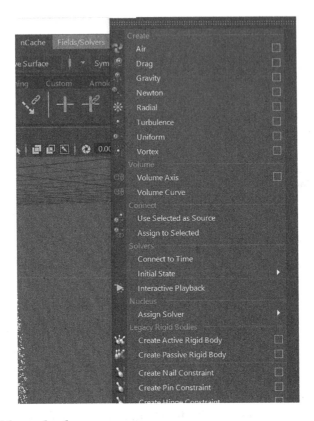

Figure 4-38. *Fields and solvers*

If you need the particles to fall down, gravity must be applied. If the direction of the particles needs to be altered, the air system must be added separately. If you are working with multiple nodes, it is best to use the Relationship Editor. You'll learn about the Relationship Editor and the Connection Editor later in this book.

For now, go back to the nParticles that you earlier created (in Figure 4-35) and check out the Nucleus system in it. Usually, when you press Play for this nParticles system, you see the simulation happening where the gravity is by default set to ground or downward. Additionally, you can see the simulation happening for a range of frames. It's important to note that before the playback, you need to set the range of your animation along with the speed of the simulation (i.e., 24fps or 25fps). The gravity field parameter is set to 9.800 by default, which pulls the particles toward the ground. Below this option are the gravity directions, where the X, Y, and Z axes are by default set to 0, -1, and 0 values, respectively, as shown in Figure 4-39.

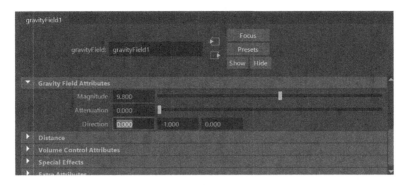

Figure 4-39. *Gravity direction parameters*

If you remove the negative value and change the y-axis to +1, you will observe the particles flowing in an upward direction, as shown in Figure 4-40.

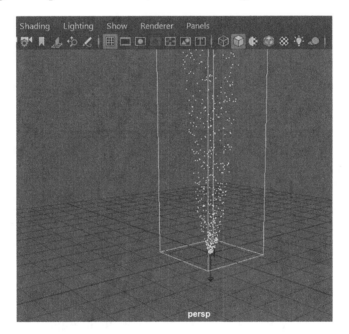

Figure 4-40. *Gravity direction for the y-axis set to +1*

Air density controls the spread of the particles, and wind speed controls the pace at which the particles flow. With the wind direction and its X, Y, and Z axes options, you can modify the path in which the particles flow, as illustrated in Figure 4-41.

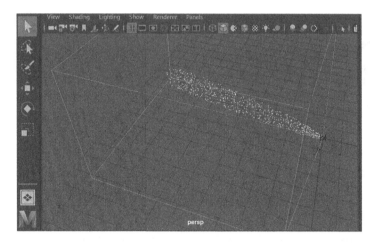

Figure 4-41. *Wind direction with +1 set for the x-axis, 0 set for the y-axis, and +1 set for the z-axis*

Now that you are familiar with these basic options, you can move to the Ground Plane section, where you can switch on the Use Plane checkbox, as shown in Figure 4-42. The Use Plane option makes the particles bounce off that surface so that there are no particles going through it. You can adjust the plane as per your requirements.

Figure 4-42. *The Ground Plane options*

Beneath the Use Plane option there are various plane options. You can bounce the particles, make them stick to the ground using the Particle Stickiness parameter, or even increase the friction of the particles with the ground plane (see Figure 4-43).

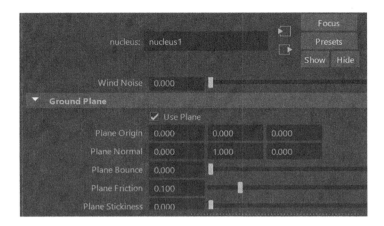

Figure 4-43. *Use Plane options*

If you want to, you can also hide the visibility of the Nucleus system in case you want to concentrate on the particle flow. you can uncheck its visibility, as shown in Figure 4-44.

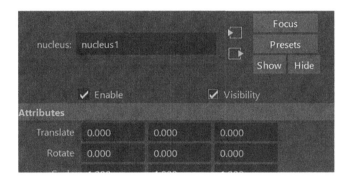

Figure 4-44. *Visibility toggle of the Nucleus system*

I hope the fundamentals of the Maya Nucleus system are now clear to you. This chapter covered how the Maya Nucleus system works, its properties, and why it's important. You should now be prepared to take up the journey of exploring the next chapter, which covers nParticles in Maya.

CHAPTER 5

Working with nParticle FX

In this chapter, you will be working with Maya's nParticles system. When you watch FX shots in films, you can see multiple dust particles or magical particles that simulate the necessary environment; these are all created with nParticles. Hence, familiarizing yourself nParticles tools will give you better insight into their use. To access nParticles, you need switch to FX mode, as shown in Figure 5-1.

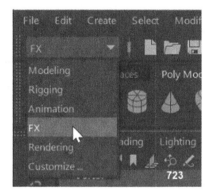

Figure 5-1. *Choose FX from the menu*

Fun with the Emitter

While working in Maya Dynamics, you need to go into Preferences and make sure that, in the Time Slider tab, the Playback speed is set to play every frame, the Playback By is set to 1, and the Max Playback Speed is set to Free. These options are shown in Figure 5-2.

© Abhishek Kumar 2022
A. Kumar, *Beginning VFX with Autodesk Maya*, https://doi.org/10.1007/978-1-4842-7857-4_5

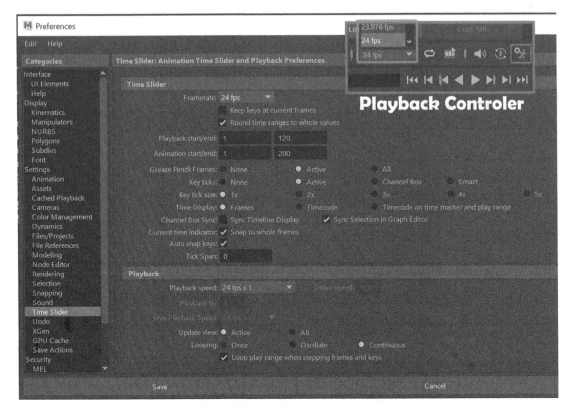

Figure 5-2. *The Preferences window in Maya*

This ensures that the dynamics are being calculated correctly for every frame that plays in the scene. Otherwise, you might find that it reacts differently. Let's look at the nParticles menu, where you can see all the various options to create nucleus particles. See Figure 5-3.

Figure 5-3. *The nParticles menu*

Let's start by emitting some particles and have them interact with objects in the scene, like a barrel and the floor, as shown in Figure 5-4.

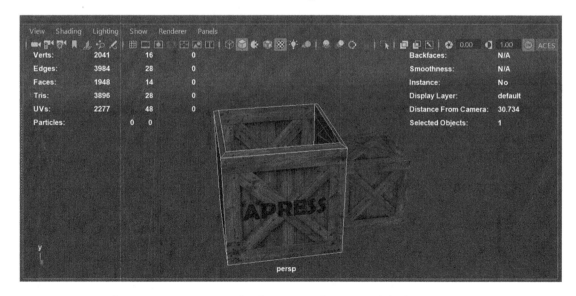

Figure 5-4. *The Maya scene to which nParticles are added*

Usually, when you add particles to your scene, you set the type before you add them, as shown in Figure 5-5. There are different types of particles, including Points, Balls, Cloud, Thick Cloud, and Water. These are simply different ways of rendering the particles for different behaviors. However, you can change the types at any point, even after you create the particles.

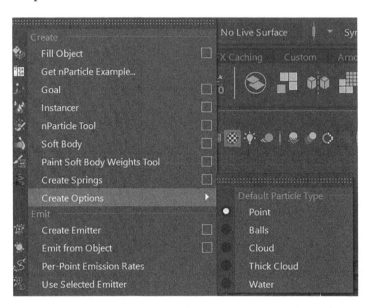

Figure 5-5. *Different types of particles*

This example leaves the type set to the default of Point. Choose Create Emitter to create an emitter. When you do so, three things are added to the Maya scene—the emitter, the nParticles object, which includes the transform node and the shape node, and the nucleus, as illustrated in Figure 5-6.

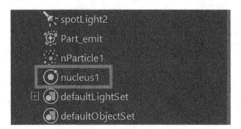

Figure 5-6. *The Nucleus node in Maya*

This nucleus is the solver for the dynamics in the scene, so if there are any additional particles added to the scene, they are tied to this nucleus solver by default. That includes any nCloth object or any nHair objects that might be created for the scene. You can add more than one nucleus solver to the scene and have different particles tied to different nucleus solvers. However, the usual flow is to keep one solver so that all the dynamics added to the scene interact with each other, but this might differ based on the situation.

Let's get started. First, you need to select the emitter from the Outline window and look at the Basic Emitter Attributes in the Attribute window. In this example, the Emitter Type is set to Volume by default, but other options like Directional, Omni, Surface, and Curve are available to choose from, as shown in Figure 5-7. This example uses Volume, but this can easily be changed at any point.

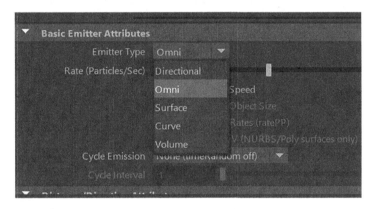

Figure 5-7. *Emitter type options in Maya*

Next, you will use the Move tool to move the emitter and place it above the barrel. Then set the Playback range to 1-100 frames and play it to observe the particle simulation. If you select nParticleShape1 from the Outliner and go to the Attribute Editor nParticles Shape node, you will find all the settings available for the particle, including Life Span, Particle Size, and Collisions, as shown in Figure 5-8.

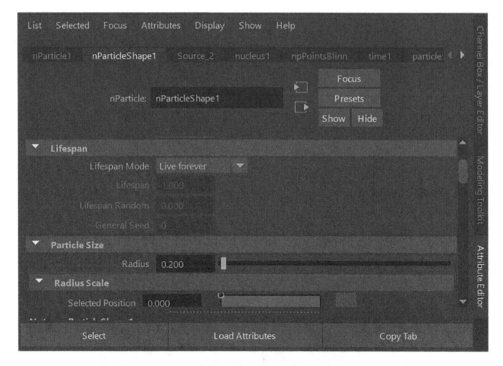

Figure 5-8. *The nParticlesShape1 options in the Attribute Editor*

For the example here, scroll down to the Shading option and decide what type of shading you want for your particles. This was initially set at Points which are just dots. You can change this to Multipoints, Multistreaks, Spheres, Spikes (spikes are like planes where you can attach a texture to make complex looks), Clouds, and so on, as shown in Figure 5-9.

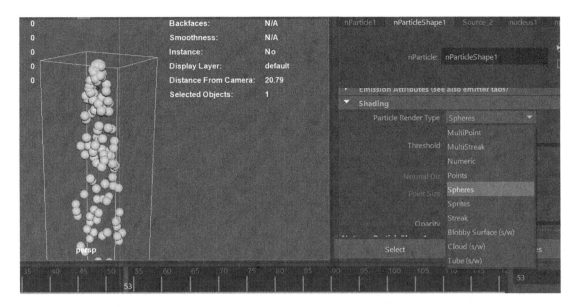

Figure 5-9. *The nParticleShape Shading options in the Attribute Editor*

For the purposes here, you will work with the Sphere and learn how to make the particles interact with other surfaces. If you play the simulation, you will find that, due to the default gravity, the particles fall down and penetrate through the barrel and through the floor beneath, as shown in Figure 5-10.

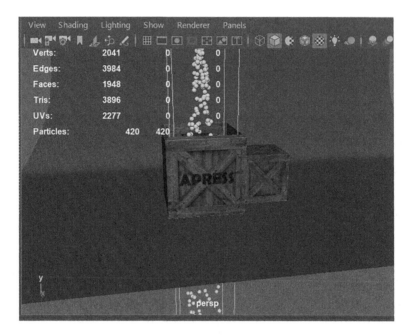

Figure 5-10. *Gravity option in the Attribute Editor of the Nucleus solver*

Gravity is controlled through the Nucleus solver, so you need to select Nucleus from the Outliner and then move to the Attribute Editor. From the Gravity and Wind option, you can adjust the gravity option. If you set it to -1, gravity goes in the opposite direction and the particles start to flow up.

Then of course you have other parameters like the Gravity Direction, Wind Speed, Air Density, and so on. As you can see, there are some dynamics built into the nucleus to control the particles. For the purposes here, we will set the air density to 1, the wind speed to 0, and the wind noise to 0. Now check out the collisions. For this, you need to select the barrel geometry and then choose Create Passive Collider from the nCloth menu, as shown in Figure 5-11. This automatically ties the barrel geometry to the nucleus solver.

Figure 5-11. *The nCloth Create Passive Collider option*

If you now play the simulation, you can see that the particles start to accumulate at the bottom of the barrel, as shown in Figure 5-12. There are no self-collisions among the particles, so they all fall on top of each other.

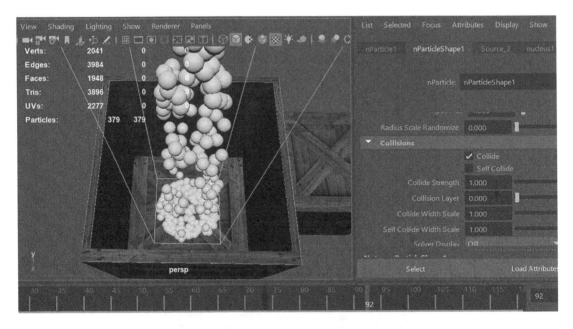

Figure 5-12. *No self-collision of particles*

If you select nParticles 1 from the Outliner and go into Collisions in the Attribute Editor and turn on Self-Collide, as shown in Figure 5-13, you can see the particles start colliding with each other and fill up the barrel.

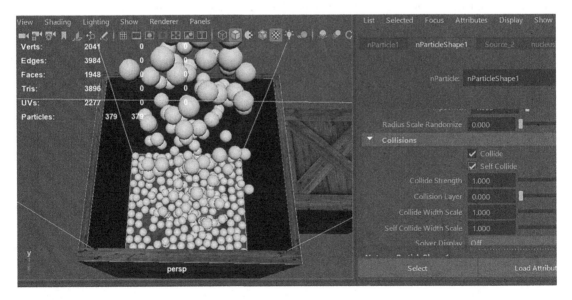

Figure 5-13. *Self-collision of particles is on*

Furthermore, you can work out the collision's thickness by turning the solver display from the default off state to the collision thickness. Then if you start modifying the scale values (for example, set it to a value of 2), there appears to be a cage around each of these particles, which determines how thick they are with regard to the colliding surfaces. See Figure 5-14.

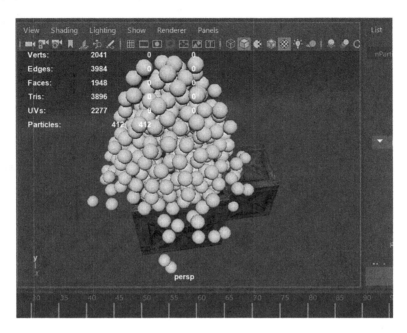

Figure 5-14. *Collision thickness set to a scale value of 2*

You can also work with the self-collision thickness and modify the scale values of the self-collision thickness to see how thick they are before colliding with each other. The self-collision thickness scale value is more like a multiplier. So, these two different levels can be tried in various permutations to get desired results.

If you want the particles to bounce off the surface as well, you need to select the floor geometry and follow the same steps. Go to the nCloth menu and select Create Passive Collider. The result is shown in Figure 5-15.

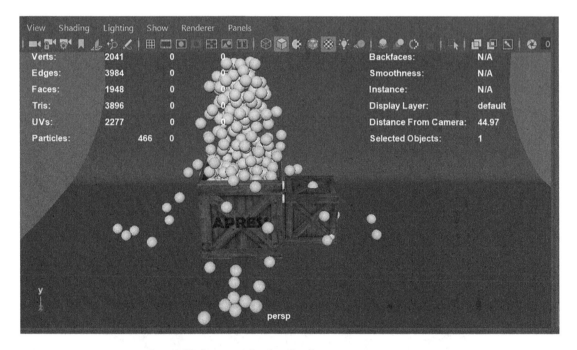

Figure 5-15. *Particles colliding with the floor*

nParticles have their own ground friction and stickiness. If you increase the
stickiness, the particles will stick to the surface.

Using the nParticles Tool and Instancer

Once you are in the FX layout, you can choose the nParticles menu to see its various
options, as shown in Figure 5-16.

Figure 5-16. *The nParticles menu*

We start exploring the nParticles tool from this menu. The nParticles tool shows the Tool Settings window shown in Figure 5-17. One important point to remember is that you must always click the Reset tool to ensure that there are no presets applied.

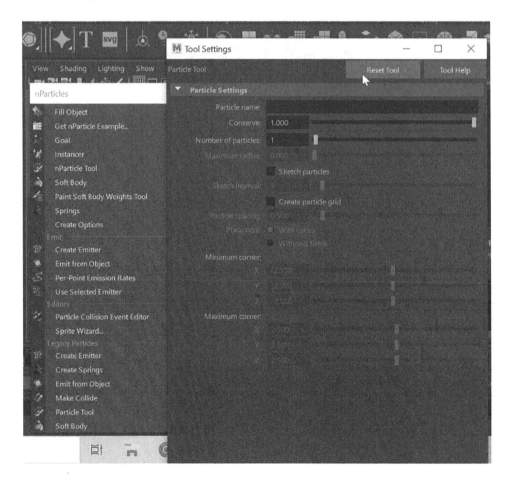

Figure 5-17. *nParticles tool settings*

Let's now explore some of these options in the tool settings. As you can see in Figure 5-18, Particle Settings shows the particle name and the number of particles.

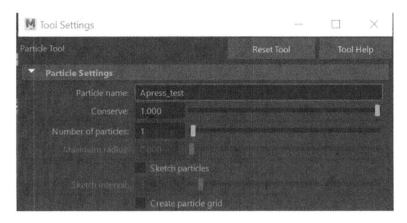

Figure 5-18. *nParticles tool settings*

When you click the viewport using these settings, it will create single particles. If you scroll below on the properties, you will find the Sketch Particles checkbox. With this option selected, you can click and drag a path on the viewport, which will create a trail of particles, as shown in Figure 5-19. This option comes with a submenu called Sketch Interval. If you increase this value, it will increase the interval between the particles.

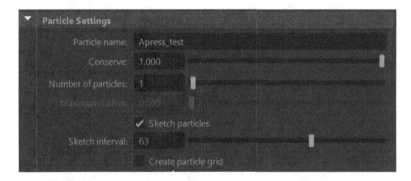

Figure 5-19. *The Sketch Particles option in the nParticles tool settings*

Your other option is to draw particles on the grid. To do this, you need to select the Create Particle Grid option, as shown in Figure 5-20.

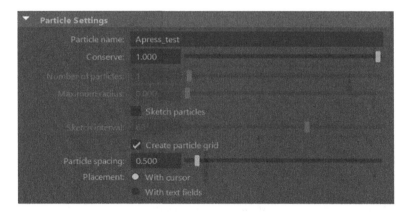

Figure 5-20. *The Create Particle Grid option from the nParticles settings*

These options create the output shown in Figure 5-21.

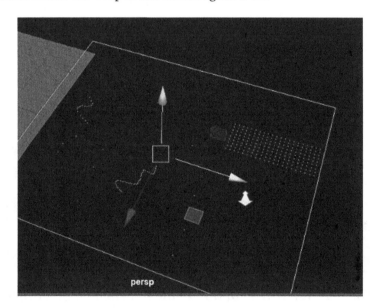

Figure 5-21. *View from the viewport*

Now let's explore the Instancer option, as shown in Figure 5-22. This example uses a model of a basketball.

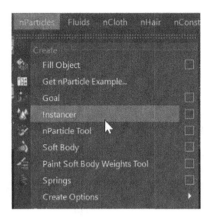

Figure 5-22. *The Instancer command*

To create the instances of the ball and assign it to the particles, you need to create the particles. Select the particles from the Outliner. Then select the Instancer from the nParticles menu, which will show the Particle Instancer Options window, as shown in Figure 5-23.

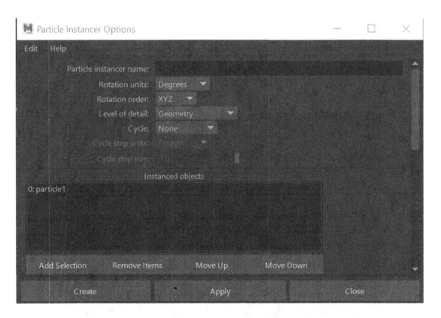

Figure 5-23. *Particle Instancer Options window*

From the Instancer Option section, select the ball in the viewport and then choose Add Selection, as shown in Figure 5-24.

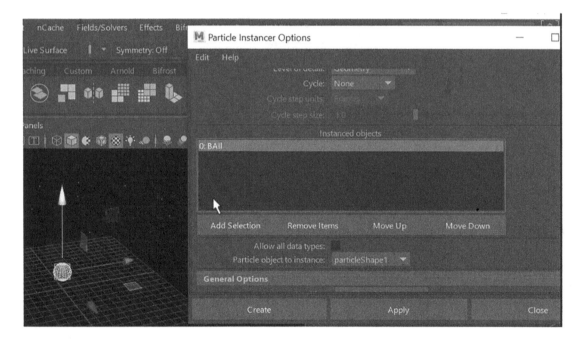

Figure 5-24. *The Instancer options*

This will add the ball into the Instancer Object window. After this, you just need to click the Create button and you will be able to see the ball placed where you created the particles. See Figure 5-25.

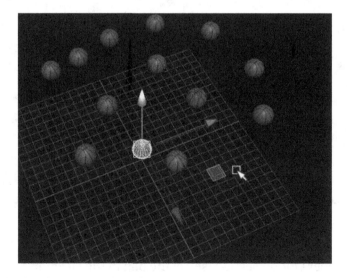

Figure 5-25. *The ball instance has been created*

You can make any changes to the properties of the main ball, which is now acting like the master particle. It affects all the instances at the same time. This is the benefit of using the Instancer.

If you want to add motion or simulation to these instanced particles, you can apply the various forces found on the Fields/Solvers menu. However, do not tamper with the main ball. To do this, you can assign a Display layer, add the main ball to that layer, and then switch off the visibility of the layer so that you don't affect the ball accidentally.

To address the simulation of the instanced balls, select Gravity from the Fields/Solvers drop-down menu, as shown in Figure 5-26. If you play the simulation, you will see that the ball falls downward.

Figure 5-26.   *Applying gravity to the particles*

To make these particles bounce against a surface, you first need to create a surface and then make the particles collide with it. The following section explains this process.

To create a colliding surface, just select a cube and create a fairly large surface below the balls, as shown in Figure 5-27.

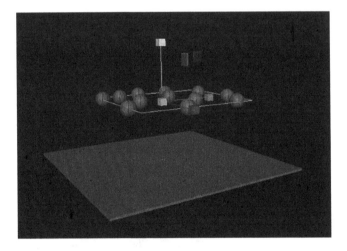

Figure 5-27. *Creating a surface for collision of particles (balls)*

To make the particles collide with the surface, you need to select the surface and the particles, and then go to the nParticles menu and choose Make Collide, as shown in Figure 5-28. Now if you play the simulation, you will see that the particles bounce against the surface.

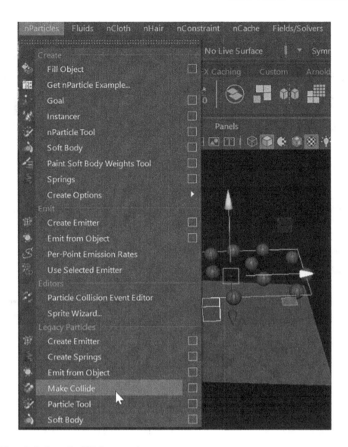

Figure 5-28. *The Make Collide option*

However, if you want to check the simulation better, you can tilt the surface and play the simulation to see the result. See Figure 5-29.

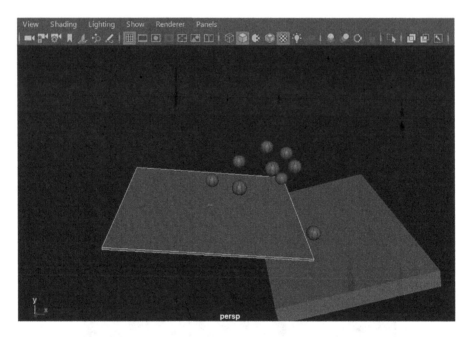

Figure 5-29. *Ball simulation*

You can see these kinds of particles in action in the film *Cloudy with a Chance of Meatballs,* where it rained hamburgers and pizza. Such effects can be achieved using instancing. Several ads also use similar effects where there is the need to create identical objects. With the Particle Instancing option, it is much easier to achieve these kinds of FX. Other examples of creating identical objects in scenes are when you need to create multiple street lights or multiple trees in a forest scene. Having to create each object separately is not only difficult but also render-heavy and scene-heavy. In such cases, using instancing is very effective.

The next chapter covers the effects and simulation of particles in detail, using the field and solvers. You learn how to create galaxy effects and real-life rain simulation effects.

CHAPTER 6

Creating Effects with Particle Emissions and Fields/Solvers

Maya's nParticles system is a simple and powerful simulation system. It is used to generate a wide range of amazing effects. Particles can be used to emulate real-life effects such as dust, sand, rain, snow, smoke, and ash, as well as create magical and energy-based effects. The best and simplest way to achieve realism with dust, snow, ash and more is to use particles.

This chapter discusses the particles and fields needed to create real-life dynamic effects. For example, you'll see how to simulate rain using solvers and fields. The chapter also covers galaxy formation and particle FX scene development.

Real-Life FX Simulations with Solvers and Fields

Real-life simulations can be used to mimic effects such as falling rain, smoke coming out of a chimney, and so on. To understand and create real-life simulations with solvers and fields, you first need to learn how to simulate a rain effect with the help of nParticles. See Figure 6-1.

© Abhishek Kumar 2022
A. Kumar, *Beginning VFX with Autodesk Maya*, https://doi.org/10.1007/978-1-4842-7857-4_6

Figure 6-1. *Real-life CGI rain FX*

The scene is created with three elements, as shown in Figure 6-2:

- The cloud plane: The plane where the rain effect starts

- The base plane: The plane where the umbrella stands; also considered the ground plane

- The umbrella

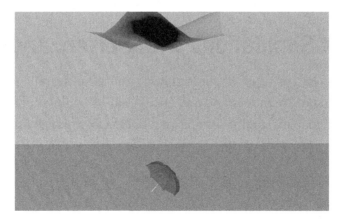

Figure 6-2. *Scene setup for the rain simulation*

The scene that you need to simulate is one in which rain is pouring down and colliding against the umbrella and against the ground plane, where the rain particles split into multiple particles. Additionally, the particles should bounce off of the umbrella and the ground plane.

If you observe the real-life scenario, you will find that when it rains, raindrops collide with surfaces and then dissipate or scatter into multiple parts. This is the effect that we aim to achieve in this section.

Start by creating the scene elements. When the scene model is ready, the scene elements need to be managed properly through the help of the Display Layer management system. You need to rename those layers appropriately, as shown in Figure 6-3.

Figure 6-3. *Layer management*

To create the rain effect, you can also use legacy particles. Go to the nParticles menu and locate the Legacy Particles area. Find the Emit from Object option, as shown in Figure 6-4. Check its option box and select the Cloud plane.

Figure 6-4. *Using a legacy particle*

A new window titled Emitter Options (Emit from Object) will pop up, where you need to set the attributes. Name the emitter cloud in this example and choose Surface for the Emitter Type. Click Create, as shown in Figure 6-5.

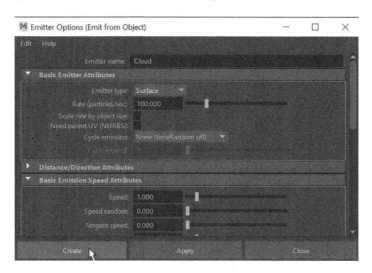

Figure 6-5. *The Emitter Option window*

After you click the Play button, the particles will start emitting. However, the raindrops need to fall toward the ground. This is a problem because you haven't set a gravitational force yet. In real-life simulations, the gravitational force is present by default and hence the particles fall toward the Earth automatically. To drag these particles down, you need to apply a gravitational force. The Gravity option is found on the Fields/Solvers tab, as shown in Figure 6-6.

Figure 6-6. *The Gravity option on the Fields/Solvers tabs*

When you apply a gravitational force, the particles will flow down toward the umbrella and ground plane, thus abiding by the law of gravity, as shown in Figure 6-7.

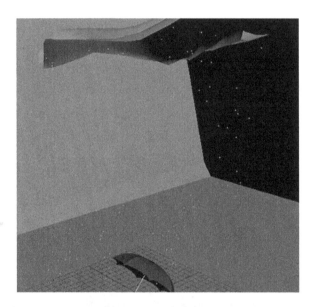

Figure 6-7. *Particle emission*

To affect the gravity value and the manner in which the gravity force works in Maya, you need to select gravityField1 from the Outliner window and press Ctrl+A. This opens the Attribute Editor, where you can adjust the emitter values.

The default magnitude value of the Gravity field is 9.800, as per Newton's Law. The direction value in the x-axis is 0.000, the y-axis is -1.000, and the z-axis is 0.000. Although the magnitude value is a positive 9.800, the particles fall down because of the directional y-axis being negative, as shown in Figure 6-8.

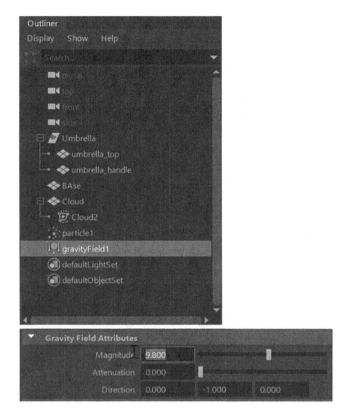

Figure 6-8. *Gravity field attributes*

If you play the simulation, you will be able to see the particle animation, but it may not give you the feel of rain. This is because the Particle Shape Type is set as a Point Particle. To create proper rain particles, the shape needs to be changed. To do this, select the particle shape (particle1) from the Outliner and click particleShape1 from the Attribute Editor. Change the Particle Render Type to Streak Particle. From the Render Attributes tab, set the Streak Particle as the Current Render Type, as shown in Figure 6-9.

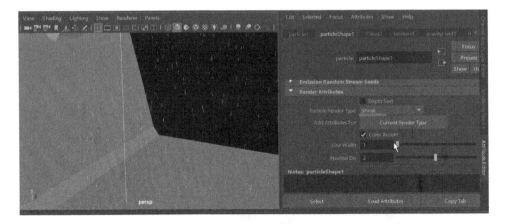

Figure 6-9. *Render Attributes tab*

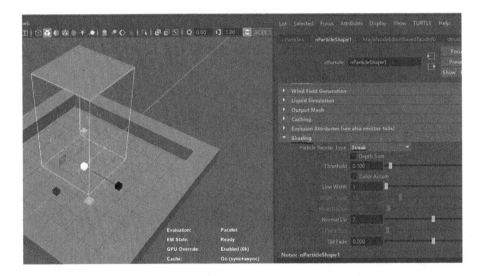

In the particleShape1 render attribute, there are many attributes you can use to achieve a realistic rain look, such as Color Accum, Line Width, Normal Dir, Tail Fade, Tail Size, and so on. These values can be adjusted according to your needs. The result, after changing the shape from point to streaks, is shown in Figure 6-10.

Figure 6-10. *Particle shape changed from point to streaks*

When it rains in real life, there is also often an element of wind. We don't typically see rain descend absolutely perpendicular to the ground. To achieve this look and feel, you need to apply some external force, such as an air field.

Just as you applied gravity in the previous section, you'll apply an air field in this section. In Maya, there are three air options—Wind, Wake, and Fan—as shown in Figure 6-11. Hence, you need to reset the air field and apply the default wind option.

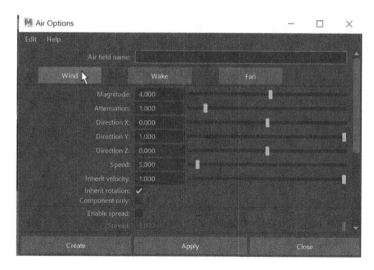

Figure 6-11. *The Air Field option window*

Air fields also have a similar kind of attribute that gravity fields have, as shown in Figure 6-12. The wind speed, flow, direction, and magnitude can be controlled according your needs.

117

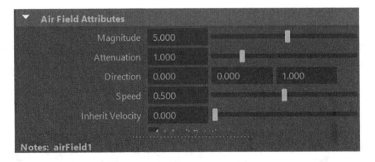

Figure 6-12. *The Air Field Attributes tab*

After adding the air field, the particles start acting against the wind force. But when it rains heavily, rain particles pouring toward the ground follow the wind direction along with some randomness in the droplets. To achieve this realistic look and feel, you need to add turbulence to the scene.

The Turbulence Field Attributes tab is shown in Figure 6-13. Note its attributes such as Magnitude, Attenuation, Frequency, Phase, Interpolation Type, and Noise Level.

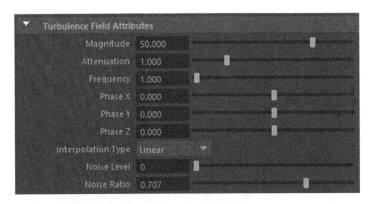

Figure 6-13. *Turbulence Field Attributes tab*

After you adjust all these attributes, particles will start acting more like real raindrops, as shown in Figure 6-14.

Figure 6-14. *Rain falling output*

After fixing the rain and adjusting its look and feel, you now need the raindrops to interact with the umbrella and as the ground plane. The raindrops should not pass through either surface. To fix that issue, the particle system needs to be selected along with the ground plane. Then you choose the Make Collide option from the nParticles menu, as shown in Figure 6-15.

Figure 6-15. *The Make Collide option*

When ground plane collision is set, the particles will not pass through the plane, rather they will bounce off it. To control their bounciness, select the ground plane, go to the geoConnector2 node attribute, and change the Resilience and Friction values, as shown in Figure 6-16. You can make these changes from the Channel Box or the Layer Editor.

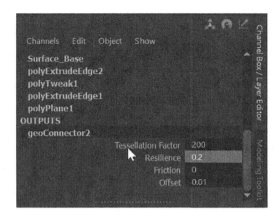

Figure 6-16. *GeoConnector options*

The particles also need to collide with the umbrella surface, albeit slightly differently. The geoConnector attribute can react differently according to different material surfaces.

When raindrops hit any surface, they split into many small droplets. For that action, a new event is required on top of those rain particles. You need to choose the Particle Collision Event Editor from the nParticles menu, as shown in Figure 6-17.

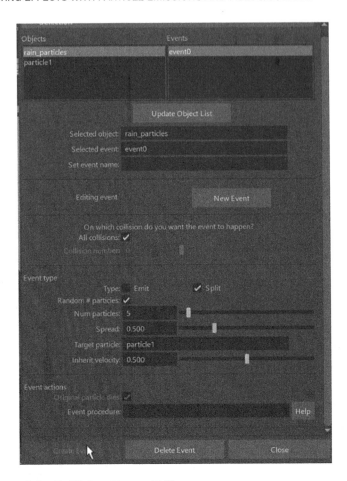

Figure 6-17. *Particle Collision Event Editor*

A new dashboard will open where all the attributes can be manipulated according to your needs. In this case, all collision events should happen. Thus, all the collide options need to be checked manually. The other option is that, when a particle hits a surface, a new particle will split or emit. In this exercise, the particles need to split into a random number of particles. After setting all these values per your needs, you can click the Create Event option, as illustrated in Figure 6-17.

When a new event is created, new particles are added to the Outliner. By default the particle shape will be a Point Particle. Hence, you have to change it to a Streak Particle from the Render Type Particle option in the Particle Shape Attribute tab. You also have to adjust the line width, tail fade, and tail size.

The new particle is not connected to the gravity solvers, so those particles will try to move upward, according to the default value mentioned earlier. Instead of creating new gravity forces, the previously created gravity force can be connected by choosing Windows ➤ Relationship Editors ➤ Dynamic Relationship Editor, as shown in Figure 6-18. A new window will open where you need to simply click the particles from the left side and from the right-side gravity field and the program will connect them automatically, as shown in Figure 6-18.

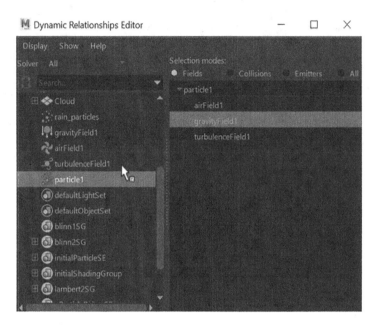

Figure 6-18. *Dynamic Relationship Editor window*

You also have to set the gravity for these new particles. Additionally, from the Channel Box, the geoConnector attributes need to change according to your requirements. These are the simple steps needed to create realistic raindrops with the help of nParticles and the Solver.

Creating Galaxy and Particle-Based Effects

A *galaxy* is a huge collection of dust, gas, and stars that are held together by gravity. In this section, you learn how to achieve the look and feel of a galaxy. In a simple way, a galaxy system can be created using an Emitter system and the Vortex Solver, as shown in Figure 6-19.

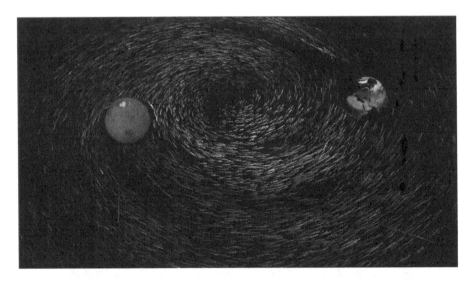

Figure 6-19. *Galaxy system*

To create a galaxy system, you need to create and scale a base plane according to your needs, with appropriate naming conventions such as Galaxy Base. You can use ALT+B to change the color of the viewport, as per the convenience of the user. Be sure that the history has been cleared by choosing Edit ➤ Delete by Type ➤ History, as shown in Figure 6-20. Also, it's best to choose the Modify ➤ Freeze Transformation option and set all values to 0.0.

Figure 6-20. *Delete by Type history*

Similar to the previous example, you use the nParticles system here too, but will not use legacy particles. Select the plane, open the nParticles tab, and select the Emit from Object option. Emit from Object needs to be reset from its option box first. The Emitter type, which is set to Omni, needs to be changed to Surface, as shown in Figure 6-21. The Particle Rate needs to be increased and the basic emission speed attributes can be adjusted. When you have set all these options to your liking, click the Create button.

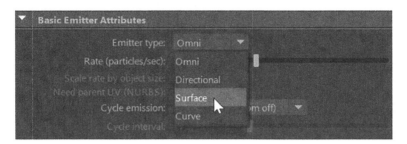

Figure 6-21. *Emitter types*

After creating an emitter system, the particle system will be falling down by default because a nucleus system has been applied. To switch off the gravitational force, open the Nucleus tab from the Attribute Editor and reduce the gravity value and the gravity direction values all to 0, as shown in Figure 6-22.

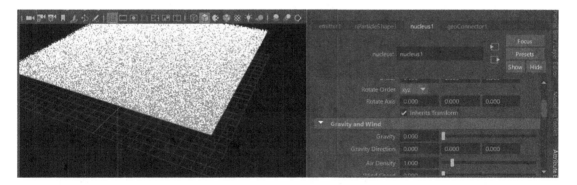

Figure 6-22. *Zero gravity*

As explained in the previous example, you need to change the particle shape from Point to Streak Particle, as shown in Figure 6-23. Choose nparticleShape1 ➤ Shading ➤ Particle Render Type from the Attribute Editor. You can also adjust the size and fade options per your needs.

Figure 6-23. *Particle Render type*

You now need to add color to the particle. This process can be done from the attribute menu bar using the Per Particle (Array) attribute, but that is a long process whereby every particle needs to be changed with the help of coding. So, this section introduces color to the particles through the texture emission of the galaxy plane. This can be achieved in a few steps. These options are Add Dynamic Attributes tab (shown in Figure 6-24) and the Visit Color option.

Figure 6-24. *Dynamic Attributes tab*

A tab will open showing the Add Per Particle Attribute and Shader options, as shown in Figure 6-25. Galaxy is a multi-color system so every particle will have a different Color attribute. In this scenario, the Add Per Particle Attribute option needs to be checked.

Figure 6-25. *The Add Per Particle Attribute checkbox*

After that, you need to visit the Emitter tab and open the Texture Emission Attributes (NURBS/Poly Surfaces Only) tab. Under this tab, the Particle Option checkbox needs to be clicked, as shown in Figure 6-26.

Figure 6-26. *Texture emission attributes used to change the particle color*

This will trigger a new tab called Create Render Node. Choose the File option, as shown in Figure 6-26. The galaxy texture can be added as a 2D file, as shown in Figure 6-27, or you can add any other similar texture according to your needs.

Figure 6-27. *Galaxy textures (Source: https://pixabay.com/)*

After choosing the texture map, you need to check the Inherit Color box, as shown in Figure 6-28, so that the particle will emit through all colors except black. The galaxy base plane should be hidden to see the particles clearly.

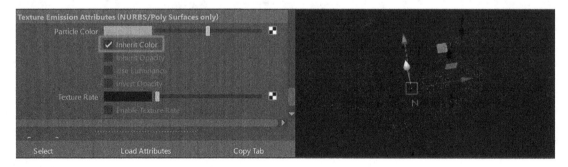

Figure 6-28. *The Inherit Color option*

Particles are reacting according to the galaxy texture, but the texture emission is not working. To see a particle's color, that same galaxy texture map needs to be added inside the Texture Rate, as shown in Figure 6-29. Texture Rate can be used with the emitter to generate more particles on the brighter part of the texture and fewer particles on the darker part.

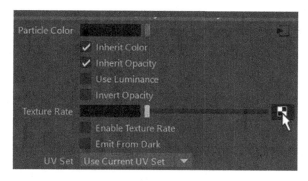

Figure 6-29.   *Texture Rate attribute color/map*

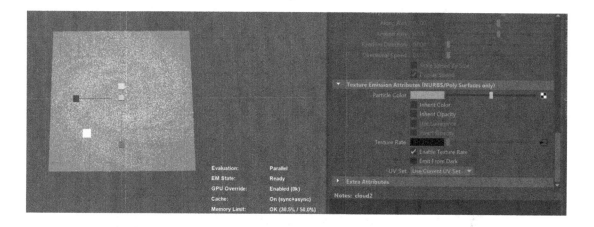

To achieve a more beautiful and more accurate color, you need to activate Depth Sort and Color Accum by choosing nParticleShape ➤ Shading tab, as shown in Figure 6-30.

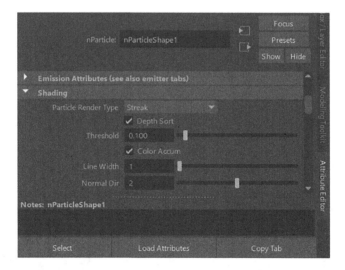

Figure 6-30. *The Shading tab*

A more realistic galaxy color and shade can be achieved by further adjusting the shading parameters.

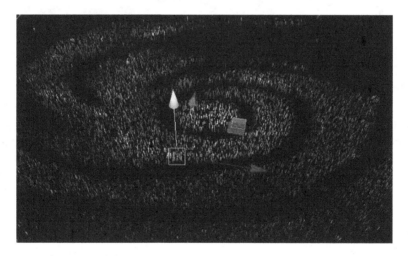

Figure 6-31. *Galaxy system pre look*

Once the galaxy look has been achieved, the particles need some rotation. To rotate the particles, Maya Dynamic has introduced the Vortex option, found on the Fields/ Solvers menu, as shown in Figure 6-32.

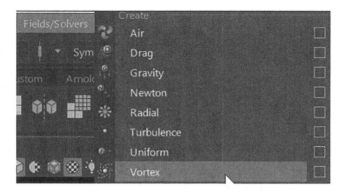

Figure 6-32. *The Vortex field*

When a vortex force is applied to a particle, it starts rotating exactly the same as the galaxy, as seen in Figure 6-33.

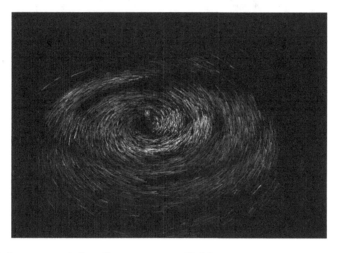

Figure 6-33. *Galaxy particle after a vortex field*

Inside the galaxy there will be some planets. Let's create those and determine how the planets will interact with the particles. This example uses Mars and Earth in a simple form of spheres and then applies a texture map. Properly name each and every element that's used, as shown in Figure 6-34.

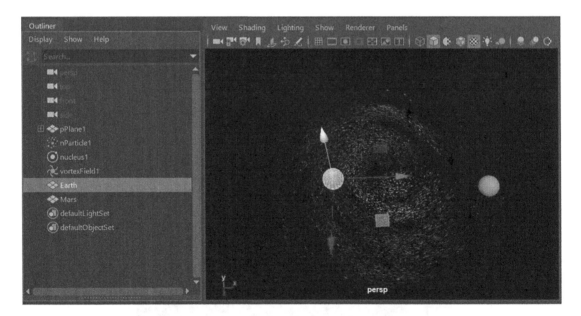

Figure 6-34. *A galaxy with Earth and Mars planet 3D model*

On top of those spheres, you need to add textures. Select the object and then MMB ➤ Assign New Material ➤ Lambert, as shown in Figure 6-35.

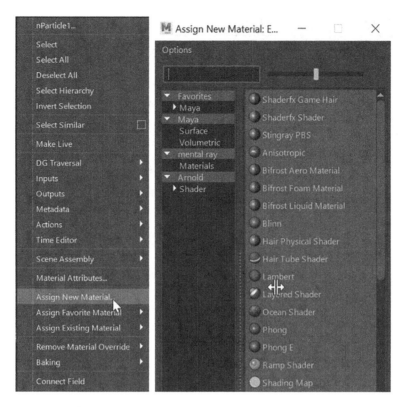

Figure 6-35. *Material projection assignment on planet 3D models*

The texture map needs to be assigned with the Lambert material. For a realistic Earth and Mars texture, you can get reference files from Google Images. A simple texture file can be added using the Attribute Editor. Choose Lambert ➤ Common Material Attribute ➤ Color Option Box ➤ Create Render Node ➤ File ➤ Choose Image, as illustrated in Figure 6-36.

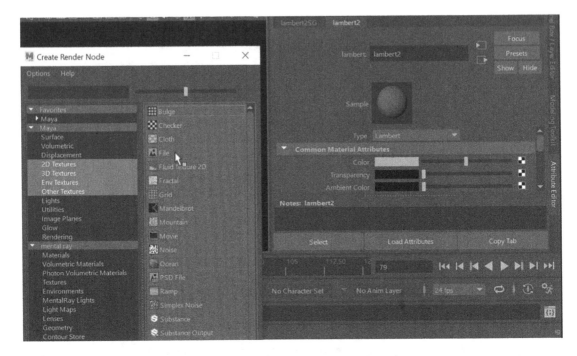

Figure 6-36. *Assigning a 2D texture map*

The texture projection output is shown in Figure 6-37.

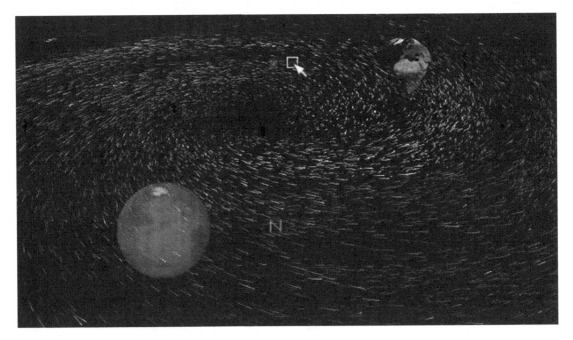

Figure 6-37. *Mars and Earth map on a 3D model*

The particle is not currently interacting with the planet; it is passing through the planet. To fix this issue, the planet mesh needs to collide with particles. You need to select the mesh of those planets and convert them into a passive collider. Selected Mesh ➤ nCloth ➤ Create Passive Collider, as shown in Figure 6-38.

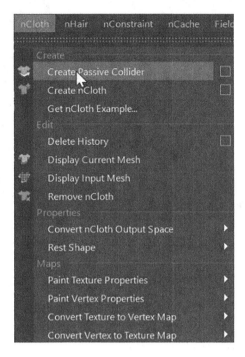

Figure 6-38. *The Create Passive Collider option*

Now the particle will start interacting with the planet, which makes it look more realistic, as shown in Figure 6-39.

Figure 6-39. *Galaxy simulation effects*

The particle is reacting with the planet according to its default rigid value. These rigid attributes can be adjusted by selecting the Nucleus node from the Outliner and going to the Channel Box. From the Input tab, you'll see Bounce, Friction, Damp, Stickiness, and so on, as shown in Figure 6-40.

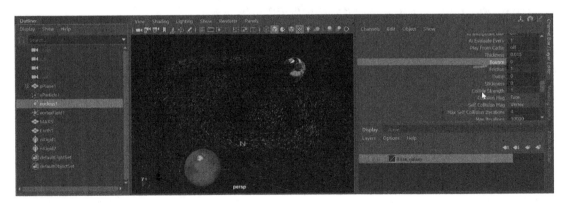

Figure 6-40. *Modifying the Nucleus attributes*

After adjusting all the rigid values, the scene in Figure 6-41 can be rendered. But the Streak Particle has been used here, so try to render this with Maya hardware 2.0 as a render engine instead of using the Maya software render.

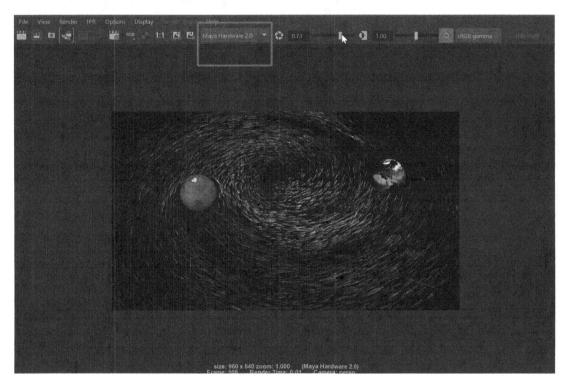

Figure 6-41. *Galaxy FX rendered with the Maya hardware render engine*

By following these steps, you can create many other magical effects, as shown in Figure 6-42. This is done using just the applied physics properties (Air, Drag, Gravity, Newton, Radial, Turbulence, Uniform) and adjusting Maya's dynamic properties.

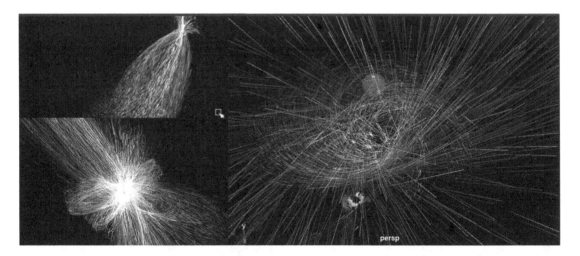

Figure 6-42. *Particle-based magical effects*

Figure 6-42 shows a small example of a magical effect over the galaxy effect. It was created using a Newton field and adjusting its attributes. In the next chapter, you learn about rigid body dynamics.

CHAPTER 7

Maya's Rigid and Soft Body Systems

This chapter unveils the power of realistic animation using Maya's rigid and soft body dynamics. You will explore the rigid body dynamics and soft body dynamics systems using dominoes and a curtain example, followed by rigid and soft body constraints in Maya.

Introduction to Rigid Bodies

The previous versions of Maya placed the legacy rigid bodies in the Fields/Solvers menu. This menu contains the Active Rigid Body and Passive Rigid Body options, which are the traditional rigid body systems, as shown in Figure 7-1.

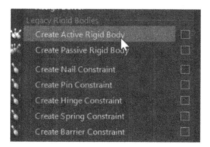

Figure 7-1. *Traditional legacy rigid bodies*

© Abhishek Kumar 2022

A. Kumar, *Beginning VFX with Autodesk Maya*, https://doi.org/10.1007/978-1-4842-7857-4_7

The new-generation rigid body simulations are known as Bullet solvers. They are available in the menu bar, as shown in Figure 7-2.

Figure 7-2. *Bullet solver menu*

If the Bullet menu option is not visible in the menu bar, choose the Windows menu, then scroll to Settings/Preferences ➤ Plug-In Manager, as shown in Figure 7-3.

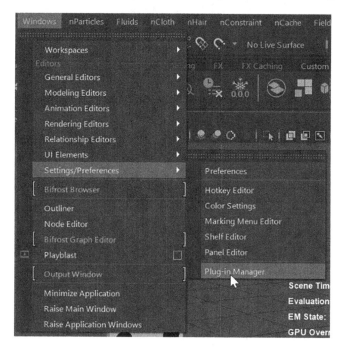

Figure 7-3. *The Plug-in Manager option*

The Plug-In Manager will open a window. Type **bullet** in the search bar to see the Abcbullet.mll and bullet.mll options. Select both checkboxes for the Loaded and Auto Load options, as shown in Figure 7-4. This will activate the Bullet menu and show it in the menu bar the next time you load Maya. Simply click Refresh and close the window.

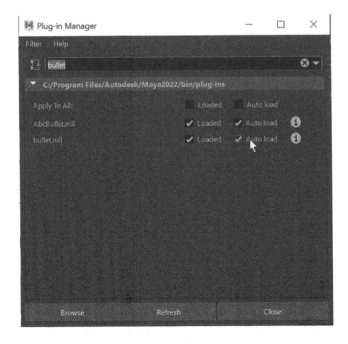

Figure 7-4. *The Bullet solver menu activation*

This Bullet solver has multiple options that enable you to create various complicated simulations in substantially less time. Simulations like the dominoes can be created fairly quickly using the Bullet options, which would otherwise be rather time-consuming if each domino had to be created manually.

To explore the basic features of the Bullet menu, start with a simple sphere and apply a ball texture to it, as shown in Figure 7-5.

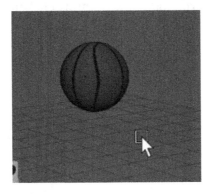

Figure 7-5. *A sphere with the texture of a ball*

Now convert this ball to an active rigid body by selecting the option from the Bullet menu, as shown in Figure 7-6.

Figure 7-6. *Select the ball and choose the Active Rigid Body option*

The Active Rigid Body option will show another window, where you need to select Sphere from the Collider Shape Type option. From the drop-down menu, select Dynamic Rigid Body. The Bullet dynamics system uses a bounding box as a collision shape for all meshes by default. Users have to identify and select the correct colliding shape based on the shape of the object. The ball becomes a dynamic rigid body, as shown in Figure 7-7.

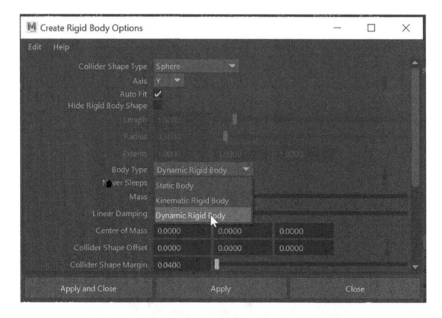

Figure 7-7. *Dynamic Rigid Body type to be selected for the ball*

Let's pause here and look more closely at the three basic rigid body types:

- ✓ Dynamic Rigid Body is a fully simulated physics-based object.

- ✓ Kinematic Rigid Body can be animated during the physics simulation.

- ✓ Static Rigid Body will not move during the physical simulation. This is good for surfaces, which will usually not move during a simulation.

The ball has been converted into an active rigid body. You now need a surface against which the ball will collide. This surface ideally should be a static rigid body, as shown in Figure 7-9. First align a surface beneath the ball, as shown in Figure 7-8.

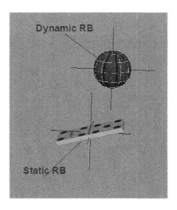

Figure 7-8. *A surface below the ball*

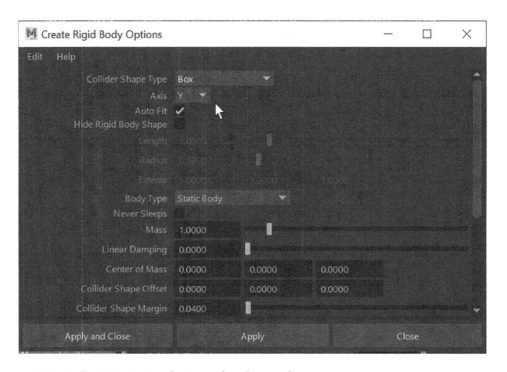

Figure 7-9. *Select Static Body Type for the surface*

Upon simulation, you will see that the ball hits this static rigid body and rolls over with absolutely no interaction with the surface, which has been set as a static rigid body.

To see the kinetic rigid body type in action, create another surface plane and convert it to a kinetic rigid body using the options shown in Figure 7-10. Animate its position over time by creating two keyframes, as shown in Figure 7-11.

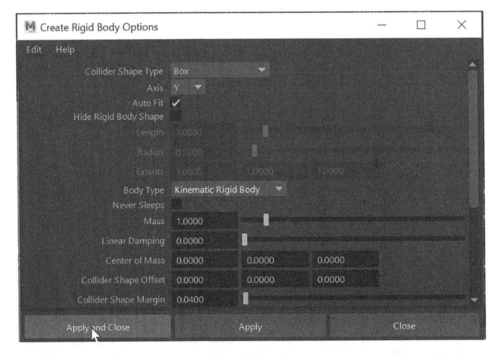

Figure 7-10. *Choose Kinetic Rigid Body Type for the second surface*

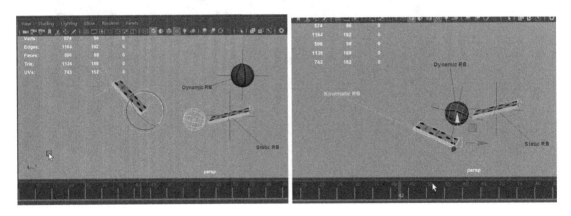

Figure 7-11. *Keyframes set at the 25th and 42nd frames of the simulation*

Finally, study the Select Bullet solver options shown in Figure 7-12.

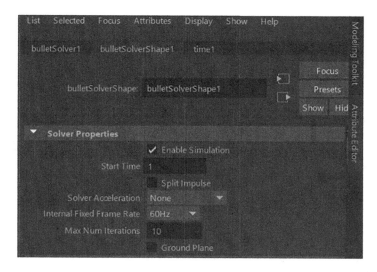

Figure 7-12. *Select Bullet options and properties*

This option shows the solver properties; you will find the Enable Simulation checkbox checked by default. The Internal Fixed Frame rate option helps you increase the speed of the simulation. Below this option, you will find the Basic Fields tab, which includes the Use Maya Fields checkbox. If you select this box, then the Maya Fields/Solvers are activated. However, if you leave it unchecked by default, you will get all the solvers, like the gravity, wind magnitude, and wind direction, as shown in Figure 7-13.

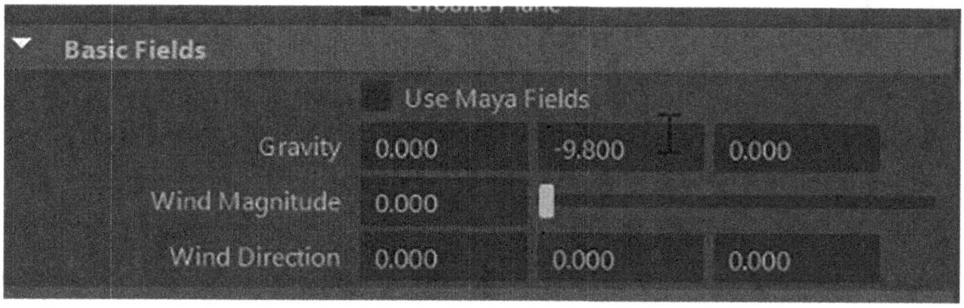

Figure 7-13. *Basic Fields options*

When activated, the Ground Plane option acts as a collider and enables the collision of the dynamic object as a static rigid body, as shown in Figure 7-14.

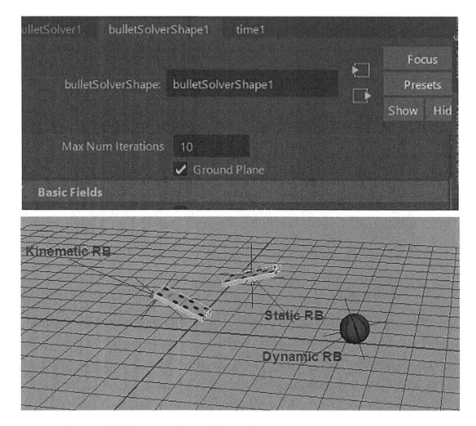

Figure 7-14. *Ground Plane option selected*

Rigid Body Simulation with Dominoes Using the Bullet Solver

This section goes through an example of using the rigid body type to create a dominoes simulation.

In continuation with the examples in this chapter, you can create a stack of dominoes, one behind the other, as shown in Figure 7-15.

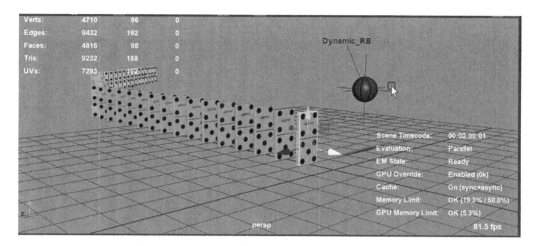

Verts:	4710	96	0
Edges:	9432	192	0
Faces:	4816	98	0
Tris:	9232	188	0
UVs:	7293	192	0

Dynamic_RB

Scene Timecode:	00:00:00:01
Evaluation:	Parallel
EM State:	Ready
GPU Override:	Enabled (0k)
Cache:	On (sync+async)
Memory Limit:	OK (19.3% / 50.0%)
GPU Memory Limit:	OK (5.3%)

persp   81.5 fps

Figure 7-15. *The dominoes scene*

Select the dominoes and put them under a group. Now select the group and go to the Bullets menu to select Active Rigid Body. Here, you should select the Collider Shape Type option and then choose Dynamic Rigid Body from the Body Type drop-down option. Scroll further down the window and check the Initially Sleeping option, as shown in Figure 7-16. This will force the boxes (the dominoes) to remain static/passive until they are hit by an external force (in this case, a ball).

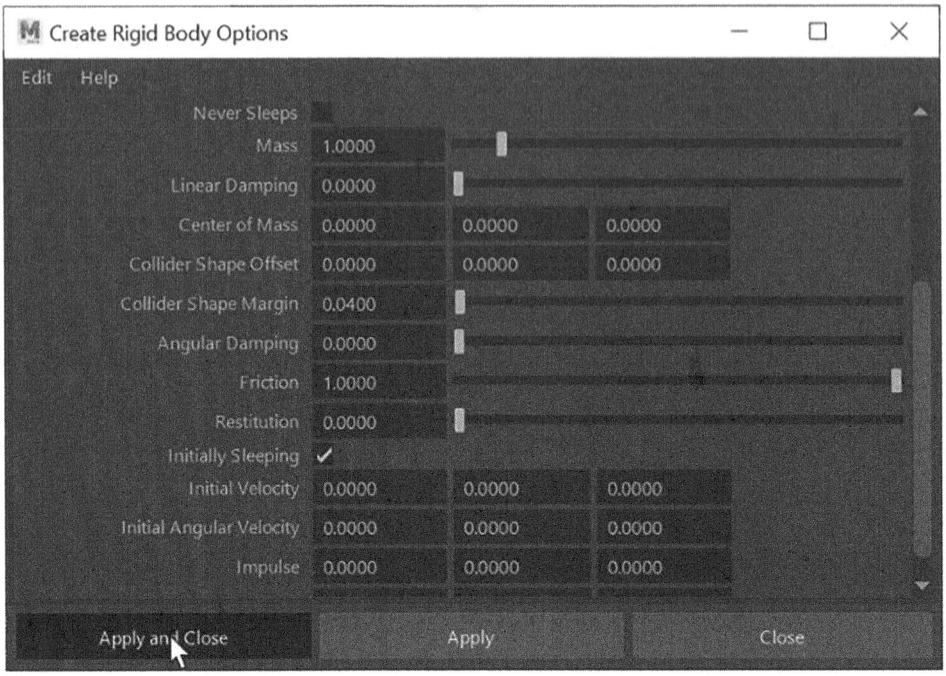

Figure 7-16. *The Initially Sleeping option must be checked*

Make sure all the dominoes are selected. The active rigid body should be applied to all the dominoes. If you press the Play button, you can see the simulation as captured in Figure 7-17. You can increase the speed of the simulation by changing the Internal Fixed Frame Rate to 120Hz or 240Hz from the default 60Hz on the BulletSolverShape1 tab, as explained in Figure 7-12.

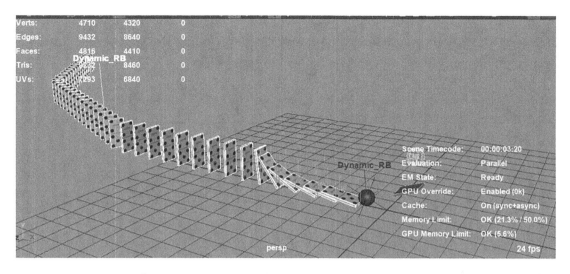

Figure 7-17. *Simulation in progress*

You can turn off the Bullet solver's Solver Display-Collision Shape option to get rid of the green boxes. Now suppose you want the domino simulation to happen from both ends. You need to apply some additional options to do that. You need to select the active rigid body, as shown in Figure 7-18, which will show the options in the Properties panel.

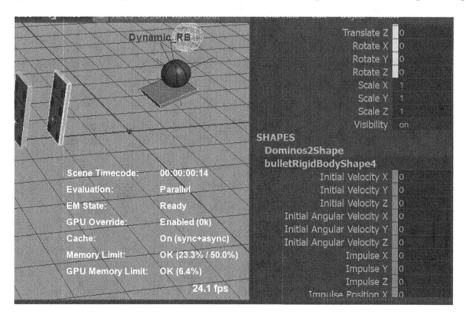

Figure 7-18. *Active Rigid Body: Initial Velocity options*

Here you will find the option for Initial Velocity. If you populate Initial Velocity on the x- and z-axes to 5 and uncheck the Initially Sleeping option, you will see that the simulation happens from both ends, as shown in Figure 7-19.

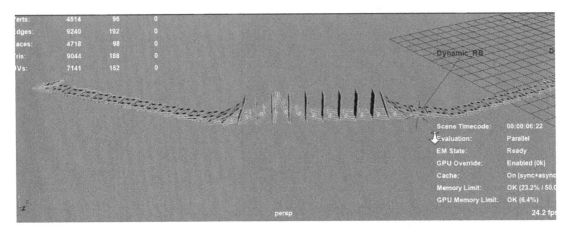

Figure 7-19. *Simulation in progress from both ends*

Bullet Rigid Body Constraints

This section explores the Bullet Physics Render engine-based dynamics system. It focuses on the use of constraints by specifically locking an object to a point, such as nailing a particular object to a location or creating a slider or a knob. These constraints can be very useful.

The Constraint option is found in the FX layout, in the Bullet menu, as shown in Figure 7-20.

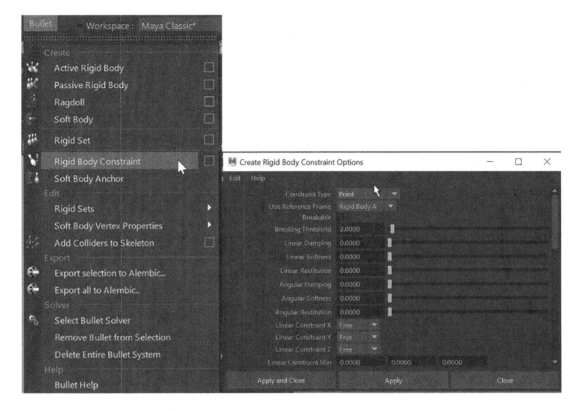

Figure 7-20. *Rigid Body Constraint options*

The most commonly used constrains are the Point and Hinge constraints. The types of rigid body constraints are described as follows:

- **Point:** Restricts translation so that the pivot points of the two rigid bodies coincide in world space.

- **Hinge:** Restricts the body's rotation around one axis and two additional angular degrees of freedom. The hinge axis is defined by the z-axis of the constraint.

- **Slider:** Rigid bodies can rotate around and translate along an axis. The z-axis of the constraint defines the slide axis.

- **Cone-Twist:** Useful for ragdoll upper arms. It extends the point-to-point constraint by including cone and twist axis limits.

- **6 Degrees of Freedom (DOF):** When each of the six DOFs are configured, this constraint can simulate a number of standard constraints. The first three DOF axes represent linear translation of rigid bodies, while the last three DOF axes represent angular motion.

- **Spring Hinge**: Has three positions—two degrees of rotation around the z-axis (Axis 1) and the x-axis (Axis 2), and one translation along the z-axis (Axis 1) with a suspension spring.

- **Spring 6 Degrees-of-Freedom:** Adds springs to each degree of freedom. This constraint precludes the use of springs and motors.

To further explore the constraint's options, you'll work on a particular example that will clarify the way these constraints work with rigid bodies. For the purposes here, you will explore the chain simulation.

You need to create or model the chain. Select all the objects of the chain and merge them into a group called Chain_Seq, as shown in Figure 7-21.

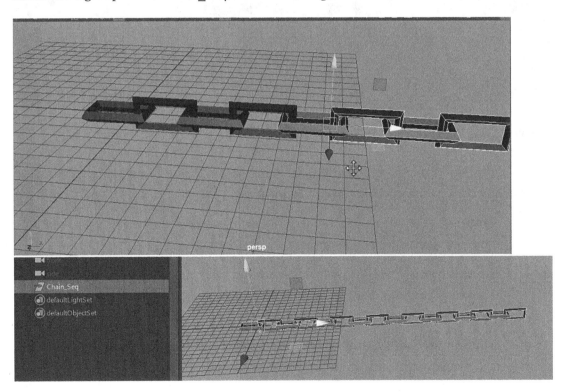

Figure 7-21. *Chain model*

To make this chain look like it's modeled for a purpose, add a cylinder or sphere to the end of the chain to make it look like Figure 7-22. Add it to the Chain_Seq group.

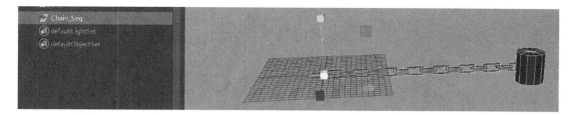

Figure 7-22. *Cylinder added to the chain*

You now have to convert this to a rigid body system. You need to choose the Active Rigid body option from the Bullet menu and convert the Collider Shape Type option to Auto Compound, as shown in Figure 7-23, since the shapes are not the same.

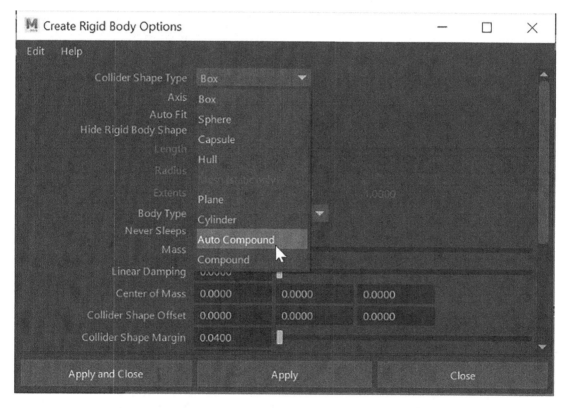

Figure 7-23. *Select the Auto Compound option*

With the Ground Plane on, press the Play button to see the simulation. You will see the Chain_Seq falling/colliding with the ground plane while the cylinder seems to move in a separate direction, as shown in Figure 7-24.

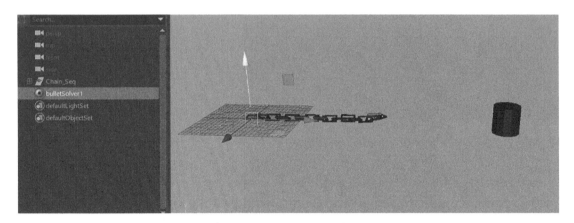

Figure 7-24. *No constraints attached*

In order to fix this issue, you need to add a constraint to the cylinder. You need to select the cylinder and the one block of chain that is attached to the cylinder. Then select the Rigid Body Constraint option from the Bullet menu, as shown in Figure 7-25.

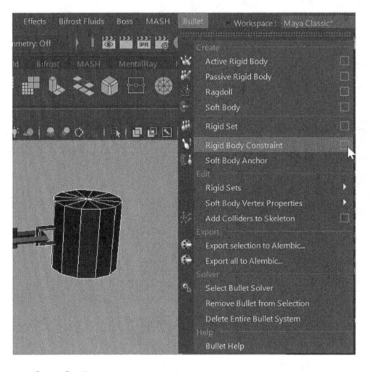

Figure 7-25. *Rigid Body Constraint option*

From this menu, you need to select the Hinge constraint, as shown in Figure 7-26.

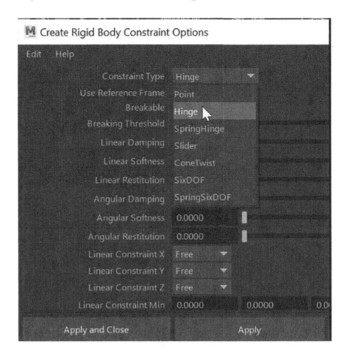

Figure 7-26. *Select the Hinge constraint type*

If you play the simulation, you will see that the cylinder sticks to the chain, as shown in Figure 7-27.

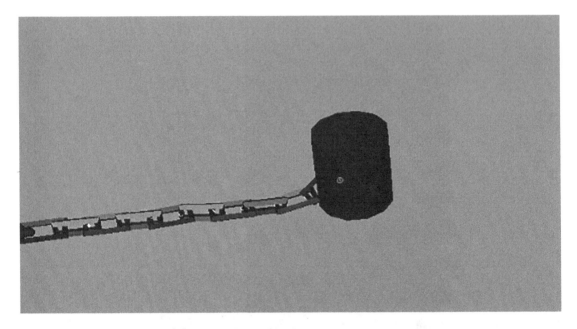

Figure 7-27. *Output of the Hinge constraint*

However, in this output, you can see the entire Chain_Seq gravitate down to the ground. But it should be locked at the top so that it has a swing motion.

You need to select the first block of the chain sequence and, from the Attribute Editor, change this to Static Rigid Body or change the Mass value to 0, as shown in Figure 7-28.

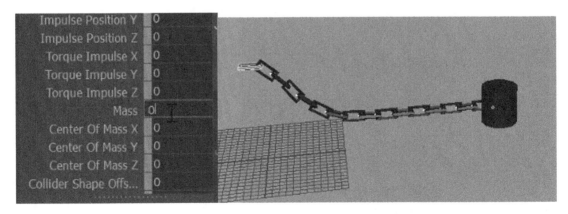

Figure 7-28. *The Mass is set to 0*

Recall that you had switched on the Ground Plane option, so the whole chain collides against the ground. If you want the swing motion, you need to switch off the Ground Plane option. After you do this, play the simulation to check for the swinging motion, as shown in Figure 7-29.

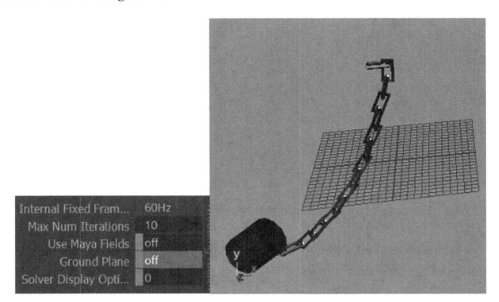

Figure 7-29. *The Ground Plane is set to off and the swinging motion is achieved*

So let's summarize. You can use constraints when you have to lock or create a relationship between two rigid body objects. Point constraints are used when an object to object position needs to be locked.

Let's make this a little more interesting. I created a cube, scaled it up, and placed another cube just above it, without merging the two surfaces, as shown in Figure 7-30.

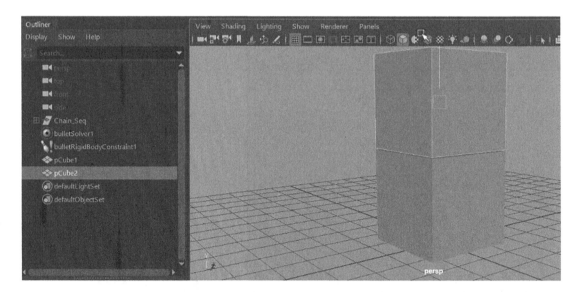

Figure 7-30. *The cubes are placed on top of each other but don't merge*

You need to create a block of wall, as illustrated in Figure 7-31, and group it together. Name it Wall in the Outliner.

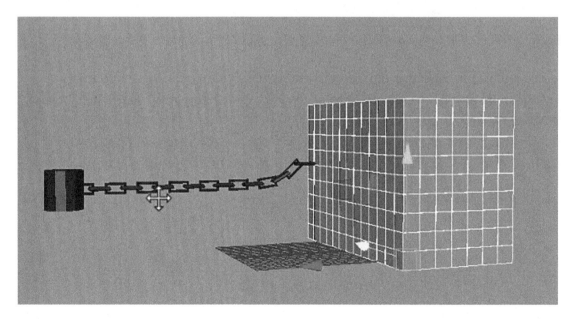

Figure 7-31. *The cubes grouped to form a wall*

Now you need to Shift+select all the cubes in the group and convert them to an active rigid body with the Collider Shape Type set to Box. Check Initially Sleeping, as shown in Figure 7-32. Recall that the Initially Sleeping option will make the object static unless it collides with another object/active rigid body simulation.

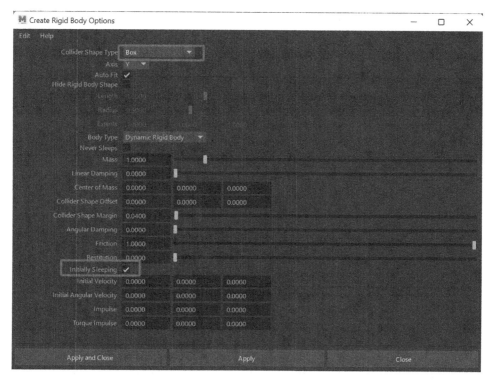

Figure 7-32. *The Create Rigid Body Options window for the wall*

If you play the simulation, you will see something similar to Figure 7-33.

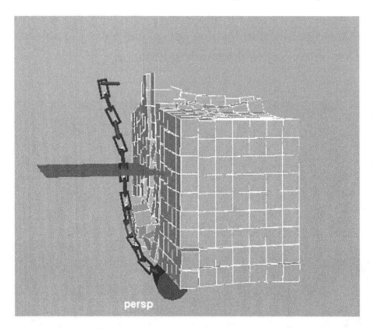

Figure 7-33. *The simulated output*

To make this more complicated, you can place a large sphere below the wall, as shown in Figure 7-34, and convert it to a static rigid body from the Attribute Editor.

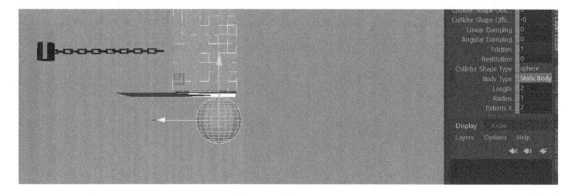

Figure 7-34. *The sphere is added as a static rigid body*

If you play the simulation, you will see all the objects in the scene beautifully collide with each other. See Figure 7-35.

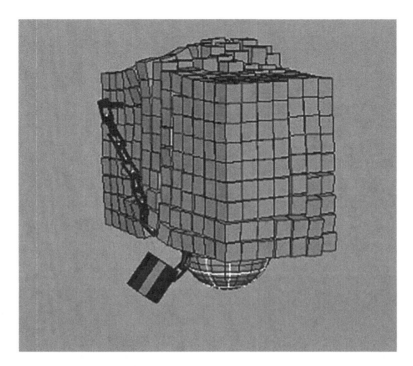

Figure 7-35. *The final simulation*

Having seen the rigid body options in action, you are now set to explore the options for soft body simulations, which are covered next.

FX Simulation with Soft Bodies

This section explores Maya's soft body using the Bullet solver. While working on any soft body, it is best to use the Maya nCloth system, which is covered in upcoming chapters, as it helps you achieve better details and more realism in the simulation. However, Maya's soft body options also help you achieve a fairly good result when simulating a soft object.

To understand how the soft body options work in Maya, you will be creating a ball and applying soft body dynamics to it.

First create a sphere and apply the Lambert shader with any ball texture, as shown in Figure 7-36.

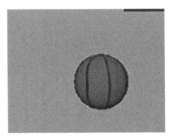

Figure 7-36. *Ball with a basketball texture.*

You need to apply the soft body to it. To do this, select Bullet from the menu bar and choose Soft Body, which will open a dialog box. You need to click Apply and Close without changing any options, as shown in Figure 7-37.

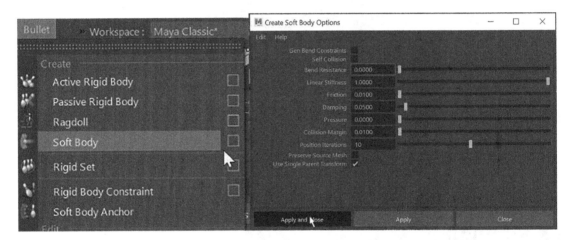

Figure 7-37. *Select Soft Body, then click Apply and Close*

You now need to go to the Bullet solver Attribute Editor and activate the Ground Plane option, as shown in Figure 7-38.

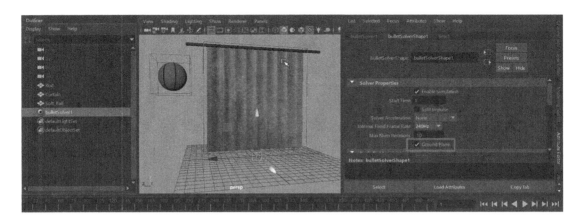

Figure 7-38. *Select the Ground Plane option*

This will make the ball, which is now a soft body, collide with the ground plane. The output will look like Figure 7-39.

Figure 7-39. *Simulated output*

There are other soft body properties that you can change to vary your results. For example, you can add mass to the soft body so that it appears to be heavier and falls more quickly to the ground, as shown in Figure 7-40.

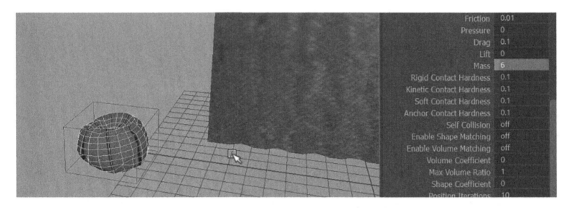

Figure 7-40. *A value of 6 applied to the property of Mass for the soft body ball*

Similarly, if you want a smooth or silky material, you can change the Linear Stiffness value to 0.05; the resultant simulation is shown in Figure 7-41.

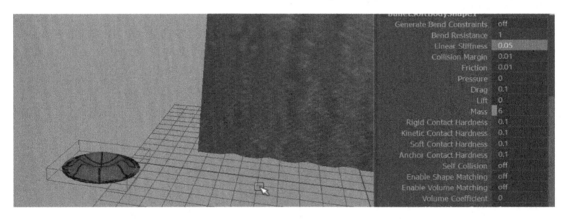

Figure 7-41. *A value of 0.05 applied to Linear Stiffness*

This ball is acting like a cloth now, and if you want it to respond like a rubber ball, you need to activate the Generate Bend Constraints option, as shown in Figure 7-42. This will give each vertex its own constraint value so that each vertex preserves its shape.

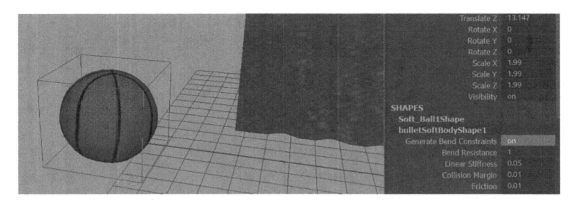

Figure 7-42. *Turn on the Generate Bend Constraints option*

You can go to the Attribute Editor of the bullet soft body shape and switch on the Self Collision option as well, as shown in Figure 7-43. This will make the ball collide with the surface and roll away.

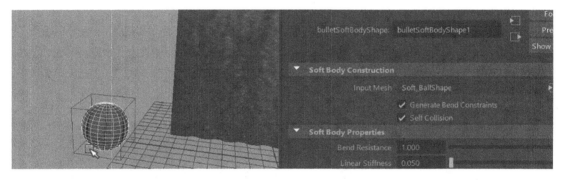

Figure 7-43. *Switch on Self Collision*

Similarly, you can experiment with other properties in the Soft Body and Aerodynamics options of Pressure, Drag, and Lift. These options help you control the air pressure. As you scroll down, you will find the soft body solver. If you decrease the Collision Margin to 0.001 and increase the Position Iterations to 20, as shown in Figure 7-44, the collision will be smoother and more precise.

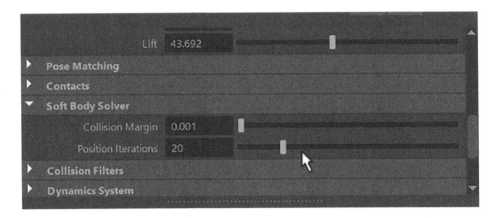

Figure 7-44. *Soft Body Solver options*

If you increase the friction value of the soft body properties, you will find the ball colliding with the surface and then sticking to the ground.

So far, you have explored the options for the soft body. Now you will see how to use these options on the curtain model in the scene.

First select the curtain and select the Soft Body option from the Bullet menu. Switch on the Gen Bend Constraints and the Self Collision checkboxes and then click Apply and Close, as shown in Figure 7-45.

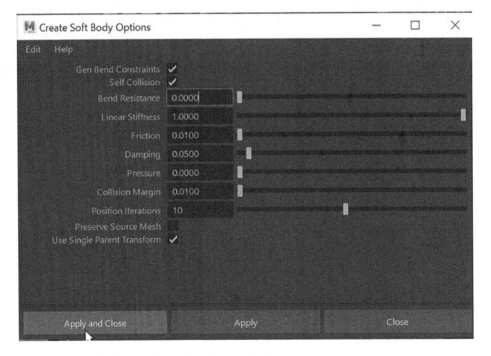

Figure 7-45. *Soft Body options for the curtain*

If you play the simulation, you will find the curtain falling to the ground and behaving like a cloth. You can tweak the rigidity of the curtain material for more smoothness in the flow. Right now it looks like a crumbling paper effect. Let's work toward making a curtain simulation effect.

You need to affix the cloth to the rod that holds it. Create a locator and fix it to the top corner of the curtain. Then hide the rod geometry and switch to Vertex mode. Select the vertices in the top corner and Shift+select the locator. Go to the Bullet menu and select Soft Body Anchor, as shown in Figure 7-46.

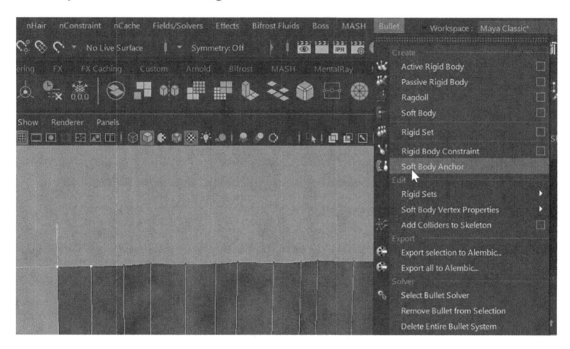

Figure 7-46. *The Soft Body Anchor option*

Similar to the rigid body constraints in a soft body, this is called a Soft Body Anchor. The anchor will lock the selected vertices to the locator. The simulation will look as shown in Figure 7-47.

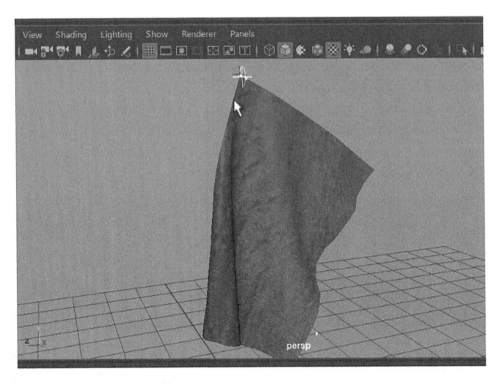

Figure 7-47. *Soft Body Anchor applied*

Similarly, you need to lock more vertices of the curtain, as shown in Figure 7-48, and align them to the curtain.

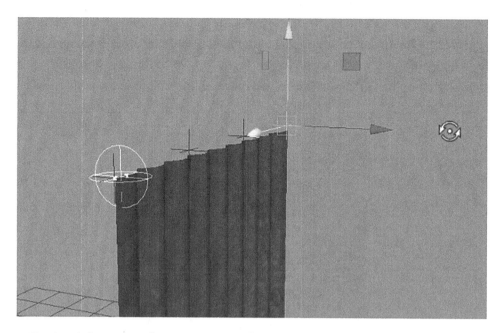

Figure 7-48. *A few more locators created*

Repeat this process. Switch to Vertex mode, select two vertices, Shift+select the locator, and apply the Soft Body Anchor. The curtain will be locked to the rod, as shown in Figure 7-49. If you play the simulation, you will see the curtain moving lightly.

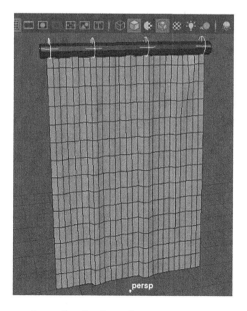

Figure 7-49. *Soft body anchors locked to the curtain vertices*

To increase the movement of the curtain, you need to introduce some air fields.

First select the bullet solver shape. From the Basic Fields tab, increase the wind magnitude to 5 and the wind direction in the x-axis to 1. Additionally, from the Aerodynamics tab of the curtain bullet solver, increase the lift value to 10, as shown in Figure 7-50.

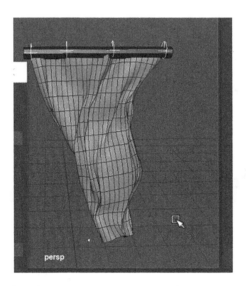

Figure 7-50. *Aerodynamics lift value 10 applied*

You can modify the Pressure value to 2 and the Drag to 1 and see the simulation as shown in Figure 7-51.

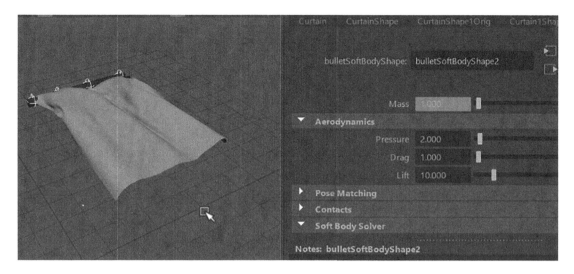

Figure 7-51. *Aerodynamics pressure and drag values applied*

Now that you've reached the end of this chapter, I hope it is clear how you create beautiful soft body simulations simply by tweaking values at various levels. In the next chapter, you learn about the fluid simulation system in Maya.

CHAPTER 8

Working with Maya Fluids

This chapter explores the concepts of fluid dynamics. It explains the meaning of fluids with respect to Autodesk Maya, taking into consideration the voxels and fluid containers. It also covers fluid emitters and explains the ways that fluids can be manipulated, such as via their density, velocity, turbulence, temperature, and fuel characteristics.

Understanding Fluid FX

Let's get started by reviewing the fluid dynamics system in Autodesk Maya. In simple terms, a *fluid* is the motion of a substance, whether in a liquid or gaseous state, with respect to forces like gravity and other external forces.

People often generalize fluids as a liquid state, but fluids are not limited to the domain of liquids. They have another branch, the study of aerodynamics, which refers to the utilization of fluids in terms of gases, because gas itself is a fluid. Software programs like Autodesk Maya, Houdini, and FumeFX have intelligent solvers and algorithms based on real-life physics that are capable of mimicking the behavior of fluids. Fluids used in the visual effects industry can calculate the motion of smoke, liquid, fire, explosions, and more. This chapter focuses on the study of the Maya Fluids system by creating examples from scratch and explores the capabilities of the Maya Fluids. The principles of fluid dynamics can be applied to other software programs, like Houdini and FumeFx, as well.

Maya Fluids dynamically simulate the motion of fluids, which are based on the laws of real-world physics. Maya uses its Native Fluids solver, which is based on the Navier-Stokes equations. Navier and Stokes were two great scientists who studied fluids based on Newton's Second Law. The most important part of this equation is the vector feed of the velocity inside the flow of the substance. That's where the Navier-Stokes equation is focused. The Maya Fluids solver can compute the calculations of fluid dynamics for each

© Abhishek Kumar 2022
A. Kumar, *Beginning VFX with Autodesk Maya*, https://doi.org/10.1007/978-1-4842-7857-4_8

frame on the timeline as you play through it. Fluid dynamics has been used to create stunning visual effects for major blockbusters, such as Superman emitting heat waves from his eyes, Iron man's metallic suit igniting, and the impact of Thor's hammer.

Fluids are created inside the limited domains of fluid containers. These containers are basically three-dimensional cubes made of voxels and fluid emitters. Voxels are volumetric (3D) pixels as opposed to the two-dimensionalities of typical pixels. Since they exist in the fluid container, each of these pixels has an X, Y, and Z grid, called a voxel. Voxel density or voxel distribution represents resolution. The more voxels you have in the container, the more dense it is and the clearer the effect will be. However, that will require additional processing and more calculations.

The voxels are essentially the DNA of the fluids; they store all the values of the density, velocity, temperature, fuel, etc. In fact, voxels are basically responsible for the look and feel of the fluids.

I have been using some important terms like density, velocity, temperature, and fuel, so let's look at these very simply for a basic understanding. Consider the smoke effect. The density of the smoke refers to its thickness. It will travel upward because of its velocity, its speed will be determined by the temperature component, and if there is a fire below the smoke, fuel has added to the overall reaction. This was a very simplistic description of the four very important elements of fluids, but you will see a detailed study as you go deeper into this chapter and will create some specific effects.

Fluids Containers in Autodesk Maya

There are two types of containers in Autodesk Maya, a 2D container and a 3D container. We will first discuss the 2D container and then move on to the 3D container. The attributes and properties used with the 2D container simply extend to the 3D counterpart. The only difference is that the 3D container is a volumetric container, so it has a few extended options. A visual representation of a 2D and 3D container is shown in Figure 8-1.

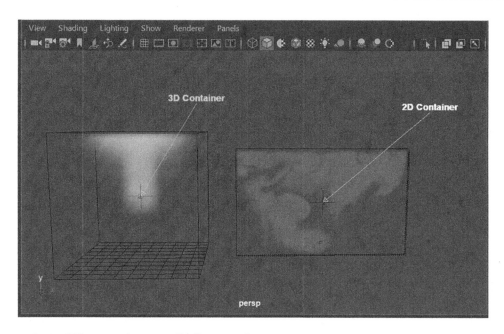

Figure 8-1. *2D container and 3D container*

To enable the 2D container, you need to go to the Fluids menu and select the 2D Container option, as shown in Figure 8-2.

Figure 8-2. *The 2D Container option*

The Fluid 2D Container looks like a rectangular shape in the viewport, as shown in Figure 8-3.

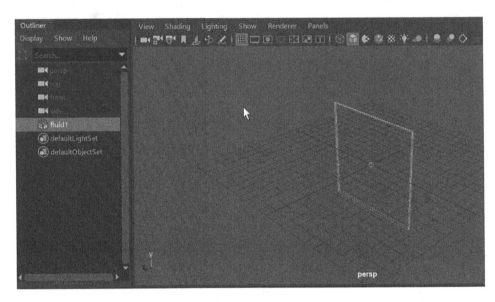

Figure 8-3. *A 2D container on the viewport*

Each 2D Container contains an emitter in the center of the container, as shown in Figure 8-4.

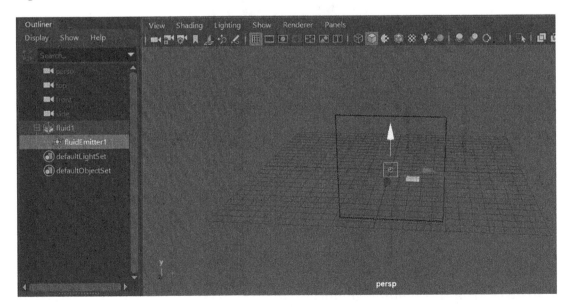

Figure 8-4. *The emitter in the 2D container*

The emitter is basically the point where the fluid emission will happen. If the emitter is at the center, the fluid emission will happen from the center, as shown in Figure 8-5. You can place the emitter at any position within the 2D rectangular container.

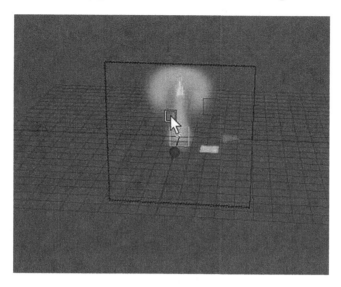

Figure 8-5. *The simulation*

Let's now move on to discuss the attributes of the fluids. These attributes are similar to that of the 3D container. In the Attribute Editor, you will find the Density/Voxel/Second property within the Fluid attributes. This attribute increases and decreases the thickness of the fluid. You can set the value to 10 and play the simulation to view the differences, as shown in Figure 8-6.

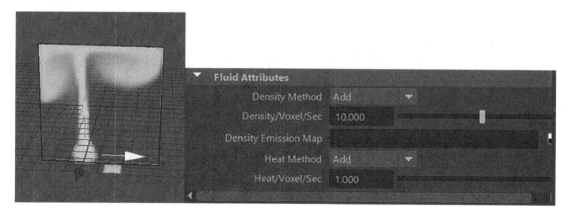

Figure 8-6. *The Density increased to 10*

In the Fluid Shape node, you will find the Container Properties tab. There, the Base Resolution is set to 40 by default. The Base Resolution option helps increase the quality of the simulation, as shown in Figure 8-7. The more you increase this value, the more Maya will smoothen the flow of the fluid emission. However, this does come at the cost of computational speed.

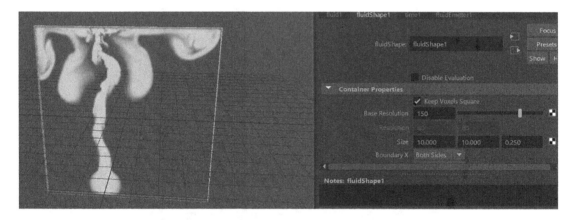

Figure 8-7. *The Base Resolution option set to 150*

As you scroll down the attribute properties, you will find the Auto Resize checkbox. This option resizes the container's boundaries based on the simulation, as shown in Figure 8-8. This speeds up the computation and preserves the details.

Figure 8-8. *The Auto Resize option is selected*

Moving farther down, there are other attributes, like the Turbulence, Density, Velocity, and Temperature options. If you increase the turbulence strength, you will find turmoil or unsteady movement in the flow of the fluid simulation, which helps in making it aesthetically more appealing. See Figure 8-9.

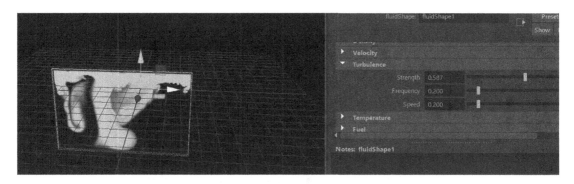

Figure 8-9. *The Turbulence options*

You can also explore the Shading section and work with the Color option, as shown in Figure 8-10. We will explore this more in the 3D Container section.

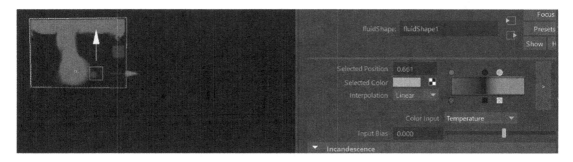

Figure 8-10. *The color section*

You should now clearly understand how the 2D Container Fluid system functions. Let's now explore these properties with an example.

As discussed, the 2D Containers reside in the Fluids menu. In this example, you will create a 2D Container, which comes with an emitter. If you need to add more emitters, you can do so. Select the container and then go to the Fluids menu. Select the Add/Edit Contents option, then choose Emitter, as shown in Figure 8-11.

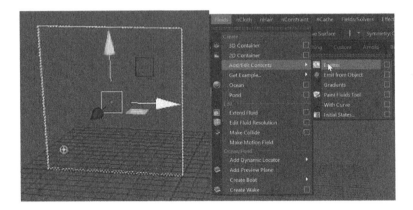

Figure 8-11. *Adding more emitters*

Once the emitters have been positioned in the two corners or wherever you need them, you can play the simulation to see the emission. It's shown in Figure 8-12.

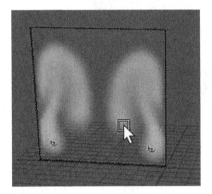

Figure 8-12. *Fluid emission from the two emitters in the same 2D container*

These two emitters are emitting at two ends. If you want the emissions to blend with each other, you can place them closer to each other; see the simulation in Figure 8-13. Similarly, you can use multiple emitters, depending on your desired output.

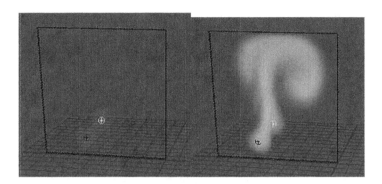

Figure 8-13. *Fluid emission using two emitters positioned close to each other*

You can also assign emissions to an object. In this example, you are creating a cylinder and resizing it, but you could create any object as needed. Then select the cylinder or the geometry that you created and select the container. Go to the Fluids menu and choose Add/Edit Contents. Then choose the Emit from Object option. This will cause the emission to emanate from the cylinder or from the geometry you created, as shown in Figure 8-14.

Figure 8-14. *Fluid emission from an object*

Next, let's explore some other emitter options. First open a new scene and create a 2D Container, as before.

This time, delete the emitter in the container by selecting it from the Outliner.

Now go to the Fluids menu and choose the Add/Edit Contents option again. This time, select the Paint Fluids Tool option. This will enable you to paint the fluid emission path, as shown in Figure 8-15.

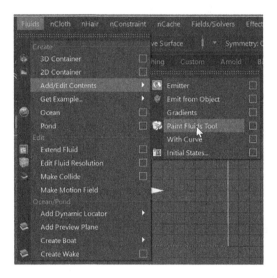

Figure 8-15. *The Paint Fluids Tool option*

When the Paint Fluids tool is active, the cursor changes to a paintbrush icon, the size of which can be increased or decreased pressing b on the keyboard or by holding down the left mouse button and dragging it left or right. Using the brush, you can paint a name, as shown in Figure 8-16.

Figure 8-16. *Painted text using the Paint Fluids tool within the 2D Container*

When you play the simulation, you can see how the name disappears into smoke. One point to remember is that the Base Resolution must be set higher for a smooth simulation. These kinds of FX are commonly used in Hollywood movie titles and can be easily created using Maya's Paint Fluids tool.

The options in the 2D Container are all present in the 3D Container, with additional handlers that you will study in the next sections of this chapter. The following sections delve deep into each of these attributes.

Working with the Emitter and the 3D Container

This section of the chapter discusses the other components of 3D Containers, namely Fluid Emitters. Fluid Emitters are responsible for modifying the properties of the voxel inside the containers. As the name suggests, you might think that this emitter is responsible for adding fluids to the container. But that is not the case. The fluids are already there in the container. The container resides under the Fluids menu, as shown in Figure 8-17.

Figure 8-17. *3D Container*

The 3D Container's settings must first be reset before starting a new fluid simulation, as shown in Figure 8-18.

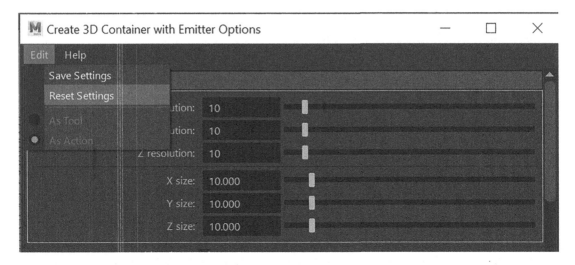

Figure 8-18. *Reset the 3D Container's settings*

This replaces the properties of the voxels. The generic objects of the Maya Fluid Container enable the flow of the density, temperature, fuel, and velocity. The Emitter emits the values of density voxels inside the containers. Go ahead and create the container first. You will need to switch off the Add Emitter checkbox and click the Apply and Close button, as shown in Figure 8-19.

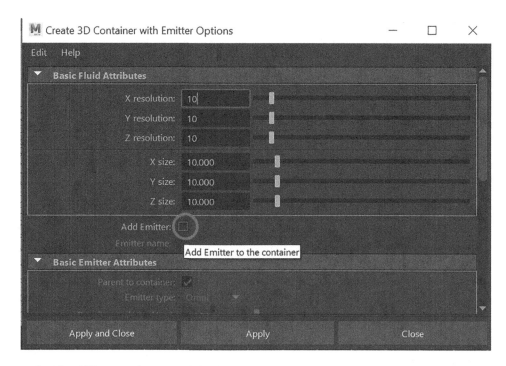

Figure 8-19. *3D container settings*

This will create the 3D Container in the viewport, as shown in Figure 8-20.

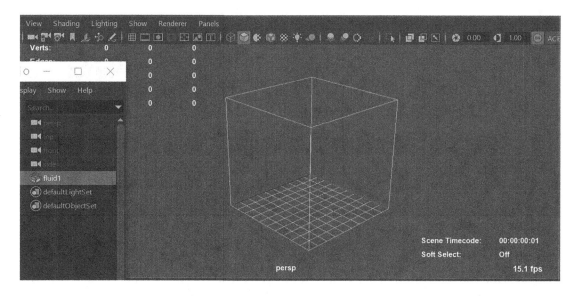

Figure 8-20. *3D Container in the viewport*

Technically, the container is already filled with voxels. The grid at the bottom of the container represents the voxels, as shown in Figure 8-21.

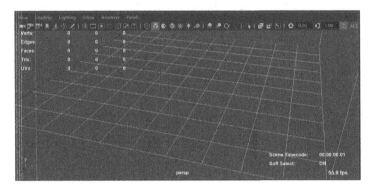

Figure 8-21. *Voxels in the 3D Container*

They just update the properties of the fluids. The rate of emission is represented by "contents" per voxel per second, where "contents" can be the density, temperature, fuel, or velocity. Hence the voxels are three-dimensional and in order to see that, you need to go to the Attribute Editor of the 3D container and switch to the Fluid Shape tab. Set the Boundary Draw option in the Display section to Full. This will then display all the voxels in the 3D space within the container, as shown in Figure 8-22.

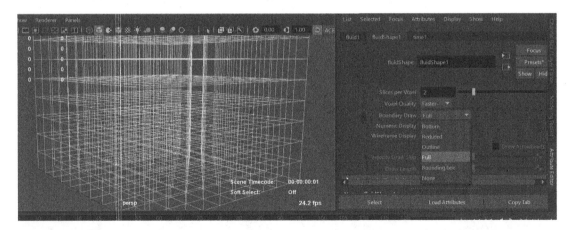

Figure 8-22. *3D voxels of the 3D container*

However, the resolution of the voxels in the default setting is 1 cm for 1 voxel, which is fairly low. To increase the resolution, you can modify the Basic Resolution settings in the Container Properties section. Set them to 100, as shown in Figure 8-23. This now indicates that each voxel is 100 the in x-, y-, and z-axes, which makes the resolution 100*100*100 = 1000000.

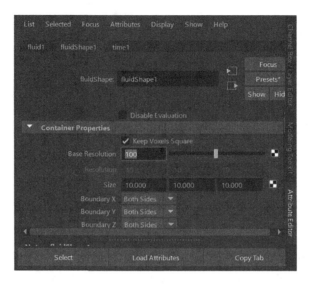

Figure 8-23. *Basic Resolution setting of the 3D container increased to 100*

This setting will make it very difficult to visualize the fluids in the container when the voxel density is so high. Set the Boundary Draw option in the Display section to Bounding Box, as shown in Figure 8-24.

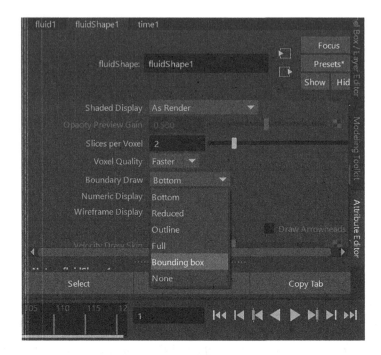

Figure 8-24. *The Boundary Draw setting of the 3D container is set to Bounding Box*

Now you add the emitter inside the container. Remember that the emitters are not adding the voxels inside the container. The voxels are already there. The emitters will just be modifying the properties of the voxels. Let's bring in an emitter. You need to go to the Fluids menu and select Add/Edit Contents. Then choose the Emitter option, as shown in Figure 8-25.

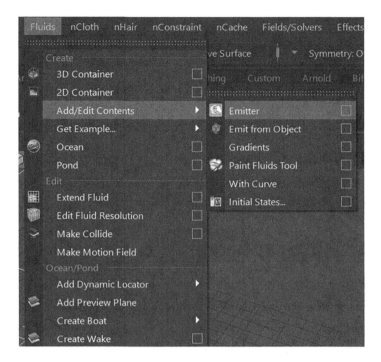

Figure 8-25. *Adding the emitter to the 3D Container*

Fluid Emitter Types

There are several types of fluid emitters, each with its own benefits and contributions:

- **Point emitters**—They are 2D emitters that emit fluid from a point that has a distance through which a fluid will flow. These are one of the basic or the default emitters.

- **Surface emitters**—As the name suggests, you will have the emission taking place from polygonal or Nurbs surfaces. For example, if you need to burn a piece of wood, the entire surface of the wood should emit the fire, which is when surface emitters are useful.

- **Curve emitters**—Fluids can be emitted from any of the curve tools.

- **Particle emitters**—You can utilize the classic particles as well as nParticles as a kind of emitter. Wherever the particles move, the fluid will inherit and flow accordingly.

- **Surface emitters (emission maps)**—This is similar to the surface emitter but has a special property. If you want to restrict the burning of the wood to a particular section of the surface, for example, you need to select the particular surface UVs and assign a grayscale alpha map to them, wherein the white pixels depict the area they should be burning as opposed to the receding black area that should remain unaffected.

- **Volume emitters**—This is the default emitter and you can work with the spherical, cylindrical, conical, and torus types.

Maya Fluids Container Details

Having discussed the emitter types, you now explore the Maya Fluids Container details. You already know that the Maya Fluids are described with various elements of container properties such as Density, Velocity, Turbulence, Temperature, and Fuel. The following section discusses these individual parameters, including their attributes, importance, roles, and relevance pertaining to Fluid effects.

Density

Density can described as mass per unit volume. When a container is filled with a liquid or a gas, the area occupied by this fluid is the density of the fluid. It represents the surface of the fluid. These concepts are important to understand before entering the practical phase, so that you know which attributes produce the desired result.

Let's look at the various attributes of the Density parameter.

- **Density scale**—A multiplier of all the attributes under it; should never be scaled to the value of 1.

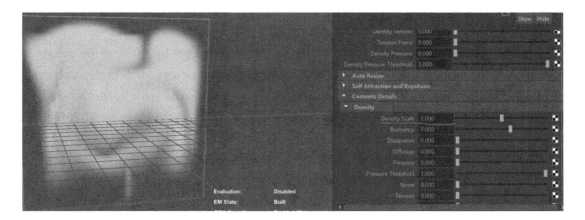

- **Density pressure**—The outward force that Maya Fluids applies and will work toward expanding the fluid. k

- **Buoyancy**—A positive value of the buoyancy will keep the fluids above the surface, whereas a negative value will make the fluids flow below the surface. For example, the positive buoyancy value could be applied to a wispy smoke and a negative value could be dry ice, which tends to flow downward.

- **Gradient Force**—Applies the force in the x-, y-, and z-axes within the voxels of the container.

- **Dissipation** —The naturalistic behavior of the fluid when it tends to dissolve in the atmosphere.

- **Density Tension**—Could be related to the surface tension inside water, which tries to preserve the water into tiny droplets. Even with gaseous effects, it could help give shapes like clouds and smoke puffs.

- **Diffusion**—Helps to spread out the fluids in the neighboring voxels. It spreads inside the container.

- **Density Tension Force**—Tries to create some stretchiness inside the fluid and is useful in creating wispy smoke.

- **Noise**—Helps create randomness in the voxel values of the density. Helps in introducing some bumpiness within the smooth flow of the fluid.

Velocity and Turbulence

The velocity field has both direction and magnitude, and it helps by pushing the values of density, temperature, and fuel. Velocity is represented by vectors. With fluids, you can visualize the directional arrows. This means that if you disable the velocity, nothing is going to work even though the density, temperature, and fuel parameters are all intact, because the fluid will remain where the emitter is located.

The velocity is required to push the fluid to the other voxel values. Turbulence creates disturbances in the flow of the velocity, causing it to change directions with respect to frequency and speed. The smaller the value of frequency, the bigger the impact of the flow, which means the smoke, for example, will have larger waves with a smaller value of frequency. With a larger value of frequency, the waves will be reduced; how often they repeat is determined by the speed. The higher the speed value, the more frequent the repetition. Let's take a quick look at the various attributes of velocity:

- **Swirl**—Controls the vortices or the amount of "blow" inside of the smoke, for example.

- **Velocity Scale (X, Y, Z)**—Controls the individual dimensions of the container.

- **Turbulence Strength**—Controls the overall amount of the turbulence. A lower value will have a lesser effect on the disturbance of the smoke as opposed to higher ones.

- **Noise**—A property with respect to velocity that controls the randomness in the voxel values of the velocity in the dynamic grid.

- **Frequency and Speed**—Indicates that once you use the turbulence, the frequency will decide how big the disturbance will be and the speed will decide how often the disturbance repeats.

Temperature

The Temperature option helps raise the fluids and ignites the fluids to burn quickly. The reactions of fire and explosions are achieved using the temperature. Temperature is very useful with shading as well. Linking the temperature and incandescence attributes creates a self-illuminating property for the substance. The attributes of temperature is as follows:

- **Temperature scale**—The universal multiplier for all the attributes underneath temperature.

- **Diffusion**—Controls the spread of the voxels within the container.

- **Buoyancy**—Helps raise the fluids. The positive values make the fluid rise higher and vice versa.

- **Pressure**—Helps to expand the voxels.

- **Dissipations**—A naturalistic behavior of the fluid in which it diminishes itself with respect to time. Higher values of dissipation will tend to cool off the temperature quickly and thereby vanish away and vice versa.

- **Tension**—Controls the stretchiness in terms of shading.

- **Noise**—Brings about randomization within the temperature values.

- **Turbulence**—Indirectly linked to the velocity inside the fluids and controls the aggressive behavior of the fluids.

Fuel

Fuel acts as an accelerator and helps to achieve a reaction with a faster rate. Fuel combines with density, and when exposed to temperature, it will add more heat to the final reactions. It is useful for creating spontaneous fire and explosions. By introducing this property inside the voxels, the rate of reaction for the fluids thereby increases. Let's take a quick look at the attributes of the Fuel option.

- **Fuel Scale**—This is the universal multiplier for all the attributes underneath Fuel.

- **Reaction Speed**—One of the most important attributes of fuel. Decides how fast the reaction takes place. However, this depends on the following two attributes of Air/Fuel ratio and the Ignition temperature.

- **Air/Fuel Ratio**—Determines the percentage of fuel that is mixed in the air; goes with the density. This helps to achieve a more realistic behavior for the explosions.

- **Ignition Temperature**—This is the minimum temperature at which the fuel will start burning, which also depends on the maximum temperature.

- **Max Temperature**—The moment it reaches this value the entire fluid will be burnt away. Hence, you can deduce that the fuel will burn between the two values of the ignition temperature and the max temperature.

- **Heat Released**—Once the entire fuel is burnt away, the heat is automatically released and will show the output in the attributes of Light release and Light Color with respect to the incandescent map.

Emitting Fluids from Point Emitters

Let's get started with the Point Emitter, also called the Omni, as shown in Figure 8-26.

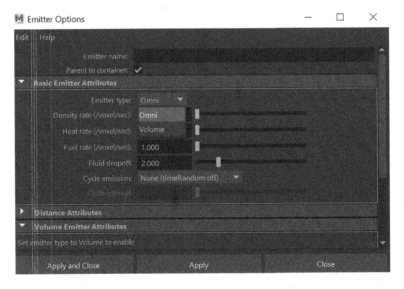

Figure 8-26. *Adding the Omni Emitter to the 3D Container*

You can select the Point Emitter and position it at the bottom of the container. Make sure it is inside the container, as shown in Figure 8-27.

Figure 8-27. *Placing the Point Emitter to the bottom of the 3D container*

You can now simply play and see the simulation of the fluid, which looks like Figure 8-28.

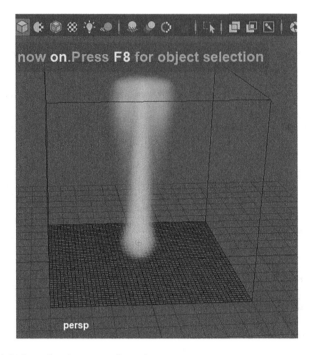

Figure 8-28. *Fluid simulation on the viewport*

The density (or in simpler words, the thickness of this smoke) can be increased or decreased using the Density property in the Fluid Attributes section, as shown in Figure 8-29. The Density Method parameter needs to be set to Add and the Density/Voxel/Second can be set to 10 to see the effect in Figure 8-29.

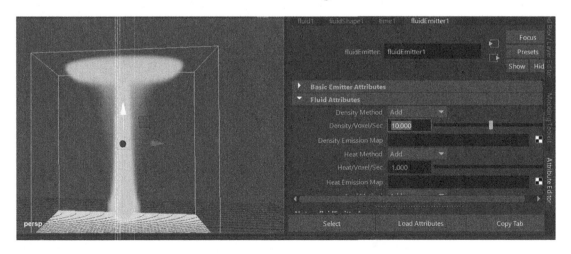

Figure 8-29. *Fluid density attribute increased to 10 from the default of 1*

Emitting Fluids from Volume Emitters

This section covers the Volume Emitter. Add the Volume Emitter from the Add/Edit Emitter option on the Fluids menu, as shown in Figure 8-30.

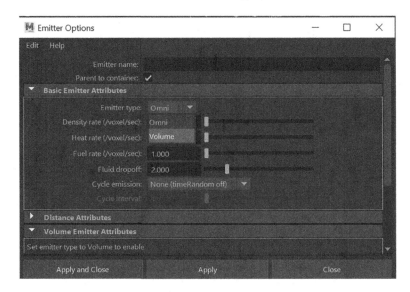

Figure 8-30. *Select Volume instead of Omni for the Emitter type*

When the Volume Emitter is selected, its options are loaded. There are various volume shapes like Cube, Sphere, Cylinder, Cone, and Torus, as shown in Figure 8-31. This section explains all the options one by one. For now, select the Cube option and click Apply and Close.

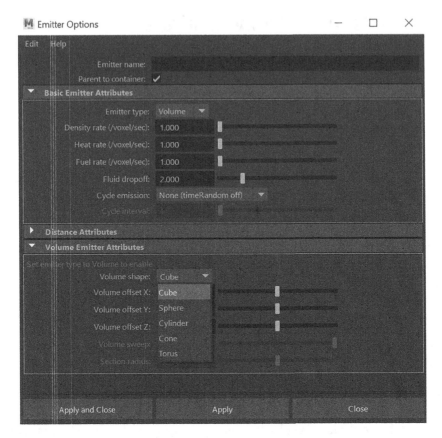

Figure 8-31. *Volume Shape selected as Cube*

With these options are selected, the Volume Emitter looks like Figure 8-32. Play the simulation to view the emission.

Figure 8-32. *Volume shape on the viewport*

As you move lower in the Fluid Emitter attribute, similar to the previous example, keep the Heat and Fuel method to No Emission for the time being. You could tweak the Fluid Dropoff value to view the effect, as shown in Figure 8-33. However, since this is reducing the volume of the fluid emission, revert to the default of 0.

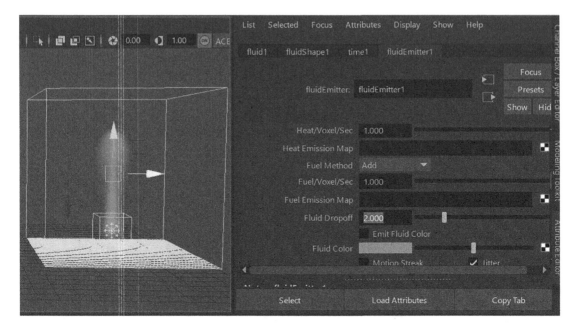

Figure 8-33. *Volume Dropoff set to 2 (fluid amount decreases)*

Let's now discuss the Fluid Emission Turbulence options. It is from these options that the disturbance or noise will be generated inside the fluids or the fluid container. Change the Turbulence to 10, the Turbulence Speed to 0.5, and the Detail turbulence to 1.

If you play the simulation, you can see some random noise being generated in the fluid emission, as shown in Figure 8-34. This helps break the regular flow of the fluids to make them it realistic. You can increase the value of the turbulence, but that needs to be adjusted based on the needs of the scene.

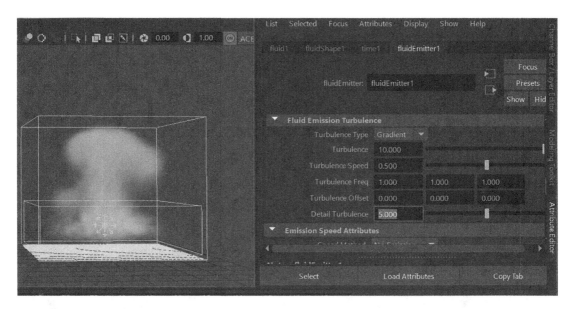

Figure 8-34. *Fluid Emission Turbulence options modified for random noise in the emission*

Another effective attribute is the Emission Speed attribute. This is linked to the Velocity aspect. Make the following changes to see the effect of the simulation.

First, change the Volume Emitter Type from Cube to Cylinder and scale it to 1. Then scale the y-axis, keeping the x- and z-axes uniformly scaled, as shown in Figure 8-35.

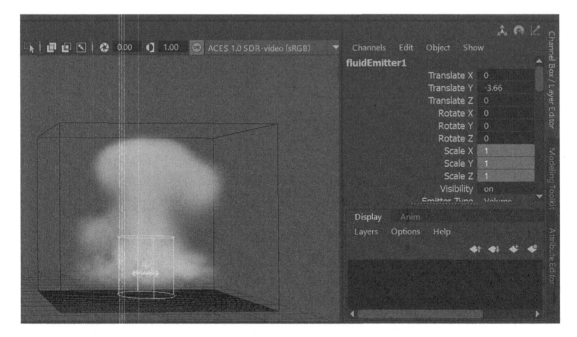

Figure 8-35. *Volume shape changed to Cylinder with scale values.*

In the Emission Speed Attributes section, set the Around Axis value to 35 to see the effect captured in Figure 8-36.

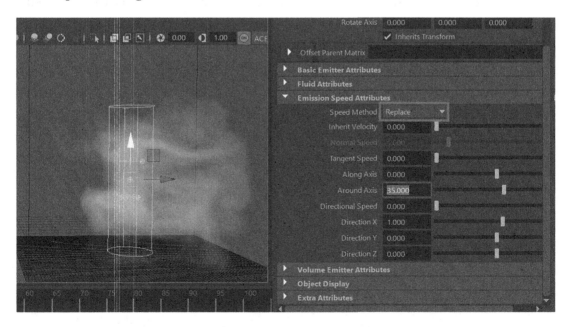

Figure 8-36. *Emission Speed Attribute: Around Axis set to 35*

Emitting Fluids from Polygonal Surfaces

In this section, you explore the fluid emission from a polygon primitive geometry.

Start by creating a basic polygon primitive with a Torus and place it in the 3D Fluid Container, as shown in Figure 8-37.

Figure 8-37. *Polygon geometry and 3D container*

But that's not enough. You need to go to the Fluids menu select Add/Edit Contents. Click the Emit from Objects option. Shift+select Torus and then the Open option, as shown in Figure 8-38.

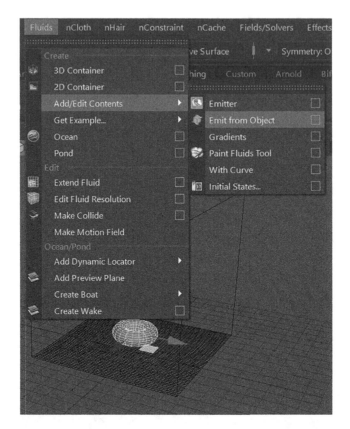

Figure 8-38. *Emit from Object option*

This will reveal another window, which will show the Surface option, as shown in Figure 8-39. Click Apply and Close. This results in making the torus primitive the emitter for the fluids.

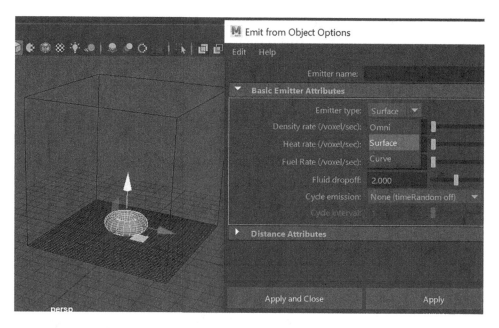

Figure 8-39. *Emit from Object popup window with Surface set as the emitter type*

Now you can see that the emission is coming from the torus, as shown in Figure 8-40. Let's dive into the interesting parameters of this emitter.

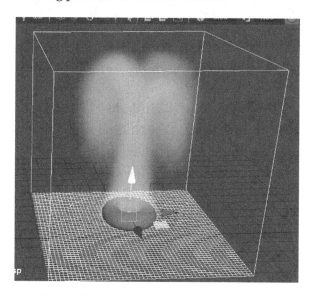

Figure 8-40. *Emission from the torus*

In the Fluid Attributes, you need to switch off the Heat and the Fuel methods. Then you can get into the Fluid Emission Turbulence section, set the Turbulence property to 10, and increase the Detail Turbulence value to 1. When you play the simulation now, you can see a better variation than the previous one. See Figure 8-41.

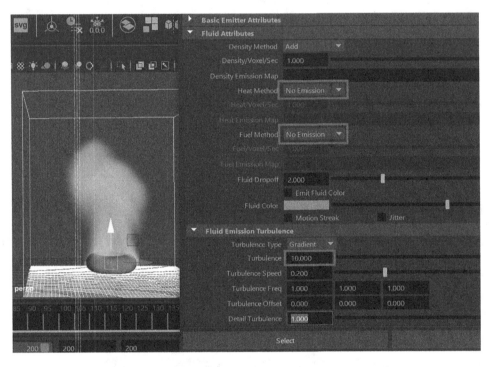

Figure 8-41. *Emission from the torus with the turbulence attributes*

Now let's delve into the Emission Speed attributes, where you modify the speed method to Replace. In this section, there is the Normal Speed property. This "normal" represents the normals of the polygon represented in the geometry, which is a reference vector perpendicular to the center of the base. If you increase this property to 10, you can see that the fluids will be emitted from the sides of the polygon based on the angle of the normals, as shown in Figure 8-42. However, the Speed Method can also be set to Add, whereby the fluids emitting from the normals of the geometry will add to the original emission.

Figure 8-42. *Emission from the torus based on the surface normal*

Emitting Fluids from Textures

This section dives into the simulation of fluids from the geometry, but this time you will also be utilizing the emission maps. This means utilizing the UV textures of the geometry. A point to note in this context is that, for texture maps with white or high pixel values, the fluid emission will be compared to the gray areas and there will be no emission in the black areas.

Let's get started.

For this demonstration, you need a polygonal surface with its UVs. Go to Hypershade and get the Ramp texture assigned to the geometry. (A plane in this example.) See Figure 8-43.

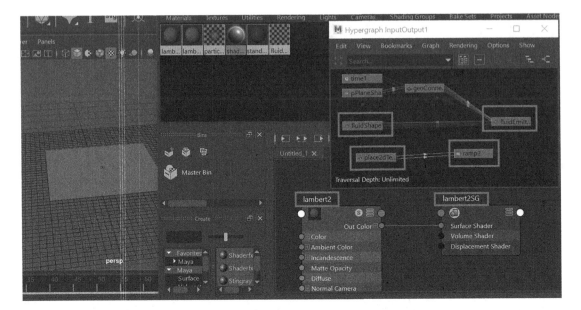

Figure 8-43. *The plane surface with ramp and lambert materials assigned*

Now, you could modify the ramp to remove any gray areas. Put the interpolation of the material attribute is set to none, which means you get a crisp demarcation of black and white areas, as shown in Figure 8-44. As discussed earlier, the emission will happen from the white areas. Set the type to Circular instead of the default Linear.

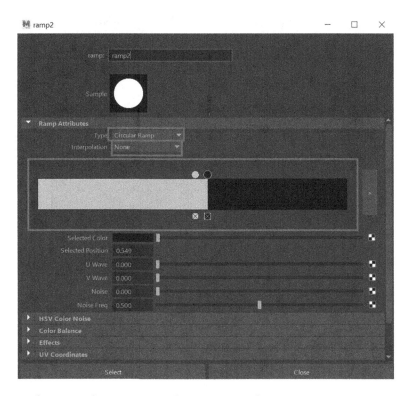

Figure 8-44. *The Circular ramp with no interpolation*

You need to select the polygonal plane and the fluid container. Go to Add/Edit Contents and select the Emit from Object option. This is similar to what you did in the previous section of emitting from the polygon surface.

Next, go to the fluid emitter Attribute Editor and scroll to the Fluid Attribute section. Switch off the Heat and Fuel methods to no emission. Then, in the Density Emission Map, you can type the name of the texture map assigned to the plane/the geometry. In this case, the texture map is called Circle. When you play the simulation now, you'll see the emission happening from the circular white section only, as shown in Figure 8-45.

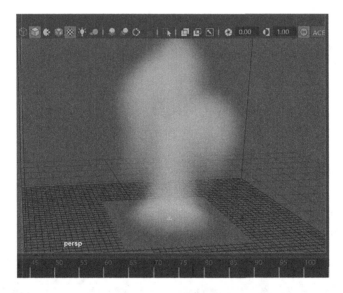

Figure 8-45. *The Circular Ramp emitting fluids*

Emitting Fluids from Particles

This section covers the emission of fluids from particles. You could just sketch particles, as shown in Figure 8-46.

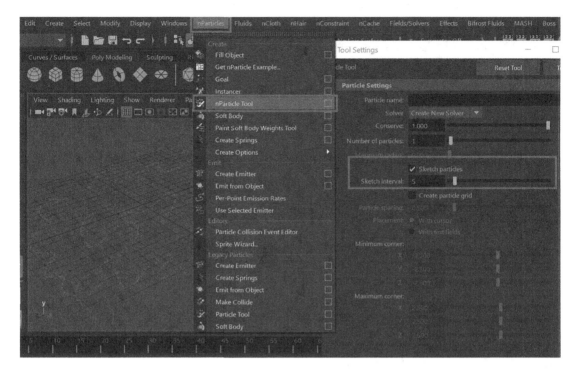

Figure 8-46. *The particle sketch*

Now you can add the Fields/Solvers. For the purposes of this demonstration, choose Turbulence and set the values of Magnitude to 30, Remove Attenuation to 0, and Frequency to 0.25. At this point, before you play the simulation of the particles, remember to make some changes to the preferences. The Playback Speed must be set to 24fps. When you play the particles, you will see them as shown in Figure 8-47.

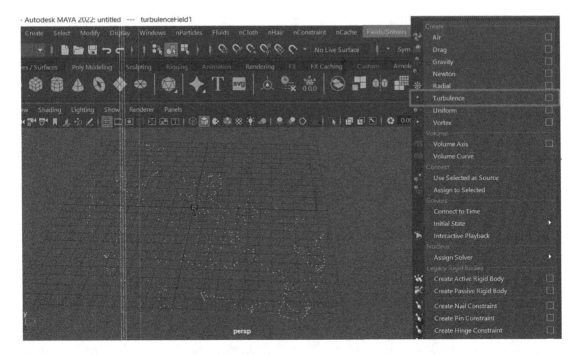

Figure 8-47. *The particle simulation*

It seems to be all over the place. So, to fix that, reduce the Conserve to 0.9, modify the Age to Random Range, reduce the Lifespan to 0.75, and set the Lifetime Random value to 0.25. In the Render Attributes, reduce the Point Size to 1. This will make the particle simulate and dissipate, which is what you want.

Now you need to select the particles and the 3D container. Go to the Fluids menu, scroll to Add/Edit Contents, and click Emit from Object. Then click Apply, as shown in Figure 8-48.

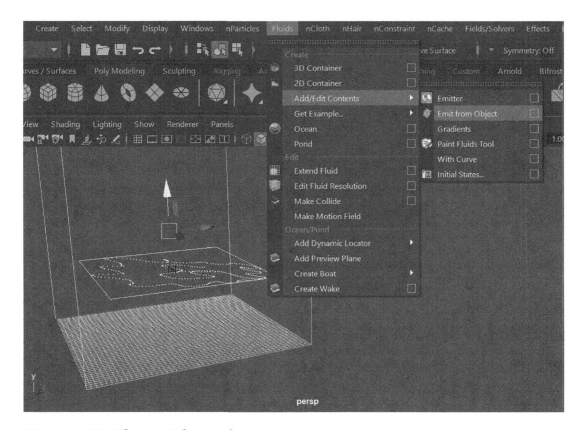

Figure 8-48. *The particle simulation*

Next, you can hide the particles to see only the fluid emission. But before you can play it, you need to tweak the Fluid Emitter. Since there is animation in the particles, you need to use Motion Streak. You need to set the Speed Method to Replace and set the Inherent Velocity to 5. You also need to alter the Max Distance to 0.1 and set the Rate percentage to 1000 to counter the Max Distance modification. You can also increase the Fluid Resolution to 100 for better render quality. If you play the simulation now, it will look like Figure 8-49.

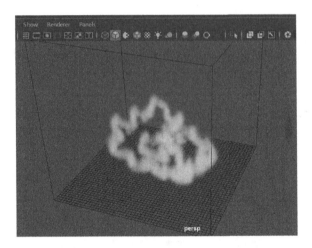

Figure 8-49. *Fluid emission from the particle simulation*

Emitting Fluids from Curves

This section explores the method of emitting fluids from the Nurbs curve.

Create the basic curve using the CV Curve tool. You can tweak the vertices on the y-axis to create variations, as shown in Figure 8-50. This creates some randomness in the fluid emission.

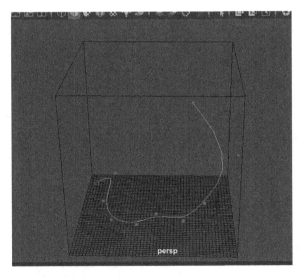

Figure 8-50. *Curve created using the CV Curve tool*

Now you need to create the 3D Fluid Container and place the curve in the container. Alter the size of the container as needed. Select both the curve and the container. Go to the Fluids menu and scroll to Add/Edit Contents. Select Emit from Object. This time, make sure Curve is selected for the Emitter Type and then click Apply and Close, as shown in Figure 8-51. When you play the simulation, you will be able to view the fluid emission.

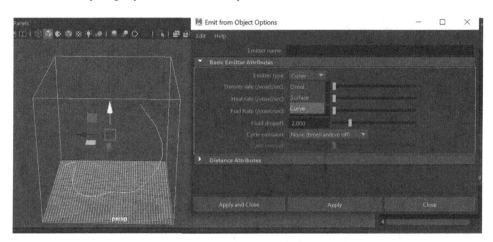

Figure 8-51. *Curve-based emission*

One specialty of the curve emitter is its tangent speed, which is found in the Emission Speed Attributes section. Set the Speed Method to Replace and the Tangent Speed to 30, as shown in Figure 8-52.

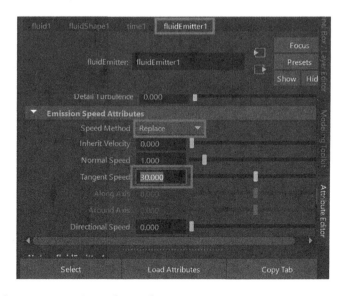

Figure 8-52. *The Tangent Speed attribute*

217

With some more tweaking of the Motion Streak—reducing Max Distance to 0.25 and increasing the Rate Percentage to 250—you can produce a more convincing result, as shown in Figure 8-53.

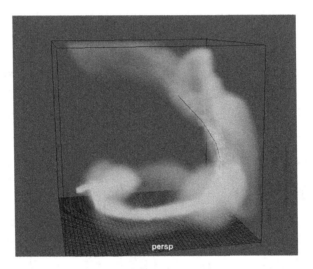

Figure 8-53. *The fluid emission from a CV curve*

You have learned all about the Maya Fluids system. The next chapter explores the predefined effects available in Maya, their purposes, and their effective uses. You will also learn about using the Attribute Editors and see how to play with values to generate interesting VFX.

CHAPTER 9

Magical FX Using Maya

This chapter discusses how to create fire, fireworks, lightning, shatter, and smoke effects using Autodesk Maya. You will also learn how to use Attribute Editors and how to manipulate values in order to create visually intriguing effects.

Creating Fire, Fireworks, Lightning, Shatter, and Smoke Effects

So far you have learned about particle systems and fluid systems in Autodesk Maya. Now you will dive into the effects available in Maya. This chapter explores simulations you can create using the default effects in Maya. To access these effects, you need to switch to the FX layout and select Effects from the top menu bar, as shown in Figure 9-1. Here you will find the default effect options, including Fire, Fireworks, Flow, Lightning, Shatter, and Smoke.

Figure 9-1. *Effects menu set*

© Abhishek Kumar 2022

A. Kumar, *Beginning VFX with Autodesk Maya*, https://doi.org/10.1007/978-1-4842-7857-4_9

In the previous chapter, you created fire using the Maya Fluids simulation. Similarly, to create fireworks, you can manually work with the Maya Particles system. Also, for shatter and smoke, you can use nParticles or even fluids to get this effect.

However, these effects have auto-simulated set parameters and can be achieved with a single click in the Effects menu. Let's start exploring the Fire effects. For this, you first need to create a geometry. Switch to the Modeling layout to create two torus and combine them into a single model, as shown in Figure 9-2.

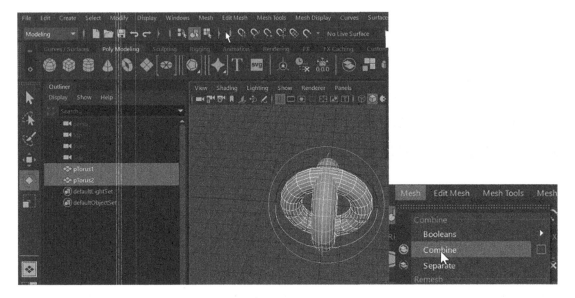

Figure 9-2. *Modeling the torus*

After you create the model but before you switch back to the FX layout, delete the history, as shown in Figure 9-3.

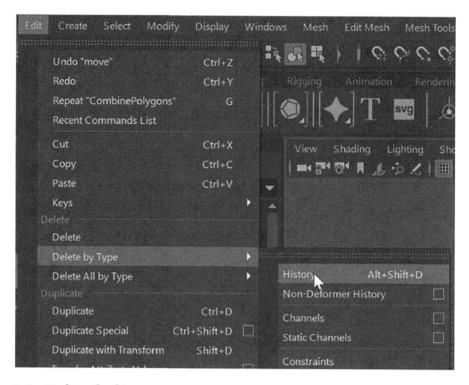

Figure 9-3. *Delete the history*

Name this geometry `Emitter` from the Outliner window. You can switch to the FX layout and select the Fire option from the Effects menu. This will open another window showing the fire attributes. From the Fire Emitter Type drop-down menu, select the Surface option, since you are to emit the fire within the polysurface you just created. Now modify some of the parameters—such as increase the Fire Density to 30. Leave the Fire Start Radius and Fire End Radius set to the defaults and decrease the Fire Intensity to 0.2. There are other parameters—like the Fire Speed, Direction in x-, y-, and z-axes, and the Fire Turbulence and Scale—which you can keep set to the default values for now. Click Create, as shown in Figure 9-4.

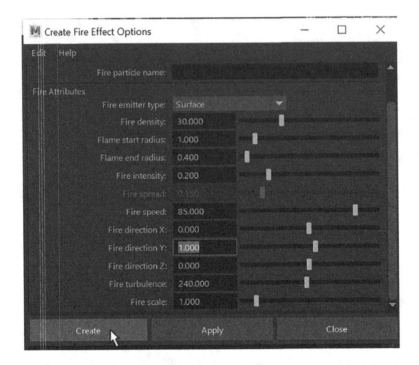

Figure 9-4. *Fire attributes*

This will create particle, drag field, and gravity field in the Outliner, as shown in Figure 9-5.

Figure 9-5. *Fire attributes*

If you play the simulation now, it will look like Figure 9-6.

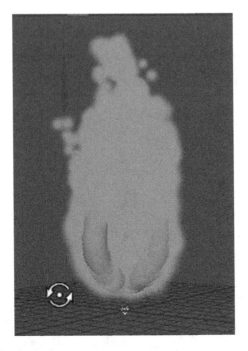

Figure 9-6. *Fire simulation*

The effects can be further modified in the particle clouds and in the emitter attribute windows. However, the color of the simulation looks gray. To view how this actually looks, you need to render it. Open the render settings and switch the Render Using option from Arnold Renderer to Maya Software, as shown in Figure 9-7.

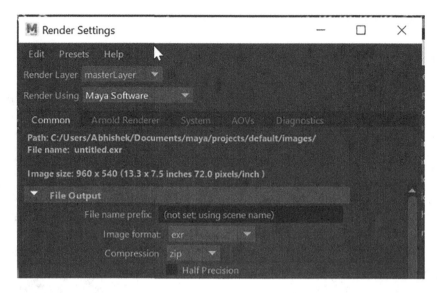

Figure 9-7. *Fire simulation*

Click the Render button, as shown in Figure 9-8.

Figure 9-8. *The Render button*

You can now see the rendered output, as shown in Figure 9-9. You will now be able to see the color of the fire.

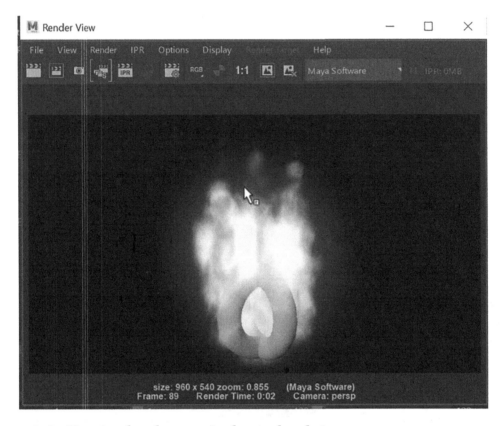

Figure 9-9. *Fire simulated output in the rendered view*

Now you can use the various attributes of the fire by selecting the particle from the Outliner view. In the Attribute Editor of the particle, modify the properties. To view the modified effect, you have to re-render the frame. In the Particle Shape Attribute Editor, there is the option to conserve. This will help with the fire's flow.

Now let's look at the Fireworks effect.

Choose the Fireworks option from the Effects menu. This will open another window with all the attributes, as shown in Figure 9-10. There are three main options—the Rocket Attributes, Rocket Trail Attributes, and Fireworks Sparks Attributes.

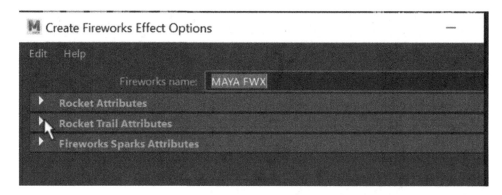

Figure 9-10. *Fireworks window*

In the Rocket Attributes, the Num Rocket specifies the number of rockets that will erupt. The First Launch Frame option indicates which frame will start the launch. Set it to 20 to make the launch start at the 20th frame. The Maxburst Speed specifies how fast or slow you want the rocket to erupt.

The Rocket Trail Attributes specify how long you want the trail to be, how fast or slow the trail should appear, the size of the trail, its intensity, and so on.

In the Sparks Attributes, you can modify the settings to determine how many sparks you want and set their length.

Once you have modified these settings, you can click the Create button and play the simulation to check the effect, as shown in Figure 9-11.

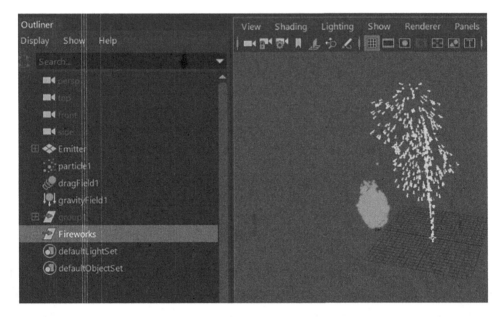

Figure 9-11. *Fireworks simulation on the viewport*

You can increase the frame range to see the simulation. You can also render the viewport to check the simulated colored output of this firework effect, as shown in Figure 9-12.

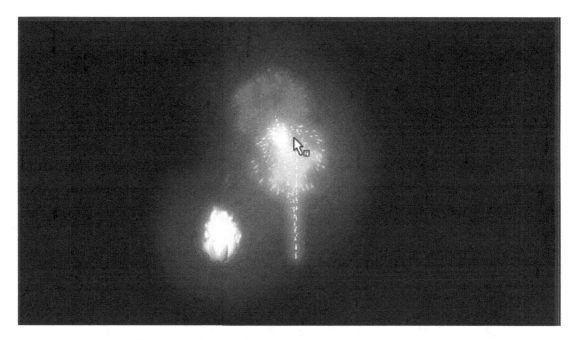

Figure 9-12. *Rendered output of the fireworks simulation*

Now, let's check out the Lightning effect. To create this effect, you need to create two objects. Use the Cylinder Primitive tool to create two poles, as shown in Figure 9-13.

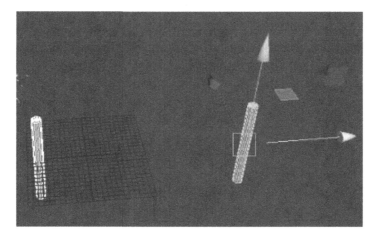

Figure 9-13. *Two poles created using the Cylinder Primitive tool*

You need to go back to the Effects menu and select Lightning. This will reveal another window showing the Lightning properties, as shown in Figure 9-14. For example, you can change the Curve Segment to 38.

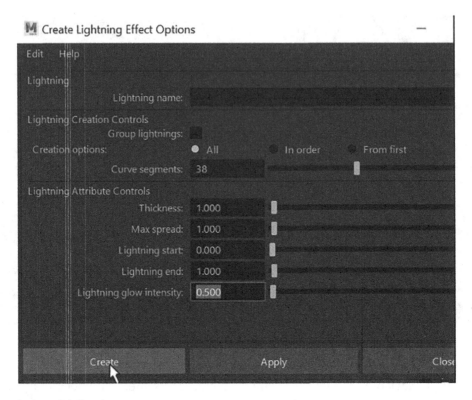

Figure 9-14. *Lightning parameters*

You can increase or decrease the thickness, the start and end of the lightning, and the amount of glow. Once you have adjusted these, you need to click the Create button, which will form the lightning from one pole to the other, as shown in Figure 9-15.

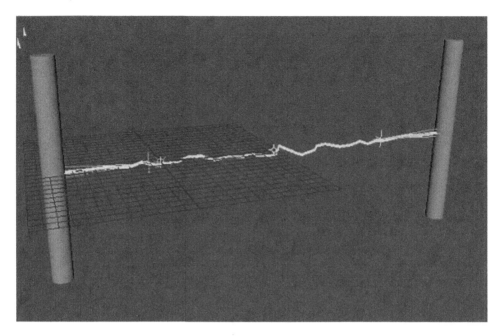

Figure 9-15. *Lightning Effect simulation on the viewport*

Moving on further, we have the Smoke effect. To work on this effect, you need to create a geometry. You can create any geometry (for example, a cube) and simply go back to Effects and apply the Smoke Effect. When you play the simulation, you will see the smoke emit from the geometry, as shown in Figure 9-16.

Figure 9-16. *Smoke effect applied*

Another default effect in Maya is the flow. To start, create a path, as shown in Figure 9-17, with the help of the Curve tool.

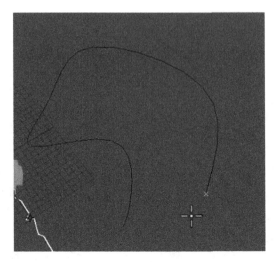

Figure 9-17. *Creating a path with the Curve tool*

The path dictates how the particle will flow. If you go back to the Effects menu now, you will find Create Curve Flow in the Flow option. Here, you can modify settings based on your needs and click Create, as shown in Figure 9-18.

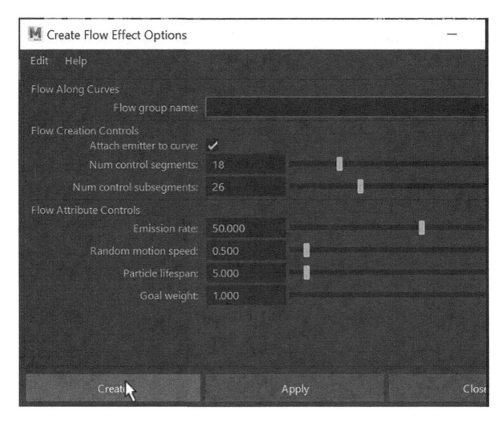

Figure 9-18. *The Flow options*

Figure 9-19 shows how the Flow effect will appear on the viewport.

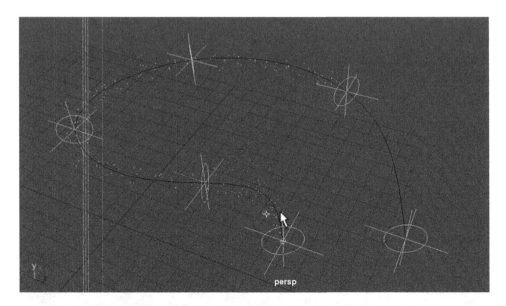

Figure 9-19. *The Flow effect applied to the curve*

The flow needs to be rendered in Maya to see the desired output. See Figure 9-20.

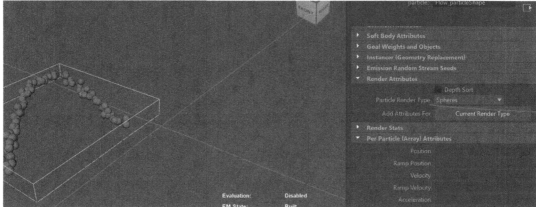

Figure 9-20. *The Rendered Flow effect with Maya hardware*

Finally, you are left to explore the Shatter effect. For this effect, you need to create the model first. For this example, create a sphere.

Tip   Remember to delete the history whenever you create a geometry. Otherwise, the new effect will not work correctly.

Once you have created a sphere, go back to the Effects menu and select the Shatter effect. This will pop up another window, as shown in Figure 9-21.

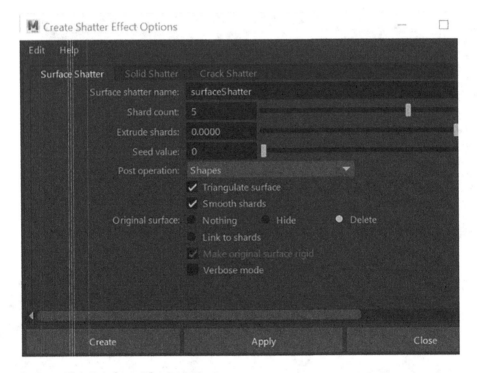

Figure 9-21. *The Surface Shatter options*

There are three types of Shatter effects—Surface Shatter, Solid Shatter, and Crack Shatter.

Surface Shatter breaks along the surface, while Solid Shatter works on the entire mass of the object, as shown in Figure 9-22.

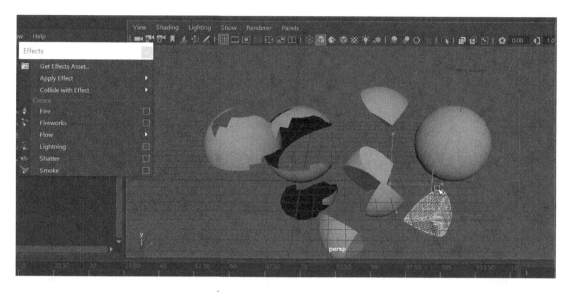

Figure 9-22. *The Surface Shatter and Solid Shatter effects after manually separating the chunks in viewport*

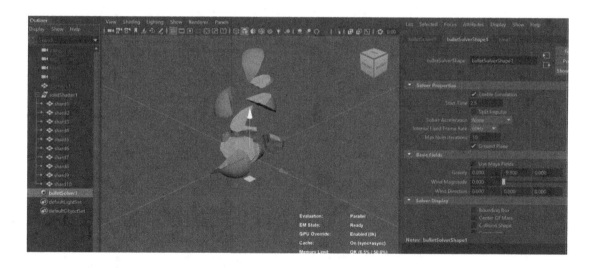

Now check out the Crack Shatter. This effect works with the vertices of the geometry, as shown in Figure 9-23.

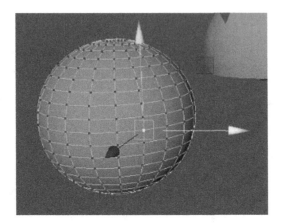

Figure 9-23. *Crack Shatter works on the vertices of the geometry*

The options of the crack surface can be manipulated to suit your scene requirements, as shown in Figure 9-24.

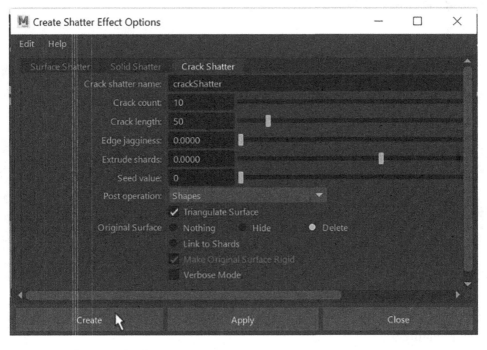

Figure 9-24. *The Crack Shatter options*

The resultant output is shown in Figure 9-25.

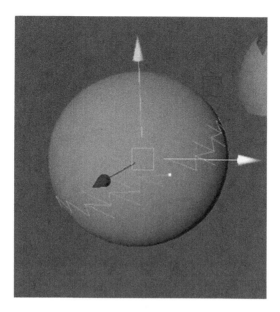

Figure 9-25. *The Crack Shatter effect applied*

By using these effects and making them active or passive rigid bodies, you can create various combinations of effects.

The Get Effects Asset Library

This section explores the Get Effects Asset option. There are several effects predefined and available within Maya. This section randomly explores a few of them along with a rigid body/soft body collision.

The Get Effects Asset library is available from the Effects menu, as shown in Figure 9-26.

Figure 9-26. *The Get Effects Asset option*

The Effects library reveals another window of effects, as shown in Figure 9-27. There are several predefined particle simulations available for direct use.

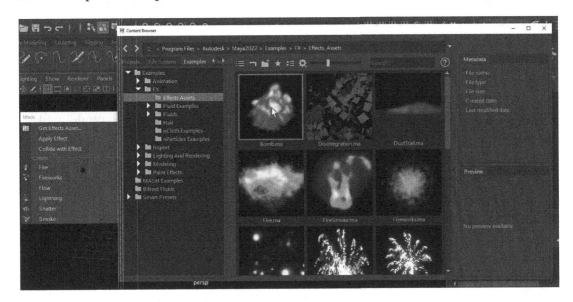

Figure 9-27. *The Effects library*

For example, if you choose the sparks and double-click it or drag and drop it on the viewport, it will be imported into the Maya scene that you are currently using, which you can see from the Outliner window, as shown in Figure 9-28. From there, you will find particle systems, locators, and so on.

Figure 9-28. *The Outliner view*

Once you have the particles in your scene, you can select them and modify the Sparks assets, as shown in Figure 9-29. Make any changes based on your requirements.

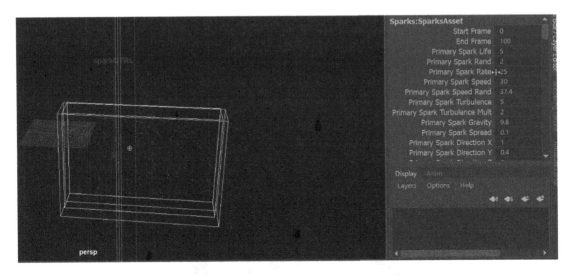

Figure 9-29. *The Sparks editing options*

Let's try the bomb effect. You can simply drag and drop this effect on the viewport and, from the Outliner, select the effect. You can modify the effects from the Attribute Editor of the Bomb asset, as shown in Figure 9-30.

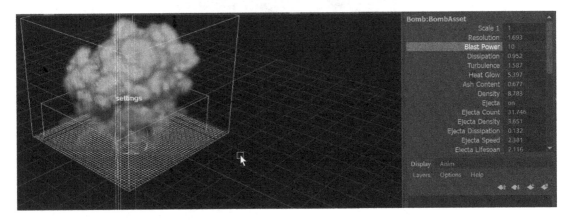

Figure 9-30. *The Bomb asset's editing options*

The rendered image of the Bomb asset simulation is shown in Figure 9-31. The quality of the output depends on the resolution value—the higher the resolution, the better the result, but that will also require a higher computational value and processor speed.

Figure 9-31. *The Bomb assets rendered output*

You can modify the values of the Turbulence, Heat Glow, and Buoyancy, which also alter the look of the blast, as shown in Figure 9-32.

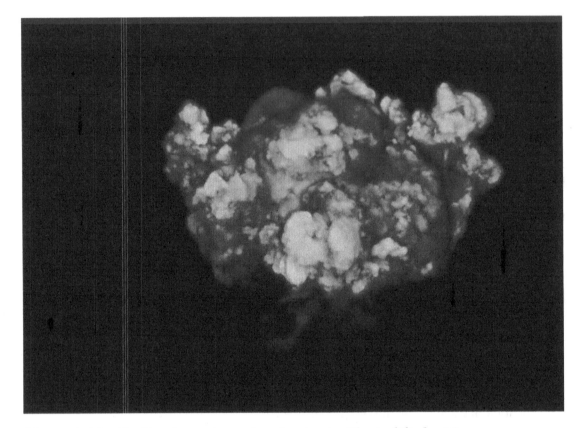

Figure 9-32.   *The Bomb assets rendered output with modified settings*

Let's check out another effect from the Assets library—the Disintegration effect.

This is indeed a very interesting effect, as shown in Figure 9-33. You can find this effect in several movies, including *Avengers: Endgame,* when (spoiler alert) Thanos is disintegrated in the final scene. That can be simulated using the Disintegration effect. In this final project section, you learn how to create this effect manually. There are also predefined effects available in Maya.

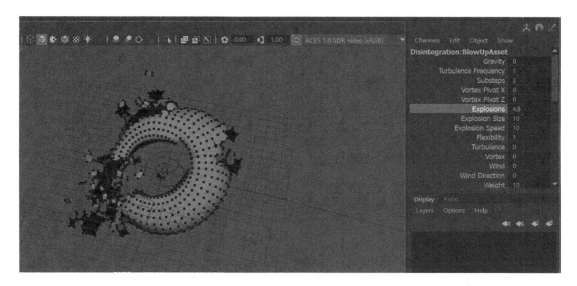

Figure 9-33. *The Disintegration effect*

By modifying the Explosion Size, Turbulence, Vortex, Wind Direction, and other options, you can create different variations in the speed of the disintegration.

Similarly, you can try the other effects like the Rocket and Fire effects, which are predefined and produce impactful results at the click of a button. With a few modifications to the attributes, you can further create hyper-realistic looks to suit your needs.

Collision with Effects

In this section, you learn how to make these effects collide with other objects. This example uses the Disintegration effect. In the previous section, you saw how the Disintegration effect made the torus break and explode away.

First, create a few barriers for the disintegrated particles to collide against. Create a wall on three sides of the torus, as shown in Figure 9-34.

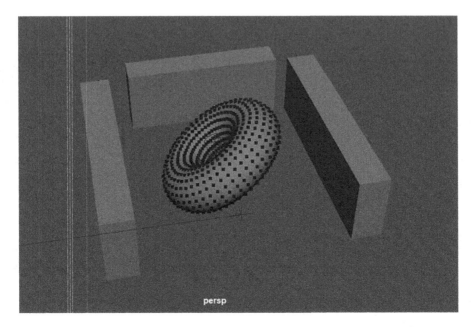

Figure 9-34. *The barriers around the torus disintegration effect*

The next steps are to select all the three objects, delete the history, and freeze the transformations.

With the three walls selected, go to the nCloth option and select the Create Passive collider option, as shown in Figure 9-35. This will turn the objects into a rigid body.

Figure 9-35. *The Create Passive Collider option*

If you play the simulation now, you will see that the particles collide with the walls, as shown in Figure 9-36.

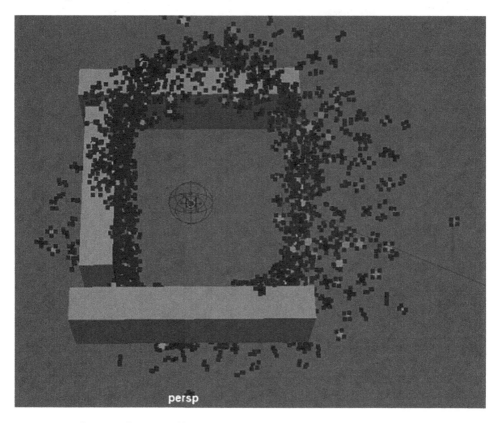

Figure 9-36. *The resultant collision*

If the collision doesn't work, select all the three objects again and choose the Collide with Effect option from the Effects menu. Then select the Disintegration effect, as shown in Figure 9-37.

Figure 9-37. *The Collide with Effect option*

Now that you have explored the various default effects in Maya, you are ready to simulate various effects easily and with impressive results in less time.

In the next chapter, you learn about the simulation of rigid and soft bodies using the nCloth system in Maya.

CHAPTER 10

Playing with Maya nCloth

In Maya, you can create dynamic cloth effects using the Maya nCloth feature. nCloth is a fast and stable dynamic cloth solution that simulates a wide range of dynamic polygon surfaces—such as fabric clothing, inflating balloons, shattering surfaces, and deformable objects—using a system of linked particles. nCloth is made up of modeled polygon meshes. You can create a nCloth object from any type of polygon mesh, which is ideal for achieving specific poses while maintaining directorial control.

Maya Nucleus is a dynamic simulation framework that underpins nCloth. A Maya Nucleus system is made up of nCloth objects, passive collision objects, dynamic constraints, and the Maya Nucleus solver. The Maya Nucleus solver, which is part of the Maya Nucleus system, iteratively calculates nCloth simulation, collisions, and constraints, improving the simulation after each iteration to produce the best cloth simulation results. This chapter covers the nCloth creation followed by collisions with passive bodies. At the end of the chapter, you will create a real-life flag simulation.

Creating nCloth

Let's get started with the creation of nCloth. To enable nCloth, you need to switch to the FX layout. You will find the Create nCloth option, as shown in Figure 10-1. Along with the Create nCloth option, you will find a whole list of other options, like Create Passive Collider, Display Options, and History Options, as well as some nCloth examples. For the examples here, select the Create nCloth option.

© Abhishek Kumar 2022
A. Kumar, *Beginning VFX with Autodesk Maya*, https://doi.org/10.1007/978-1-4842-7857-4_10

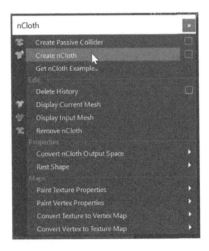

Figure 10-1. *nCloth in Maya*

Before you start creating the nCloth, you need a surface since the nCloth works on the vertices of the polygon geometry. The greater the number of vertices, the smoother the simulation will be. First create a plane geometry. You need to increase the Subdivisions of Width and Height to the value of 50, as shown in Figure 10-2.

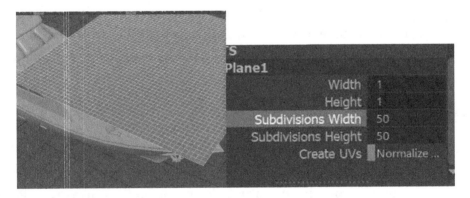

Figure 10-2. *Plane polygonal surface*

Once you create the geometry, delete the history of that object for scene optimization, as shown in Figure 10-3.

Figure 10-3. *Delete history option*

It's best to freeze the transformations using the Modify menu and selecting the Freeze Transformation option, as shown in Figure 10-4. This helps set all the values of the geometry to 0. You should also rename the plane Cloth.

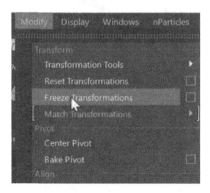

Figure 10-4. *Freeze Transformations option*

Once the plane is ready, assign the nucleus cloth to it by revisiting the nCloth menu and selecting the Create nCloth option. This will open a dialog box where you should choose Create New Solver, as shown in Figure 10-5.

Figure 10-5. *Create nCloth dialog box*

Whenever a nucleus is added, a new solver will be assigned. However, before you apply the new solver, you need to reset the settings to ensure default values.

This will create a few nodes in the Outliner—namely the Nucleus and the nCloth, as shown in Figure 10-6.

Figure 10-6. *Outliner view*

Working with the Passive Collider

Once you have applied the nCloth, you can play the effect to check the simulation.

You will notice that the cloth simply passes through the object in the scene, namely the ship in this case. To make the cloth interact with the other objects in the scene, you need to introduce the Passive Collider. So, you need to select the model and click the Create Passive Collider option that resides in the nCloth menu, as shown in Figure 10-7.

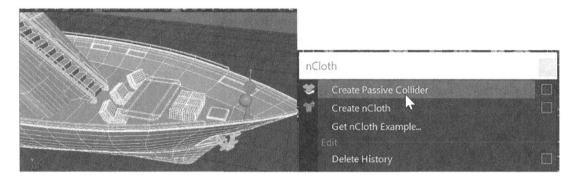

Figure 10-7. *Create Passive Collider option*

All these geometries have now been converted to a rigid body system, as you can see in the Outliner window shown in Figure 10-8.

Figure 10-8. *Outliner view with rigid body added*

When you play the nCloth simulation now, you will see a beautiful interaction with the geometry, as captured in Figure 10-9.

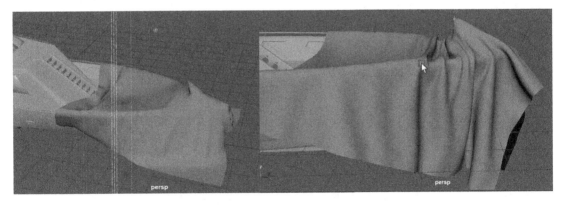

Figure 10-9. *The resultant simulation after applying the Passive Collider*

There are various options and properties associated with the Nucleus Cloth. You will learn about some challenges related to using the Nucleus Cloth in the following sections.

Play with nCloth Attributes

nCloth is the Cloth Dynamics system built into Maya. It can be used to create a wide variety of different materials types and effects. For the purpose of explanation, you will work on a tarpaulin blowing in the wind, as shown in Figure 10-10. This section explains how to set up nCloth and how to use the nCloth presets, and includes a few tips on how to work with nCloth faster and easier.

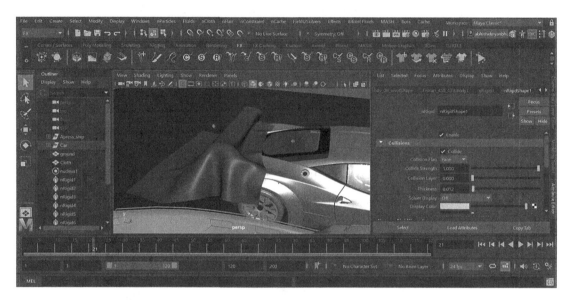

Figure 10-10.   *nCloth in Maya*

You will create the nCloth on a wreck of a car modeled in Maya and create a dynamic piece of cloth applied to it. One important point to keep in mind is that the density of your models is going to affect the calculation being used for the generation of the nCloth simulation. So, keep the model optimized for smooth simulation.

Now let's begin by creating the tarpaulin that you need to cover the car. Go to the Create menu, select Polygon Primitives, and choose Plane. Now you need to place it as shown in Figure 10-11 with the Subdivisions Parameters of Width and Height set to 50 in the Inputs section of the Polyplane. This helps you get a decent amount of deformations.

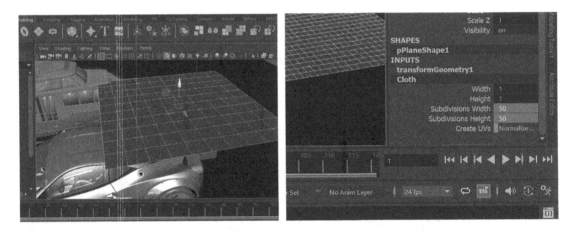

Figure 10-11. *Creation and alignment of plane with subdivisions*

Great! You now need to create the rigid bodies. To do so, select the car geometry and choose nCloth. Then click Create Passive Collider, as shown in Figure 10-12. The same thing needs to be repeated with the ground.

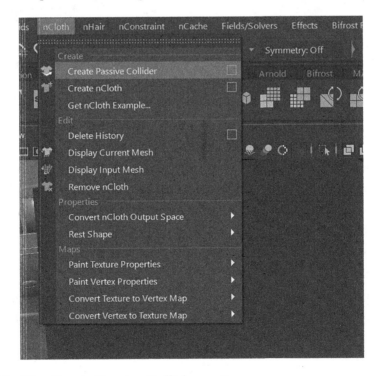

Figure 10-12. *The Create Passive Collider option*

Now you will select the tarpaulin plane that you created. Go to the nCloth menu and select Create nCloth, as shown in Figure 10-13.

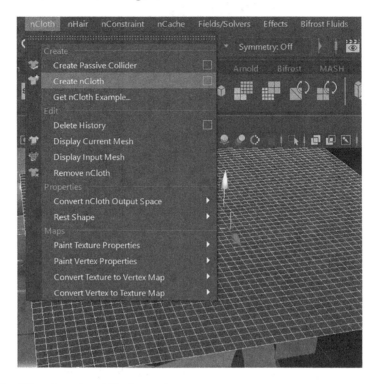

Figure 10-13. *The Create nCloth option*

Observing the Outliner window, you will see that the rigid bodies have been added, as shown in Figure 10-14.

Figure 10-14. *Maya Outliner window*

Now just play the animation to see that the nCloth slowly wraps around the car, which is our collision surface. At this point you can customize the shape, which will involve a lot of experimentation. Play the simulation and let the tarpaulin plane fall down slowly, drape, and wrap around the surface. Adjust some settings, do some tweaks, and work around with some of the presets. Then design the quality of the surface as it drapes over the collision surface. The easiest way to do that is to use the presets located in the Attribute Editor of the nCloth, as shown in Figure 10-15.

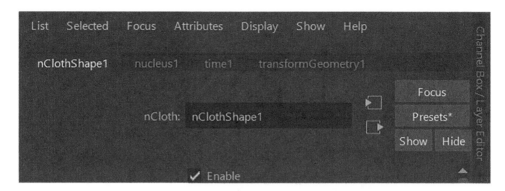

Figure 10-15. *The nCloth Presets**

There is a whole set of presets available, as shown in Figure 10-16, which you can experiment with to best suit your needs.

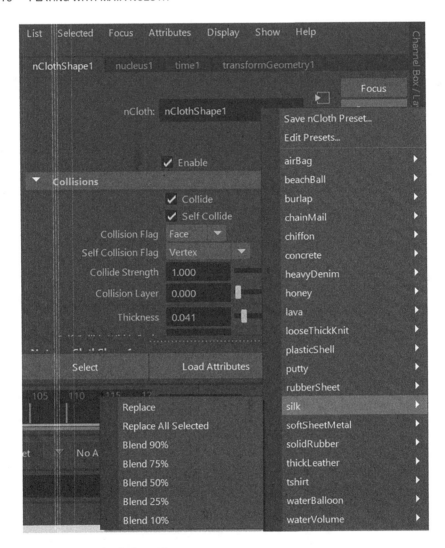

Figure 10-16. *The nCloth list of presets*

Let's say, for example, that you select the T-shirt preset, then all the settings get adjusted as per the dynamic's behavior of a t-shirt as set by the creators. So, you select T-shirt and click Replace, as shown in Figure 10-17. This will replace the existing dynamics of the nCloth with that of the T-shirt preset. However, settings can be adjusted to get alterations of the material behavior in this preset. When you play the simulation, you will see that it animates like the flow of a T-shirt. However, the dynamics calculation may be slow or fast depending on the presets.

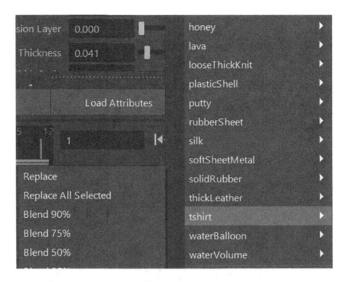

Figure 10-17. *Application of nCloth preset of t-shirt*

Again, if you want to, you can blend two different presets. Let's say you applied the Burlap and now you want to blend a silk type of material quality to it. You can select Silk and choose Blend 50%, as shown in Figure 10-18. That way, the burlap will have 50% behavior of the silk material.

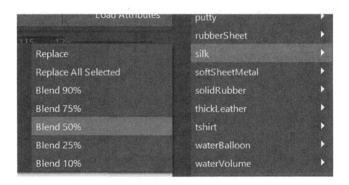

Figure 10-18. *The nCloth presets Blend options*

Now let's start working on the scene. After a few experimentations you'll see that the preset that works best for your tarpaulin is the rubber sheet. As indicated earlier, you can read the Notes section for the tips given to alter specific settings. That might be handier than blindly adjusting them.

So, you could try to adjust the damp to make it look a bit heavier and set it to 0.020 instead of the preset default of 0.010. A word of caution—adjust one parameter at a time and play it to see the effect so you can identify which property is causing the effect in your simulation. Another thing that I noticed while doing the simulation is that when I went into the Collisions tab and switched the Solver Display to Collision Thickness, the cloth appeared to be quite thick, as shown in Figure 10-19.

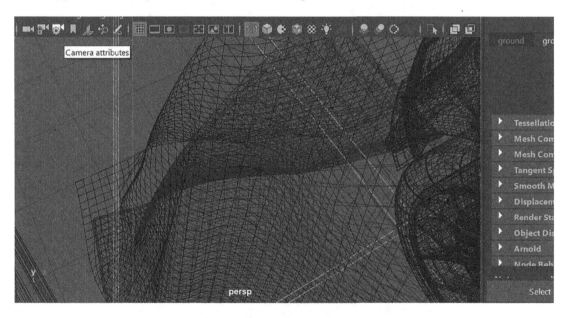

Figure 10-19. *The nCloth rubber sheet thickness*

First change the viewport settings to Wireframe by pressing 4 on the keyboard and then in the Thickness parameter, change the Collisions tab to 0.1. Then play it. You will find it to be much a better deformation with the reduced thickness. For the purposes here, you might also want to increase the friction. See Figure 10-20.

Figure 10-20. *The Friction parameter setting*

Simultaneously, increase the friction of the rigid bodies. Select nRigid 1 and in the Collisions tab, increase the Friction to 1 to make sure it doesn't slide along too easily. After experimenting with some of the settings like Stretch Resistance, Compression Resistance, Bend Resistance, and the other dynamic properties, create your own preset by selecting Save nCloth preset, as shown in Figure 10-21. Then choose a name for it and click the Save Attribute Preset button.

Figure 10-21. *The Save Attribute Preset option*

The great thing about presets is that they are set in the Maya Preferences, so if you go to a completely different scene and a completely different project, it's very simple to load presets you created previously.

Once you set your own preset, the things that are going to affect the simulations will be found in the Nucleus node. In fact, if you go to the Time Attributes, you can determine a frame to start the simulation. In that case, nothing will happen unless the animation reaches that frame number and then the simulation will start. Similarly, the Scale Attributes allow you to change the overall scale of the scene.

If you want the cloth draped over the car to be the initial state, you can first allow the simulation to happen and then stop at a frame where the cloth is draped over the car, as shown in Figure 10-22.

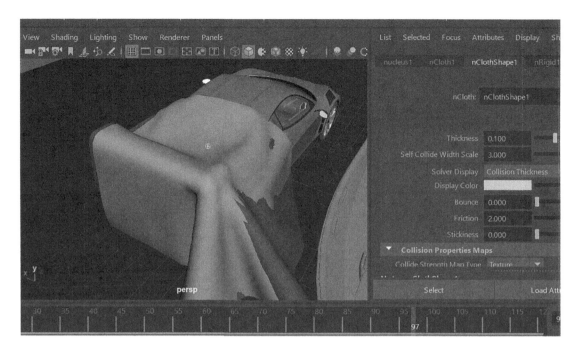

Figure 10-22. *The simulation frame at which you would want to set the initial state*

Then choose Fields/Solvers, scroll down to the Initial State, and click Set to Selected, as shown in Figure 10-23. If you rewind and play, you can see that the draped cloth is the initial state. If you need to change that, you can go back to the same option and click Clear Initial State.

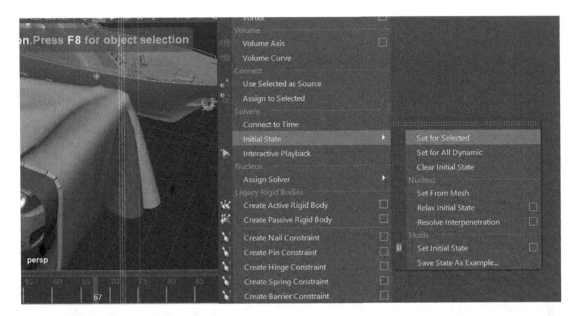

Figure 10-23. *Set the initial state*

Now you can create a field for the wind blowing effect. You can directly add wind in the nucleus node that is found in the nucleus attributes and they will affect all the nucleus objects, like nCloth and nHair. But for the purposes here, you will try independent nodes just for the flexibility so that they affect only the selected object. Select the tarp, go to Fields/Solvers, and select Air to create a nice wind effect. This creates a node in the Outliner called `airfield` and you can place it where you want the air to blow, as shown in Figure 10-24.

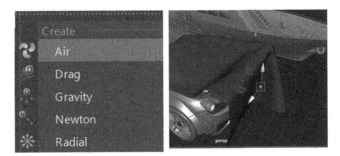

Figure 10-24. *To place the airfield*

Go into the Attribute Editor and decide how it's going to blow the tarpaulin. In the Air Field Attribute, set the Direction to x-axis (since I want the wind to blow in that direction) to 1, set Y to 0, and set Z to 0, as shown in Figure 10-25.

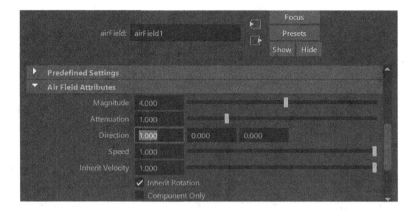

Figure 10-25. *To set the direction of the wind*

Another thing to consider is the distance. For the Air field, the maximum distance is 20 by default, which means that it is going to affect objects within 20 units of its surrounding icon. But if you want it to have a global effect, turn off the Use Max Distance, as shown in Figure 10-26.

Figure 10-26. *Use Max Distance turned off*

Now go to Magnitude under the Air Field Attribute and set it to a really high value, for example to 1000. Check how this looks, as shown in Figure 10-27.

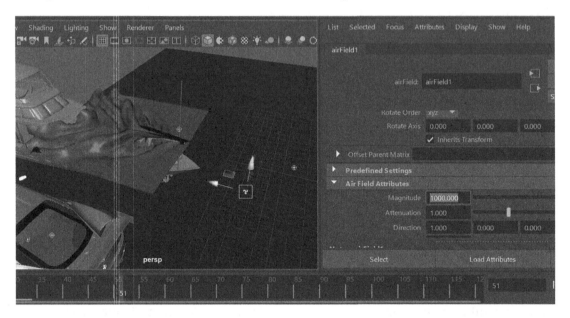

Figure 10-27. *Magnitude set to 1000 and its effect on the viewport*

Now you can see that the wind is too strong so you have to reduce it to 200 for the purposes here.

The tarpaulin should also be stuck to the car. To do that, select the nCloth and on the Collisions tab, turn the Solver Display from Collision Thickness to off.

The Power of nConstraints for Effective and Efficient Simulations

Now you need to add a constraint that basically sticks to the Ship Rod Geometry surface. There are a number of ways this can be done. For the purposes here, you will be using the Point to Surface constraint found in the nConstraint menu. Start by right-clicking the nCloth and choosing Vertex (see Figure 10-28).

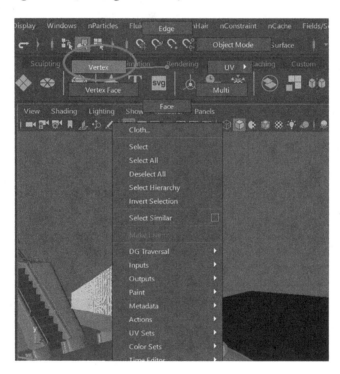

Figure 10-28. *Vertex selection mode*

Select a vertex of the nCloth and then Shift+select the Ship Rod Geo, as shown in Steps 1, 2, and 3 in Figures 10-29 through 10-31. Then go to the nConstraint menu and choose the Point to Surface constraint.

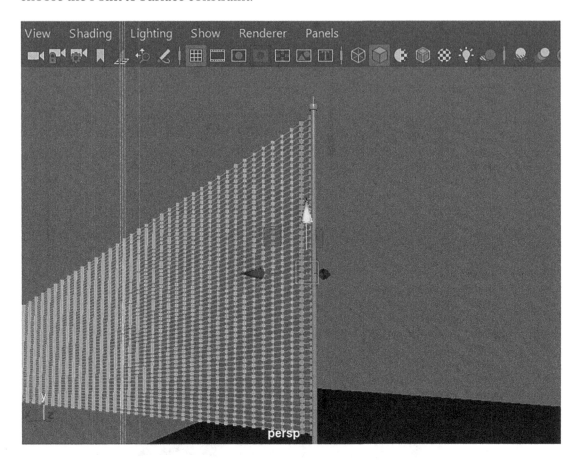

Figure 10-29. *Step 1: Select vertices*

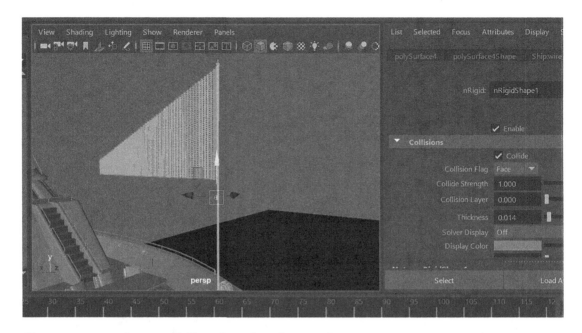

Figure 10-30. *Step 2: Shift+select the Ship Rod Geo*

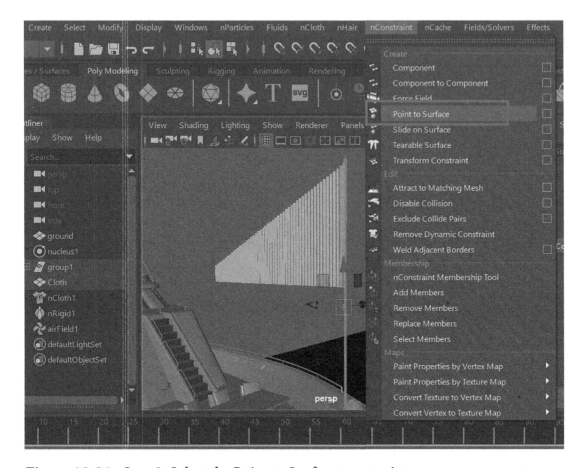

Figure 10-31. *Step 3: Select the Point to Surface constraint*

If you turn the viewer to wireframe mode by pressing 4 on the keyboard, you can see the green dot on the nCloth vertex that you selected earlier. This represents the constraint point. The Attribute Editor switches to Dynamic Constraint Shape 1. In the Dynamic Constraint Attributes, set the Constraint Method to Weld, as shown in Figure 10-32.

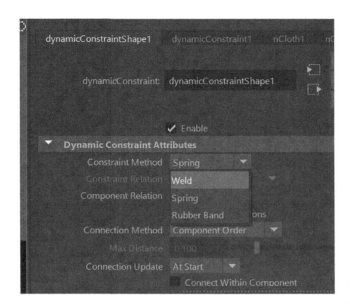

Figure 10-32. *Constraint Method set to Weld*

Now play the scene to check the dynamics. For checking purposes, you can set the magnitude higher to check how the constraint works and then again set it back to your desired value.

For the example here, set the Magnitude to 250 and play the effect. What you can see is that the wind is blowing at a constant rate. Let's bring in some turbulence here to create a more realistic effect. Select nCloth, go to the Fields/Solvers menu, and then select Turbulence. Then, in the Turbulence Field Attributes tab, increase the Magnitude to 1200, set the Frequency to 15, set the Noise level to 3, and set the Attenuation to 0.250 for a little fall off. You can also go into the Airfield option and set the settings of the Wind Magnitude to 300 instead of the earlier 250. Play the simulation now to see the combined effect.

As you keep experimenting with these settings, you will see that the real-time playback is very slow because it is calculating the settings for each frame. There are a few ways you can get around this. You can cache the playback or you can create a *playblast*. A playblast usually creates an image sequence of the scene. To create a playblast, right-click the timeline, click Playblast, go to the options shown in Figure 10-33, and click Apply. Your playblast is ready for preview.

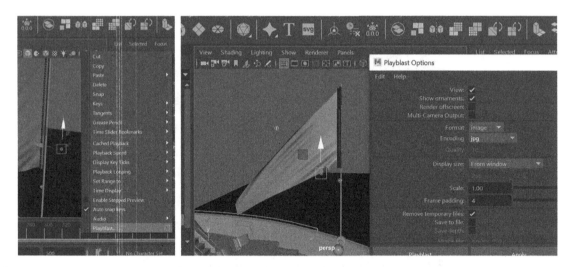

Figure 10-33. *Playblast options and realistic flag simulation*

The next chapter delves into the functions of hair and fur simulations in Maya and teaches you how to create realistic looks in Maya.

CHAPTER 11

Maya Hair FX Simulation

This chapter delves into the functions of Maya's Hair simulation and teaches you how to create realistic hair. It covers the manual techniques for transplanting hair and helps you diagnose issues and challenges during this process. Maya doesn't have a specific fur simulator, but you can decrease in the length of the hair strands so they will behave more like fur. Increasing the length of hair strands, on the other hand, makes them look and act more like hair. Let's explore the Hair simulation effect in Maya.

Foundation Concept for Hair Creation

Maya's Hair simulation program can be accessed from nHair menu (also known as the Nucleus hair system), available from the FX layout, as shown in Figure 11-1.

© Abhishek Kumar 2022
A. Kumar, *Beginning VFX with Autodesk Maya*, https://doi.org/10.1007/978-1-4842-7857-4_11

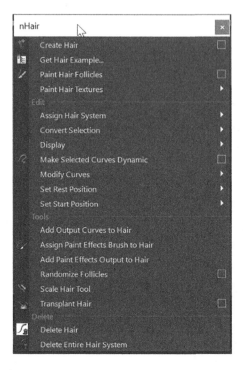

Figure 11-1. *nHair options*

Earlier versions of Maya did not have a nucleus system and hair grooming was a tedious task. You had to use external plugins to create hair and fur simulations in Maya. However, with the advent of Maya's nHair system, it's now very easy to create detailed hair without a system configuration or processor.

Let's get started!

Choose the Create Hair option from the nHair menu. This will pop up another window with the various attributes for weaving in hair follicles, as shown in Figure 11-2.

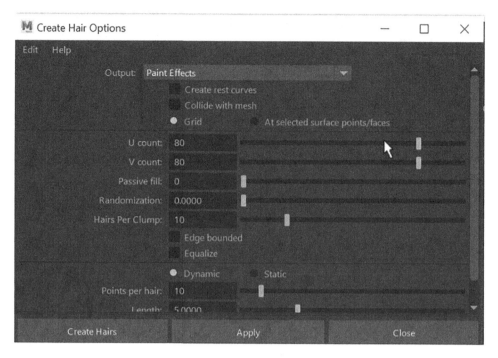

Figure 11-2. *The Create Hair Options window*

This window has three options in a drop-down menu from the output label. These are Paint Effects, NURBS Curves, and Paint Effects and NURBS Curves. Whenever you create a hair system or weave in hair follicles, there are various methods to achieve the desired effect. These three output options represent these different methodologies.

For the purposes here, you first use the Paint Effects. Choose this output effect to paint an area to make the follicles appear. You can also erase the painted areas to remove hair follicles. This can be done using the black and white paint. The black painted areas will have no hair follicles, whereas the areas painted in white will be populated with hair follicles.

To start adding hair to the character, choose Paint Effects. With all the parameters set to their defaults, select the Head model and then click the Create button. You can see the resultant output in Figure 11-3.

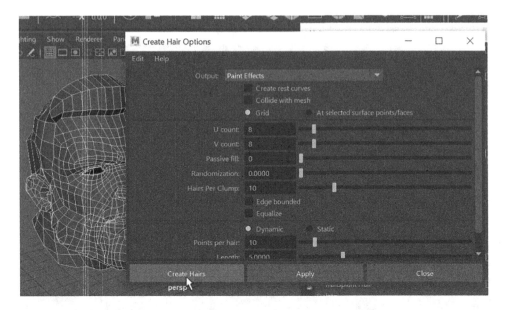

Figure 11-3. *Select the head model and click Create*

You will see the hair follicles cover the entire head's geometry. If you play the simulation, you will see something like Figure 11-4.

Figure 11-4. *Hair simulation*

Now that you can see the simulation happening, you need to revisit the Create Hair options to make some modifications and see how the various options work.

If you look at Figure 11-2, you will notice that there are two properties called U Count and V Count. The UV mapping is very important to proper distribution and creation of the hair follicles. There are options for randomizing the hair simulation. There are also options to modify the number of hair strands per clump.

However, as you can see in Figure 11-4, the hair system spreads over the entire surface (or the entire mesh of the head), since you selected the entire head rather than one particular area. Therefore, you need to correct that. First delete the existing hair system and then select a portion of the chin, as shown in Figure 11-5.

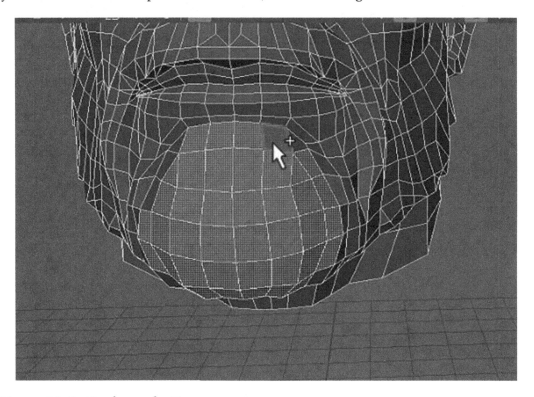

Figure 11-5. *Surface selection*

From the Create Hair options, you select the At Selected Surface Points/Faces option and reduce the length to 3, as shown in Figure 11-6.

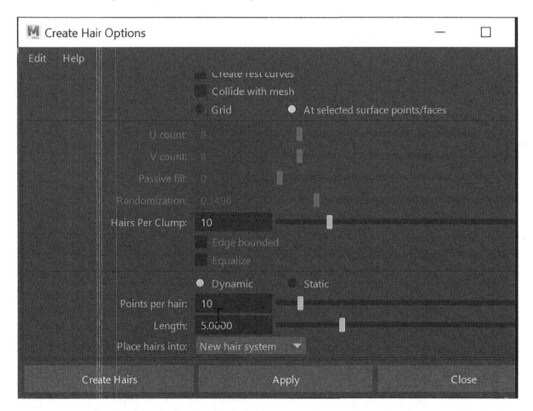

Figure 11-6. *Select the At Selected Surface Points/Faces option*

The resultant output will apply the hair follicles only to the selected areas, as shown in Figure 11-7.

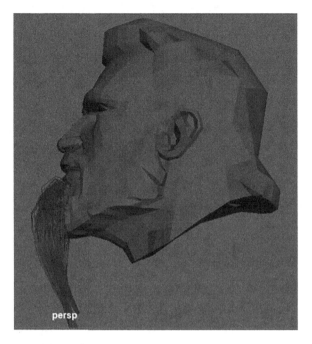

Figure 11-7. *Simulated hair follicles applied to the selected areas only*

A better method is to create a duplicate of the hair mesh like a cap and apply the hair system to it, as shown in Figure 11-8.

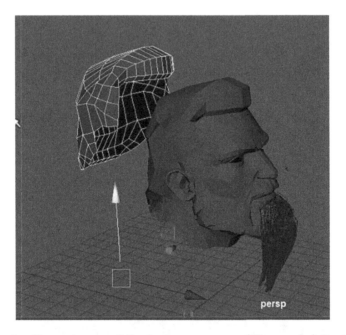

Figure 11-8. *A duplicate/copy of the hair geometry (like a cap) for hair simulation*

Now you can apply the combination of the Paint Effects and the NURBS Curves to the hair cap geometry. But before you do that, you must delete all the hair simulation on the hair cap and then set the output of the hair options to Paint Effects and NURBS Curves. In addition, increase the U Count and V Count to 30. Click Apply, as shown in Figure 11-9.

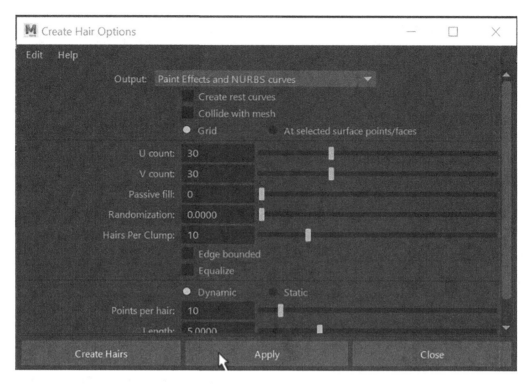

Figure 11-9. *Paint Effects and NURBS Curves option selected*

Once you apply this setting, you will see multiple hair follicles simulate beautifully. But the simulation will tend to intersect with the face geometry rather than colliding with it. This is because the Collide with Mesh option is not selected from the nHair options. Hence, selecting this option will solve the issue, right? Well, not really. The hair cap itself is a mesh and the hair follicles will tend to collide only with the hair cap mesh and not with the head mesh, which is what you ideally require. Hence, to solve this issue, you need to select the face mesh, as shown in Figure 11-10, and then choose the Create Passive Collider option from the nCloth menu.

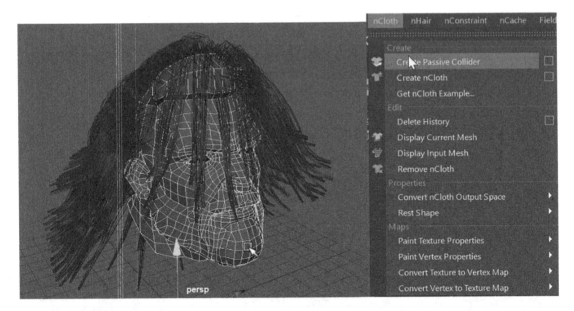

Figure 11-10. *Select the face mesh and then choose Create Passive Collider from the nCloth menu*

You can also increase the number of hair follicles and make a dense hair system for this head geometry. You need to delete the existing hair system and again select the hair cap. Go to the Create Hair options and this time increase the U and V Count to 60. Also set randomization, as shown in Figure 11-11.

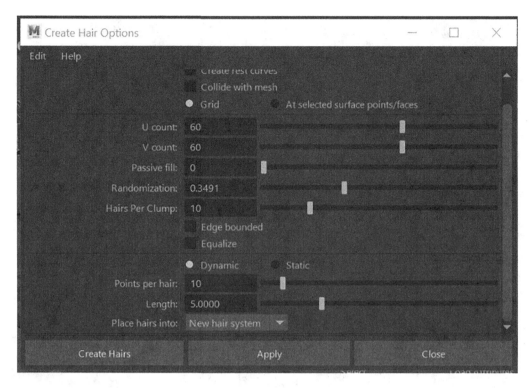

Figure 11-11. *Create hair options with new values*

This will certainly increase the number of hair follicles produced and therefore may take more computational time to generate. However, it will produce a much more effective and realistic simulation, as shown in Figure 11-12.

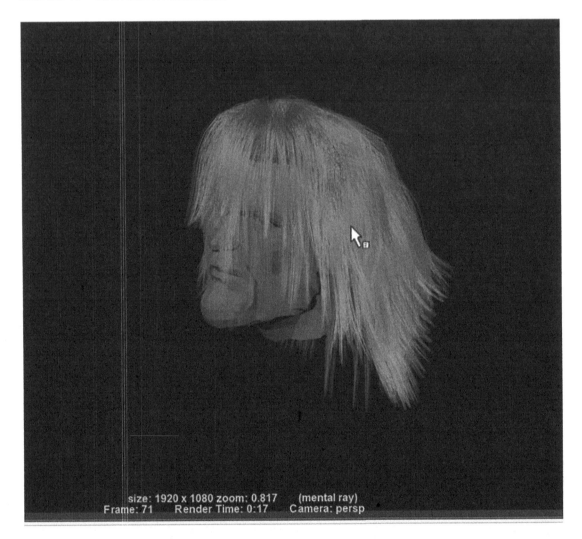

Figure 11-12. *Rendered output of final hair*

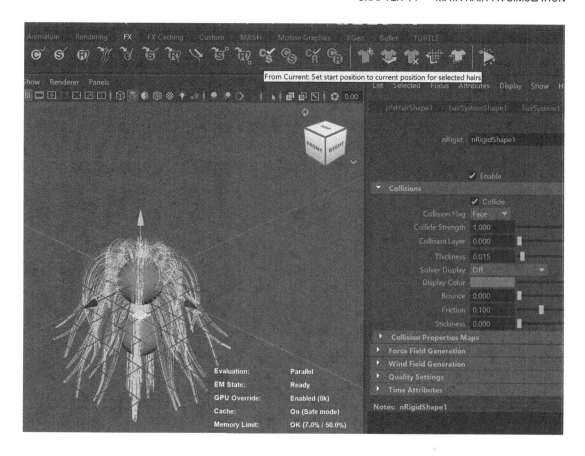

Grooming Hair

The previous section explored the basic steps in creating a hair simulation. In this section, you learn how to groom hair (in relation to the length of the hair) in the various parts of the hair cap.

As you can see, the length of the hair all over the hair cap is the same, which is not realistic. Ideally the hair near the forehead should be shorter. You need to trim a selection of the hair strands near the forehead. This can be done two ways. First, you can reduce the Display quality of the hair system, as shown in Figure 11-13, which will allow you to see the hair strands.

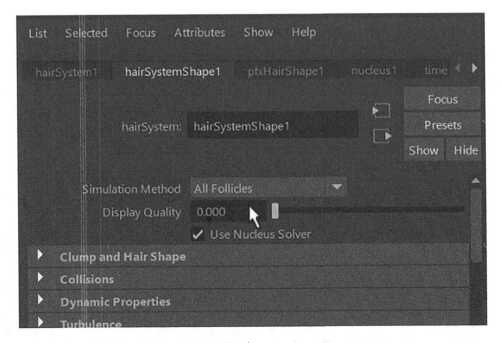

Figure 11-13. *Display quality of the hair system reduced to 0*

The other way is to select the hair system curves from the Outliner window and select the Show option. From this, you can select None and then select only the Polygon and NURBS Curve options, as shown in Figure 11-14.

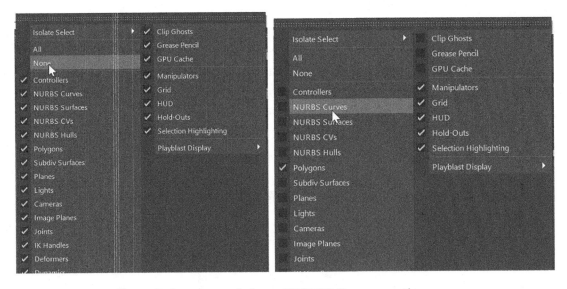

Figure 11-14. *Show Polygons and show NURBS Curves options*

Both of these options allow you to view and select strands of hair and manipulate them at a vertices level, as shown in Figure 11-15.

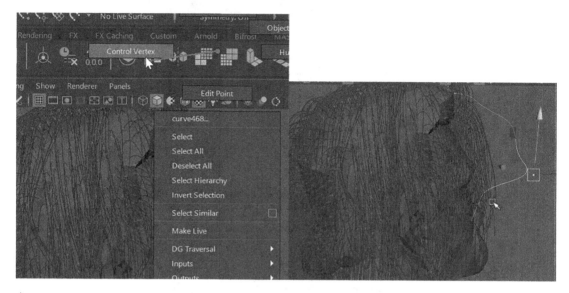

Figure 11-15. *Vertex selection for manual modifications*

Moving forward, you can see that the hair simulation starts from a standing position and falls downward due to gravity, as shown in Figure 11-4. However, that is not a realistic scenario. To fix this, you need to set the start position of the hair simulation to a rest position. You need to first identify the frame at which the hair settles. Then select the hair curves, as shown in Figure 11-16.

Figure 11-16. *Select the hair curves*

With the hair curves selected, you need to go to the nHair menu select the Set Rest Position. Set this option to the Current frame, as shown in Figure 11-17.

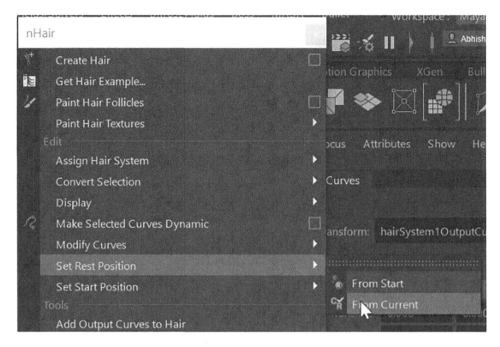

Figure 11-17. *The Set Rest Position option*

You need to do the same thing for Set Start Position, as shown in Figure 11-18.

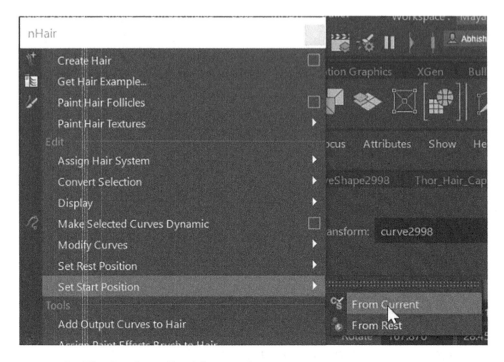

Figure 11-18. *The Set Start Position option*

When you play the simulation now, the hair simulation starts from the rest or settled position.

Let's now check out some more options of hair grooming. You need to select the Hair System Curves from the Outliner window. Then, from the nHair menu, you need to select the Covert Selection option. Choose To Start Curves, as shown in Figure 11-19.

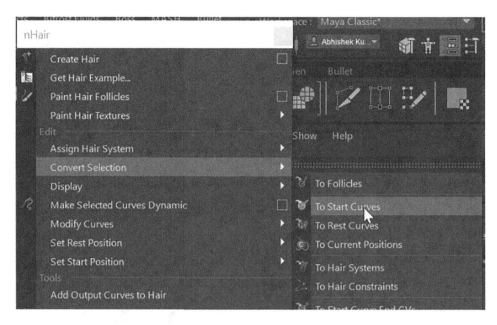

Figure 11-19. *Choose Convert Selection To Start or Rest Curves*

To add some variation to the hair style, you can select the Modify Curves option from the nHair menu. Then choose any of the options listed, such as Curl, Smooth, and so on, as shown in Figure 11-20.

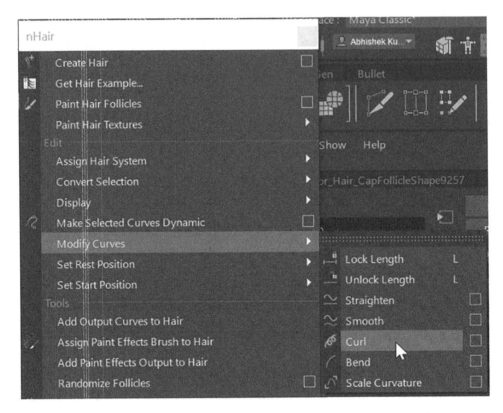

Figure 11-20. *Modify curves options*

Now let's solve the original problem of scaling the size of the hair near the forehead. To do this, you need to select the hair curves near the forehead, as shown in Figure 11-21.

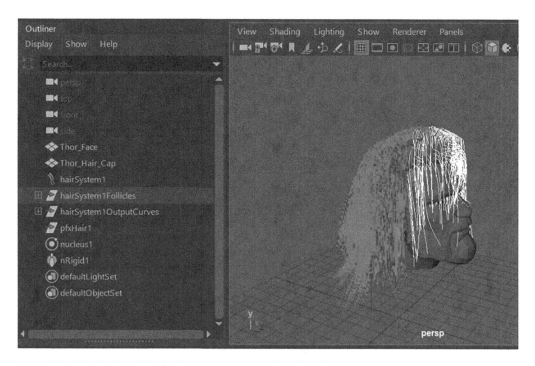

Figure 11-21. *Select the hair curves near the forehead*

With the hair strands/curves selected, go to the nHair menu and choose Scale Hair Tool, as shown in Figure 11-22.

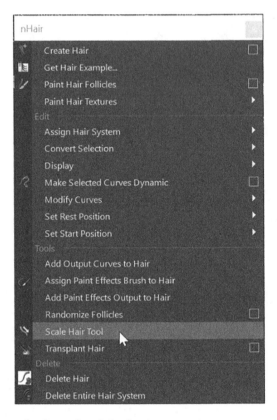

Figure 11-22. *Scaling the length of the hair*

With the left mouse button, drag left and right on the viewport. This will help you increase or decrease the length of the hair. Note that the hair seems to be intersecting with the face. To avoid this, you can go to the Modify Curves option and select the Bend option, as shown in Figure 11-21. This will pop up another window, wherein you can provide a negative value. This will make the hair bend outwards, as shown in Figure 11-23.

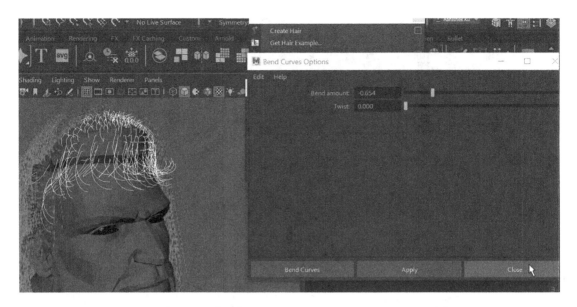

Figure 11-23. *Using the Bend option*

If you play the simulation now, you can see that hair near the forehead doesn't impede on the face. However, a point to be noted here is that each strand has an equal number of vertices. Hence, scaling the hair strands in the forehead doesn't reduce the number of vertices. Rather, the vertices come closer together, resulting in a smoother simulation of the hair, as shown in Figure 11-24.

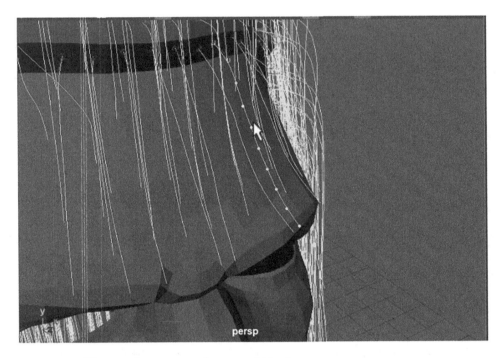

Figure 11-24. *The vertices on each strand/ hair curve*

In order to fix this, you need to use the hair trimming option, instead of hair scaling. First, select the Paint Hair Follicles option from the nHair menu, as shown in Figure 11-25.

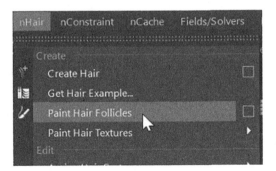

Figure 11-25. *The Paint Hair Follicles option*

This will pop up another window, wherein you need to select the Trim Hairs option, as shown in Figure 11-26. You need to select hairSystemShape1 from the Hair System drop-down. There, you can set the Points Per Hair to a value depending on the hair length. The points indicate the vertices on each of the hair strands.

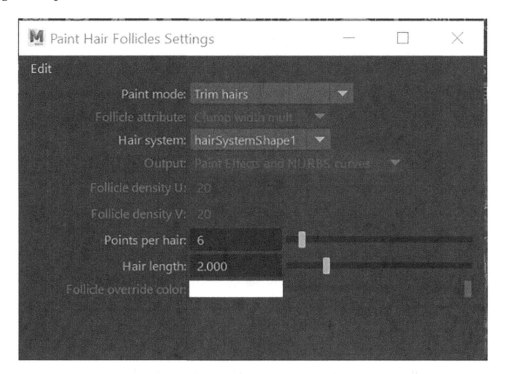

Figure 11-26. *The Paint Hair properties*

You can paint the areas near the forehead and you will notice that the strands are reduced. Upon selecting the vertices of any of these trimmed strands, you will notice that the count of the vertices reduces to 6, as specified in the Paint Hair Follicle settings.

In the next section, you see how to create longer hair.

Creating and Simulating Long Hair

So far, this chapter has explored the hair system on a geometry of the hair cap. Now you will explore how to create long hair using the EP Curve Tool, as shown in Figure 11-27. You will be doing this on a female model.

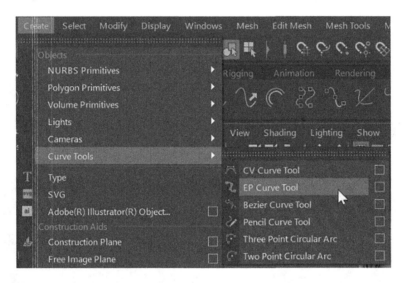

Figure 11-27. *The EP curve*

A point to remember is that the EP Curve can draw on the surface of the geometry by making the geometry Live. To do this, you need to select the part of the geometry you want to modify, as shown in Figure 11-28, and then choose Make Live from the Modify option.

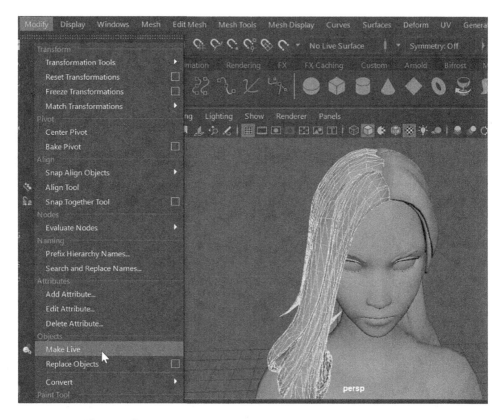

Figure 11-28. *The Make Live option*

The Make Live option works on individual sections of the geometry, one at a time, as shown in Figure 11-28. There is no way that you can select all the sections of the hair geometry together and apply Make Live. It will not work that way. The Make Live option has to be applied individually to the different sections of the hair geometry.

Using the EP Curves tool, you can draw the curve along the surface of the hair geometry, as shown in Figure 11-29.

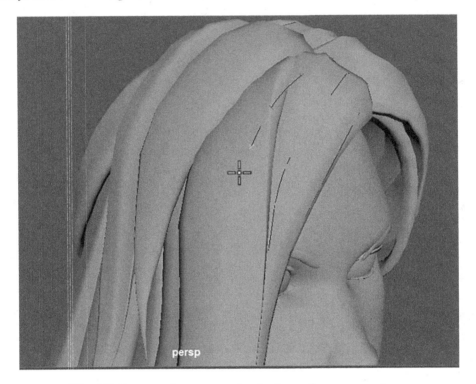

Figure 11-29. *The EP Curves drawn on the hair surface geometry*

This way, you can create a base shape wherein the hair transplantation can happen. Once the hair curves are drawn, you need to disable the Make Live option, shown in Figure 11-30. Similarly you need to draw the curves for the entire hair geometry.

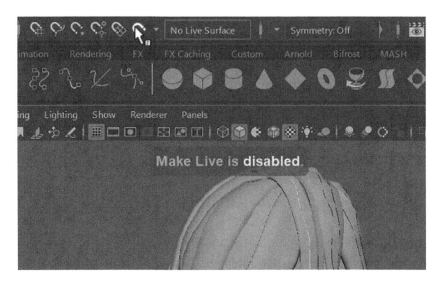

Figure 11-30. *Disable the Make Live option*

You can create a base shape wherein the hair transplantation can happen. Remember that each section of the hair geometry needs to be selected to use Make Live (as shown in Figure 11-28), then the curves need to be drawn (as shown in Figure 11-29), and then the Make Live option needs to be disabled (as shown in Figure 11-30). Follow the same process for each section of hair geometry.

Once the hair curves are drawn for the entire head, you need to make layers and assign geometry to these layers. This is required because, going forward, you will be converting the hair curves that you just created into a dynamic hair system. So you will select the entire geometry and put it in a layer and then select the hair geometries and put them in another layer, as shown in Figure 11-31.

Figure 11-31. *Assigning layers to the geometry*

This leaves the hair curves separate. You can assign a separate layer to this too. Convert these hair curves into the dynamic hair. Go to the nHair menu and select Assign Hair System. From there, Choose New Hair System, as shown in Figure 11-32.

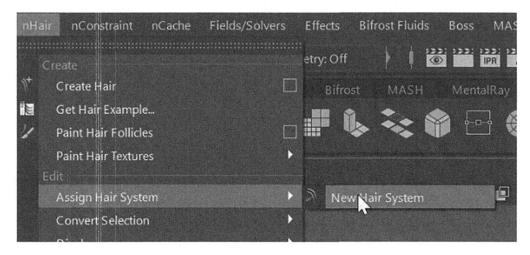

Figure 11-32. *The Assign Hair System option*

The next step is to generate the hair system. In order to do that, increase the clumps and the hair shape attribute of the hair system's Shape1 to 35 or 40. Then choose Assign Paint Effects Brush to Hair, as shown in Figure 11-33.

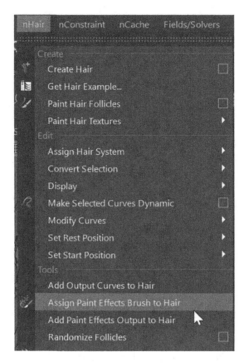

Figure 11-33. *The Assign Paint Effects Brush to Hair option*

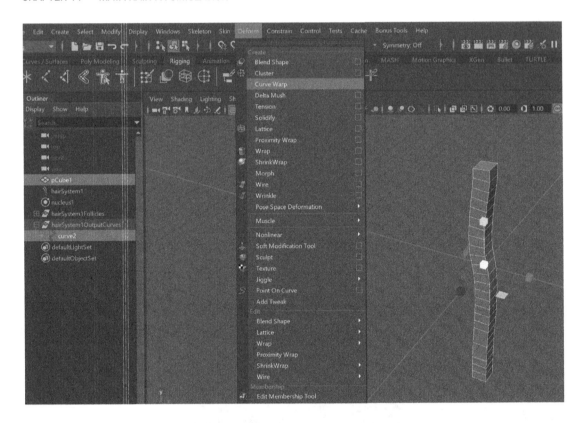

You can see the paint effects added to the hair from the viewport, as shown in Figure 11-34.

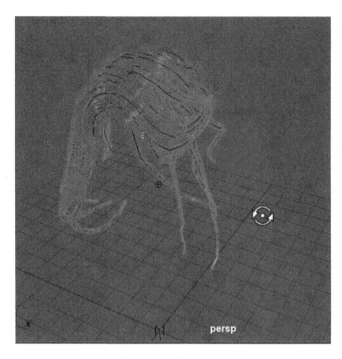

Figure 11-34. *The paint effects added to the hair*

The denser the curves, the more beautiful the hair. You can also increase the display quality and increase the clumps for more density. A rendered image of the simulated hair system is shown in Figure 11-35.

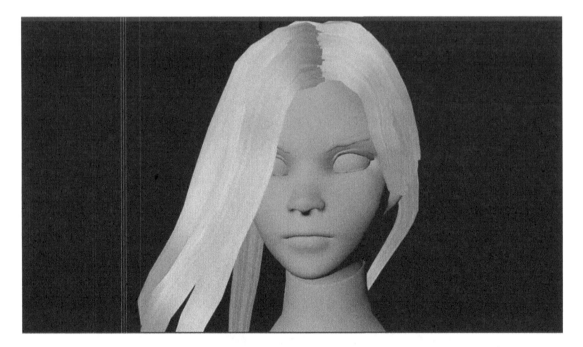

Figure 11-35. *Rendered image of the hair system*

You can now add some animation to the head to see how the hair animates with the head.

Let's go ahead and explore some of the subsections of the hair system, as shown in Figure 11-36.

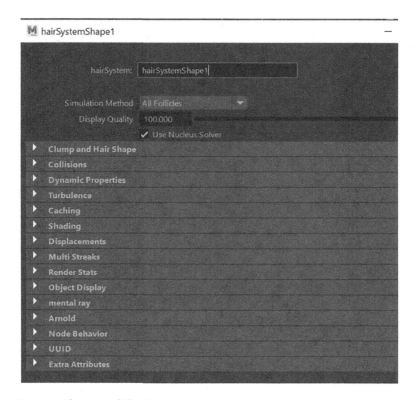

Figure 11-36. *Attributes of the hair system*

In the Clump and Hair Shape subsection, there are attributes, shown in Figure 11-37, such as the number of hairs per clump, which can be modified as needed. These attributes help smoothen the hair and taper it toward the end. The clump twist adds variation to the clumps and the clump width helps spreads the hairs in each clump.

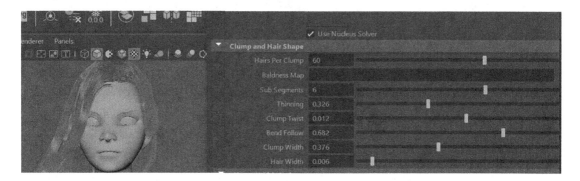

Figure 11-37. *Clump and Hair Shape attributes*

You can style the hair further by using Clump Curl and Clump Flatness, as shown in Figure 11-38.

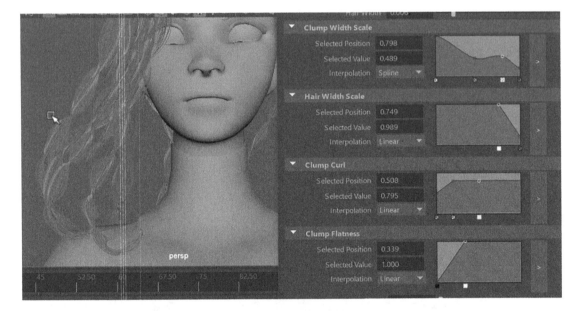

Figure 11-38. *The Clump Curl and Clump Flatness options*

Scrolling further, you'll see collision attributes. In general, the hair collides with the surface, but if you want it to collide with other hair strands, check the Self-Collide checkbox, as shown in Figure 11-39.

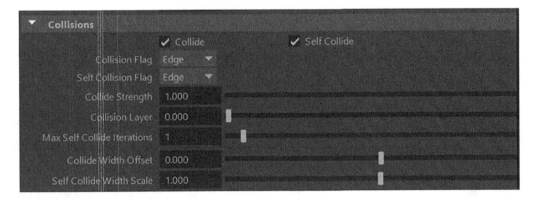

Figure 11-39. *Self-Collide checkbox*

You will also find the dynamic properties related to the stretch factor and resistance of the hair flow. The Bend option contributes to the waviness of the hair. The overall mass of the hair can be modified using the Forces option. Moving further, a major section is devoted to shading, where you can change the color of the hair, which is interactive on the viewport.

Using the Maya Hair Library

So far, you have explored the manual options in Maya's hair system . However, Maya also has some predefined hair examples that can be used to set up the hair. Then you can enhance the basic look, depending on your needs. To access these predefined options, you need to go to the nHair menu and select the Get Hair Example option.

The Get Hair Example option opens a whole library of preset hairs that you can use, as shown in Figure 11-40.

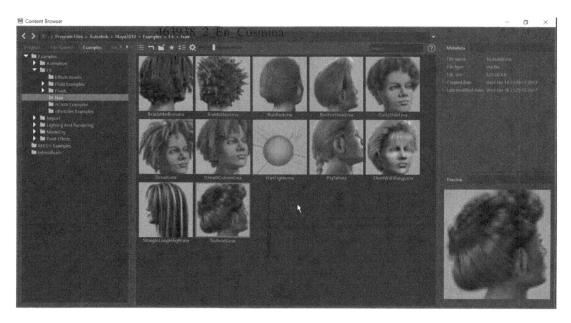

Figure 11-40. *Content Browser of the Get Hair example*

Simply drag and drop the example you want onto your scene and make alterations to suit your needs.

In this chapter, you learned about the Hair FX system in Maya. In the next chapter, you dive into Maya's Bifrost simulation system. That chapter explores how effectively and efficiently you can simulate large-scale fluid systems using the FLIP solver-based Bifrost in Maya.

CHAPTER 12

Bifrost Simulation

This chapter covers Maya's recently introduced Bifrost system for creating realistic water effects. You will learn how to use Bifrost to reproduce a big volume of water efficiently. You will use effective simulation techniques to generate a large-scale simulation shot and a waterfall shot in Maya.

Importance of Bifrost Fluids

In previous chapters, you learned about the fluid simulations in Maya. But when you deal with large body of water, like the ocean or waterfalls, where particle bodies need to collide with each other and create splashes or emanating foam, the Bifrost system is a much more effective tool. Bifrost is also known as Fluid Implicit Particles. This is not a new technology in the industry. You may have heard of FIP Solver, which is the Fluid Implicit Particle solver available in RealFlow. RealFlow is a dedicated application for creating fluid particle simulations.

Bifrost was previously used as a Maya plugin, but it's now part of the Maya system. Therefore, you no longer need to switch to other applications to create large water simulations. They can now be created in Maya using the Bifrost system. Fluid Implicit Particle solvers help convert the large number of particles into a fluid or sand animation, for example.

Let's see how the Bifrost system works in Maya.

© Abhishek Kumar 2022
A. Kumar, *Beginning VFX with Autodesk Maya*, https://doi.org/10.1007/978-1-4842-7857-4_12

For the demonstration here, you need to create nozzle section of a tap, as shown in Figure 12-1. You will be creating a water flow from that tap.

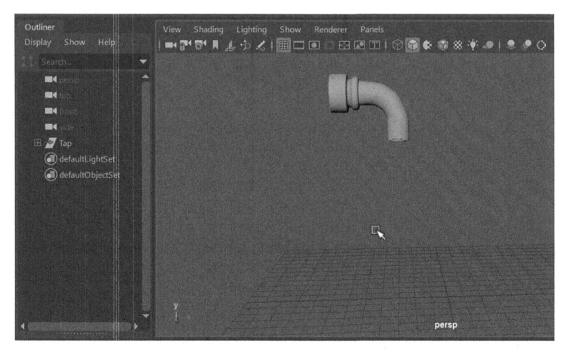

Figure 12-1. *Tap model*

From the FX layout menu, choose Bifrost Fluids, as shown in Figure 12-2.

Figure 12-2. *The Bifrost Fluids menu*

The Bifrost Fluids section has two main effects in its Create tab—Liquid and Aero. Using the Liquid effect, you can simulate large bodies of particles as fluids. Using Aero, you can simulate particles to create smoke or sand.

Let's begin by exploring the Liquid option within the Bifrost Fluids system. Go to the Bifrost Fluids menu and click Liquid. It's in the Create section of the Bifrost option, as shown in Figure 12-2.

This will generate four nodes in the Outliner, as shown in Figure 12-3.

Figure 12-3. *The Bifrost liquid applied*

Once the liquid has been created on the Outliner, you need to select the Liquid Bifrost and Shift+select the nozzle of the tap, which should be the emitter for the particle simulation, as shown in Figure 12-4.

Figure 12-4. *The Bifrost liquid and the emitter selected*

You now need to choose Emitter from the Bifrost Fluids menu, as shown in Figure 12-5.

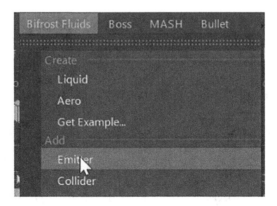

Figure 12-5. *The Bifrost emitter*

If you play the simulation now, you will see the particles emitting through the nozzle of the tap. However this emission does not look like a continuous flow. In order to make the emission of the particles continuous, you need to check the Continuous Emission checkbox from the emitter's attributes, as shown in Figure 12-6.

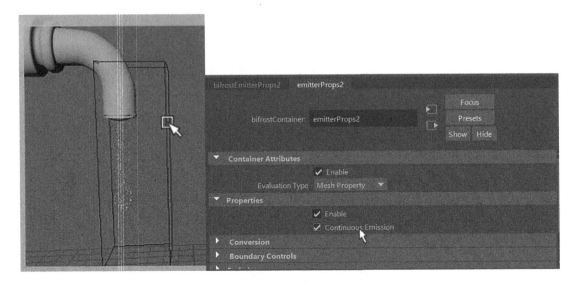

Figure 12-6. *The Continuous Emission option*

Notice that the particles are quite small. You can select the Bifrost Liquid and go to the Properties section to increase the point size. This option is found on the Particle Display window. You can also change the Type from Point to Sphere, as shown in Figure 12-7.

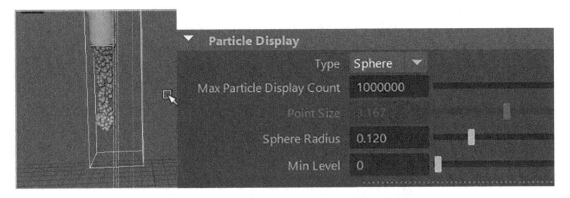

Figure 12-7. *The Particle Display properties of the Bifrost Liquid*

The water now seems to be flowing like a continuous stream. Hence, you need to create a container where the water will be stored, as shown in Figure 12-8.

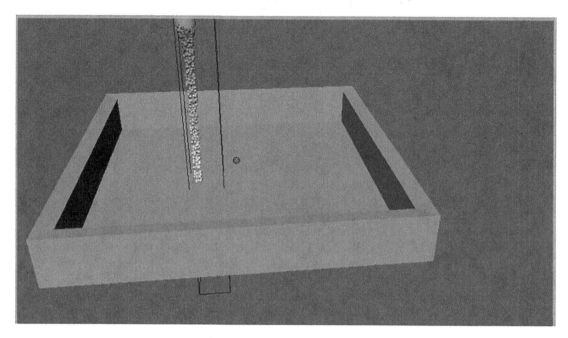

Figure 12-8. *The Particle container modeled and aligned to fetch the flowing water*

Now that you have created a container, you need the water particles to collide with this surface. To do this, you will create another surface with a cylinder and place it below the tap that is emitting the water or the liquid particles, as shown in Figure 12-9.

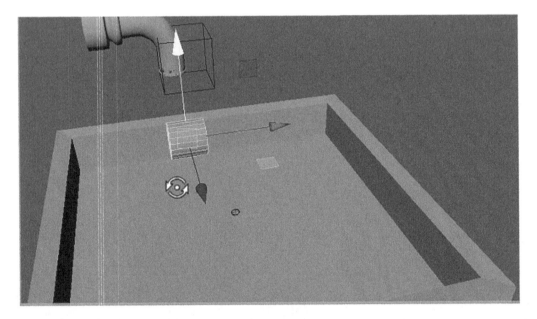

Figure 12-9. *The cylinder created for collision*

Now select the Bifrost liquid and Shift+select the cylinder. Go to the Bifrost Fluids menu and select the Collider option, as shown in Figure 12-10.

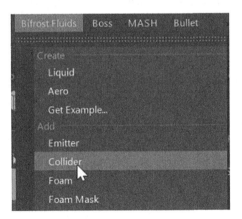

Figure 12-10. *The Collider option*

When you play the simulation now, you will see the Bifrost Liquid particles colliding with the cylinder surface, as shown in Figure 12-11.

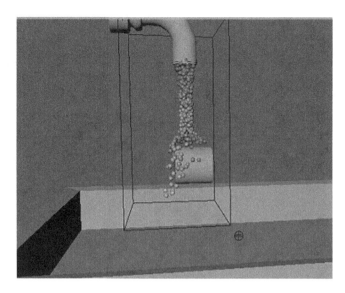

Figure 12-11. *The collision output*

Moving further, if you need to increase the density of the fluid, go to the attributes of the Liquid properties container in the Attribute Editor. In this panel, you will see the Resolution Parameter, which mentions Master Voxel Size. You learned about voxels in previous chapters. Here, the smaller the value, the more details there will be. This will also require more computational processing, as shown in Figure 12-12.

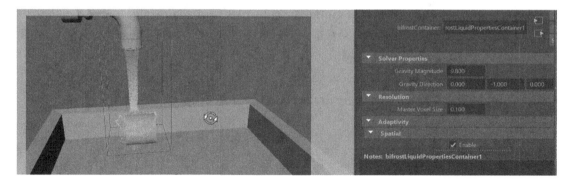

Figure 12-12. *The master voxel size set to 0.1*

With an even lower voxel size of 0.05, further details can be achieved, as shown in Figure 12-13. This kind of simulation supports in the creation of very realistic effects.

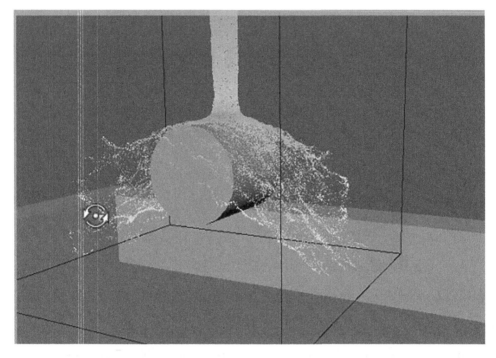

Figure 12-13. *The water simulation effect with a voxel size of 0.05*

You should now have a basic understanding of the Bifrost system in Maya.

In the following section, you will explore large-scale waterfall simulations.

This example uses a previously modeled scenery of mountains and a waterfall flowing in between the two land masses, as shown in Figure 12-14. These kinds of scenes are common in Hollywood films. Sometimes these are achieved through CGI integrated with compositing techniques. However, when you need to do scenes like spaceships colliding into waterfalls, as was done in films like *Avatar*, the scenes need to be rendered through CGI.

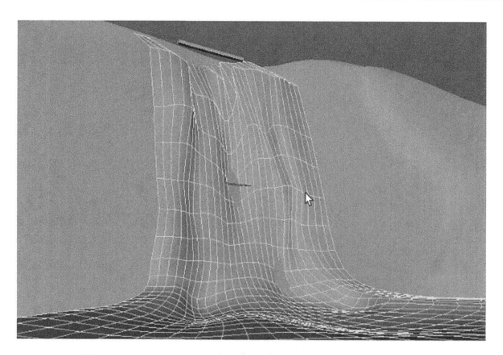

Figure 12-14. *The scene*

Follow the same steps as earlier to start the basic simulation. Select the emitter and apply the Bifrost Liquid to it. Upon playing the simulation, you will be able to see that the simulation seems to penetrate through the surface geometry. To fix this, you will need to make it collide with the geometry. This is also similar to what you did in the previous section. You need to select the Bifrost Liquid and Shift+select the water geometry. Then choose Collide from the Bifrost Fluids menu.

When you play the simulation, you may face a situation where the particles seem to be floating and not really colliding with the actual surface. In order to fix this, you will need to refer to the attributes of the collider. The attributes of the Collider property have a section on Conversion. Under Conversion, the mode needs to be set to Solid (Robust), as shown in Figure 12-15.

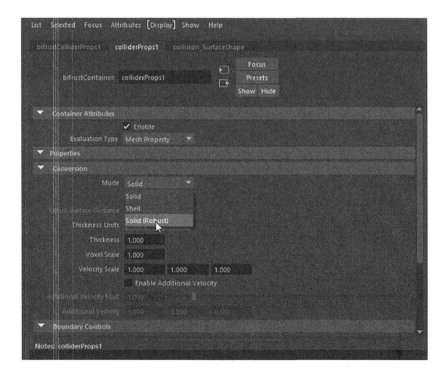

Figure 12-15. *The Solid (Robust) option is used to fix the collision*

The resultant effect is captured in Figure 12-16, where the waterfall beautifully cascades down the surface geometry to the ground plane and spreads out.

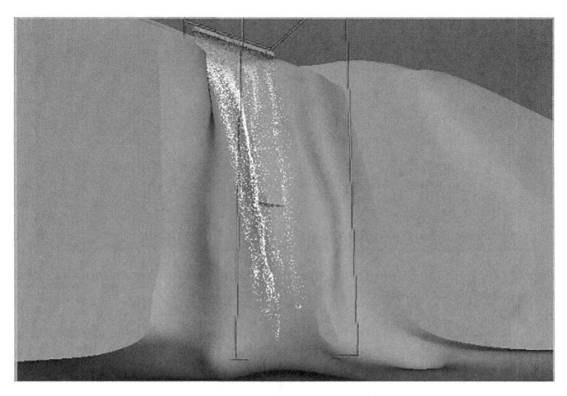

Figure 12-16. *The waterfall simulation*

The resultant effect can be even more realistic with the addition of foam. You must first change the Display property of the liquid shape to Voxels, as shown in Figure 12-17.

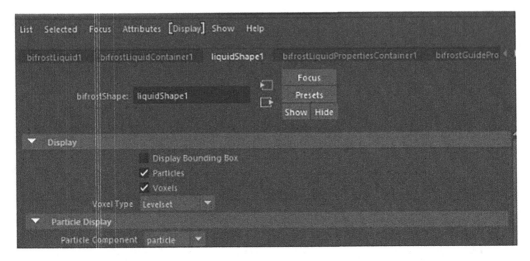

Figure 12-17. *In the Display property, the bounding box has been removed and the voxels have been added*

Additionally, select the Bifrost Liquid from the Outliner and add foam to it from the Bifrost Fluids menu, as shown in Figure 12-18.

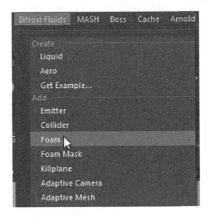

Figure 12-18. *Add foam to the Bifrost Liquid*

The resultant image is shown in Figure 12-19.

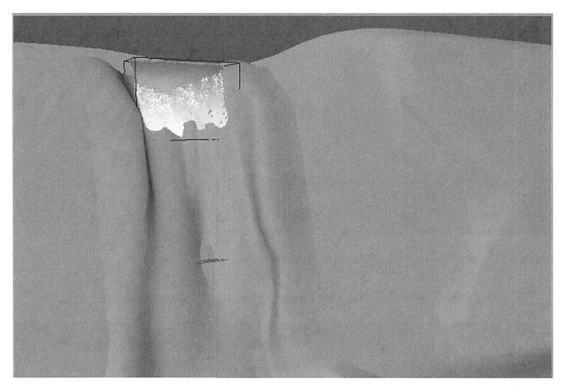

Figure 12-19. *The resultant simulation*

Computing and Executing a Water Simulation Shot

This section deals with simulations of large bodies of water. You need to model a container, as shown in Figure 12-20, and fill it with water using an emitter.

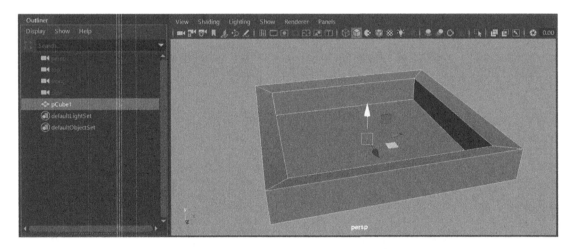

Figure 12-20. *The modeled container*

To fill the container with water, first create an emitter, as shown in Figure 12-21.

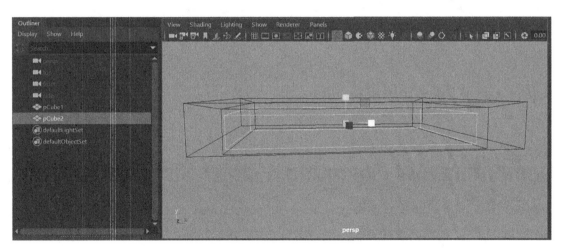

Figure 12-21. *The emitter*

Now create the Bifrost. To do this, select the emitter and then go to the Bifrost Fluids menu and select Liquid, as shown in Figure 12-22.

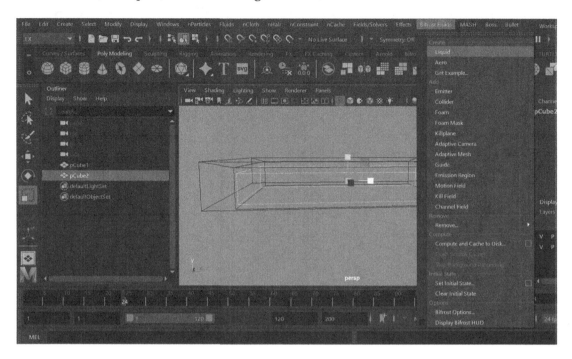

Figure 12-22.   *The Bifrost Liquid*

Once the Bifrost Liquid is applied, the water particles need to collide with the container so that the water is in the container. To do this, you need to select the Bifrost Liquid and Shift+select the container. Choose the Bifrost Fluids menu and select the Collider option, as shown in Figure 12-23.

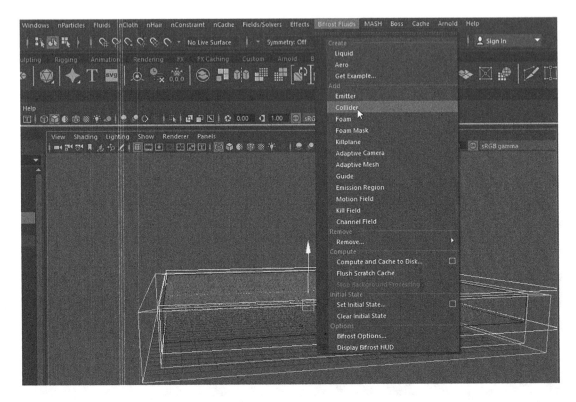

Figure 12-23. *The Collider option*

When you play the simulation now, the water particles will tend to animate in a flowing state. You need to keep the particles within the container. To do this, select the Bifrost Liquid from the Outliner and then choose the Set Initial State option from the Bifrost Fluids menu, as shown in Figure 12-24. The simulation will now maintain the same form while it runs.

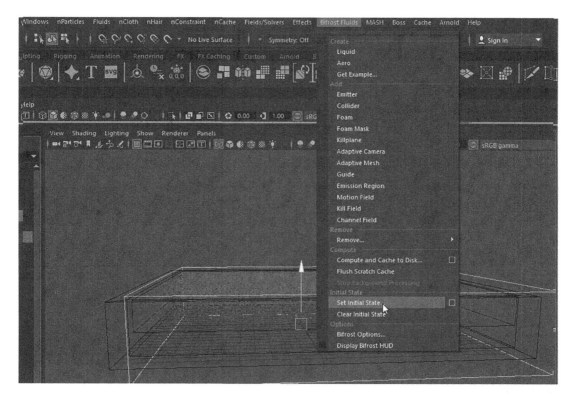

Figure 12-24. *The Set Initial State option*

Once the initial state has been applied, you can delete the emitter.

Test this effect by dropping a geometry into the water body. In order to do this, create a small sphere the size of a ball and animate it to fall in the water and bounce up, as shown in Figure 12-25. This animated ball must collide with the water body, so the collider needs to be applied.

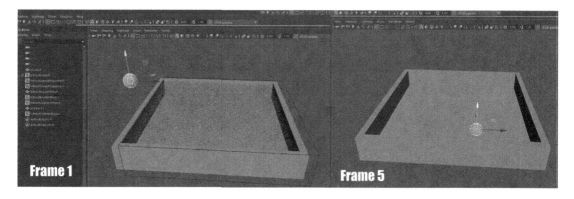

Figure 12-25. *Frame No 1 through Frame No 5*

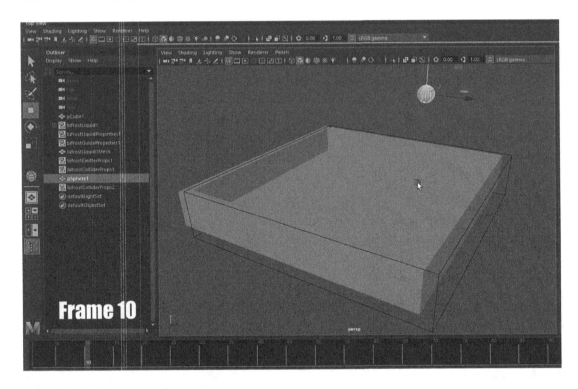

Frame No 10

The resultant simulation is captured in Figure 12-26.

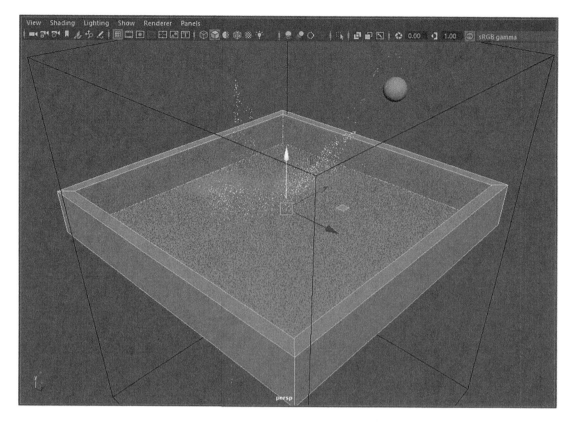

Figure 12-26. *The resultant simulation*

Additionally, if you want to add foam to the simulation, you can do that by selecting the Bifrost Liquid and applying foam from the Bifrost Fluids menu, as shown in Figure 12-27.

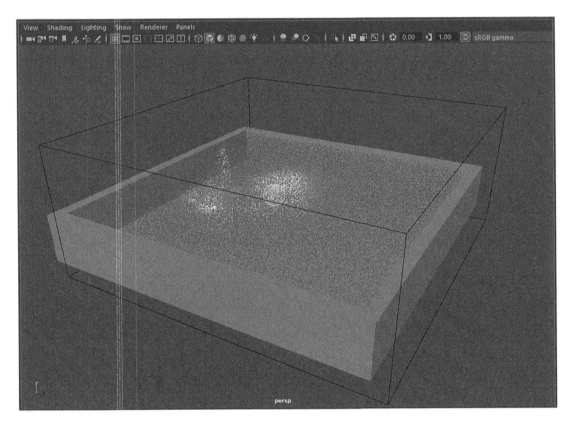

Figure 12-27. *Foam applied to the Bifrost Liquid*

This kind of effect can be applied if the scene requires multiple rocks falling in the water. To experiment further with the interaction of a model with the water, you can create another model, which could be more complicated with further animations, as shown in Figure 12-28. Before you start the animation, select the new object and the Bifrost Liquid to make them collide, as explained in the previous sections.

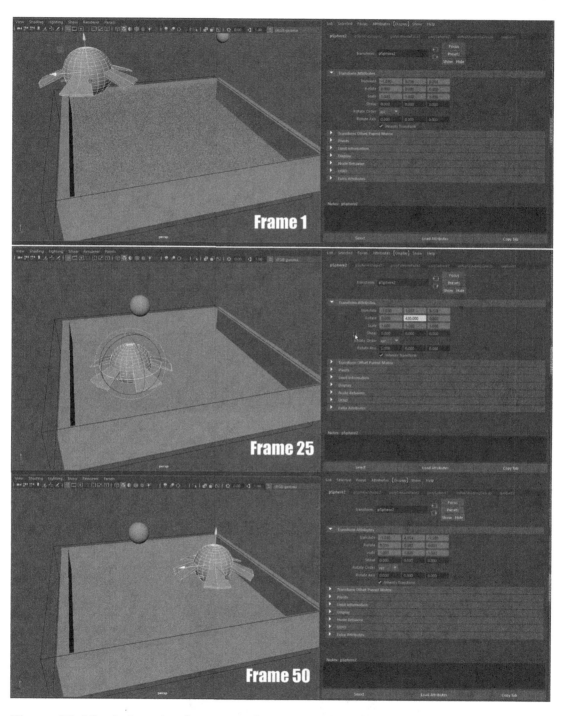

Figure 12-28. *Animation keys set to frames 1, 25, and 50*

The resultant simulation is captured in Figure 12-29. Now you can create a playblast and check out the simulation.

Figure 12-29. *The resultant simulation*

Working with the Bifrost Library

Having explored the Bifrost system, you can now check out the presets available in the Bifrost library. To access Bifrost's preset examples, choose Get Example from the Bifrost Fluids menu, as shown in Figure 12-30.

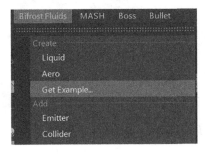

Figure 12-30. *The Get Example option*

Clicking this will open the Content Browser shown in Figure 12-31.

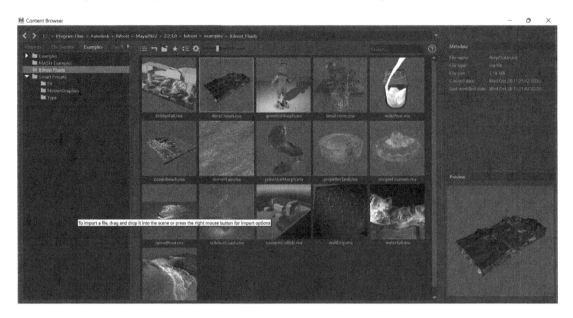

Figure 12-31. *The Get Examples Content Browser*

You can select any example by double-clicking it or dragging and dropping it into a new scene. However, you need to remember that these effects have a heavy particle count and are quite detailed. Hence, it is best to create a playblast to see such simulations rather than use the viewport render, since these detailed examples take time and computational speed.

In the next chapter, you learn some tips and tricks for using Mash FX and create a real-life, visual integrated computer graphics scene.

CHAPTER 13

Procedural Animation FX and Live Action Integration

In this chapter, you learn how to work on a complete scene in Maya using the FX system, which you learned about in previous chapters. You will create a seamless integration of live action footage in a 3D virtual world. You learn about the MASH procedural tools in this chapter.

Integrating 2D and 3D Worlds

In this section, you learn how to execute a small project with the seamless integration of the 3D CGI with live action footage. For example, films like *Terminator* and *Transformers* have scenes where CGI robots interact with real-life characters/actors in a realistic environment, with a seamless blend of environmental effects and lighting. These scenes help create hyper-realistic imagery.

You learn how you can achieve this kind of an effect with the project in this book.

For this project, you will be using a 3D CGI car model and will blend it with a real environment. A tip to remember is that you must have references to watch before you attempt such a scene, since doing so will give you a better understanding of such real-life environments. See Figures 13-1 through 13-4.

© Abhishek Kumar 2022
A. Kumar, *Beginning VFX with Autodesk Maya*, https://doi.org/10.1007/978-1-4842-7857-4_13

Figure 13-1. *Real-life footage*

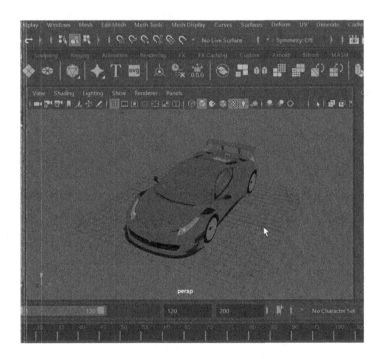

Figure 13-2. *CGI 3D car*

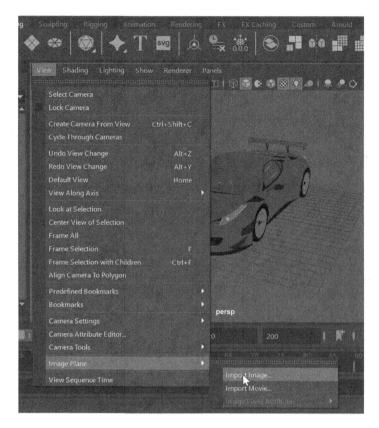

Figure 13-3. *Background plane layout in Maya scene*

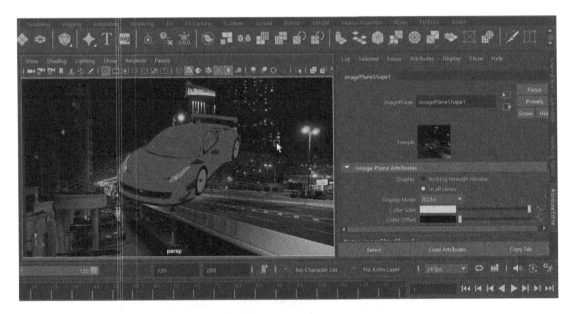

Figure 13-4. *Live 2D image and CGI 3D car*

Now let's get started!

You start by importing an image onto the image plane that you use to integrate the car model (see Figure 13-5). Then align the model to the imported scene.

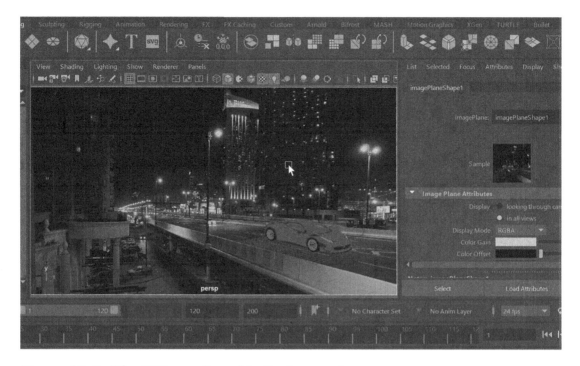

Figure 13-5. *The CGI car aligned to the image plane*

In order to blend the car into the background, you need to apply lights to it. To do this, first apply a skydome light to the car or CGI model, as shown in Figure 13-6.

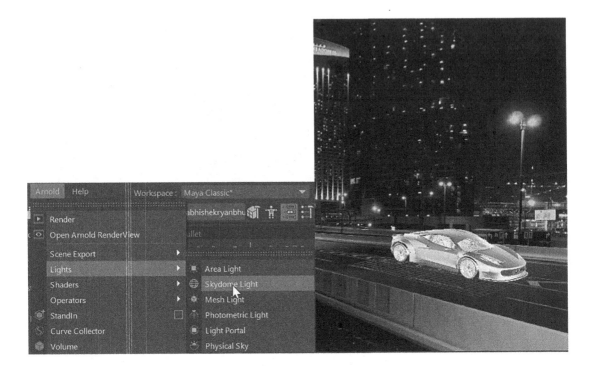

Figure 13-6.   *The CGI car with a skydome light*

This gives a white fill to the whole scene, which isn't desired. You need to visit the Skydome Light attributes and place an HDR image in the Color section, as shown in Figure 13-7. High Dynamic Range (HDR) uses technology to increase an image's color and contrast range. A High Dynamic Range (HDR) image is one that has a large contrast between the lightest and darkest tones.

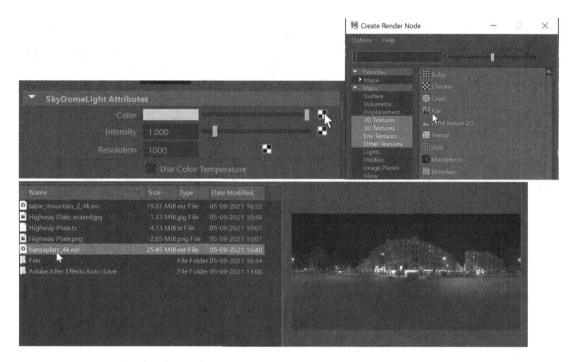

Figure 13-7. *The skydome light with the HDRI image*

Remember that, since this is a night scene, you need an HDRI image that closely represents the night light, as shown in Figure 13-7. Now the car seems to start blending with the image. However, an important part missing here is a contact shadow.

To add this, you need to create a plane below the car, as shown in Figure 13-8.

Figure 13-8. *The plane for casting shadows*

Select aiShadowmatte from the Arnold material shader to capture the shadow on the base plane, as shown in Figure 13-9.

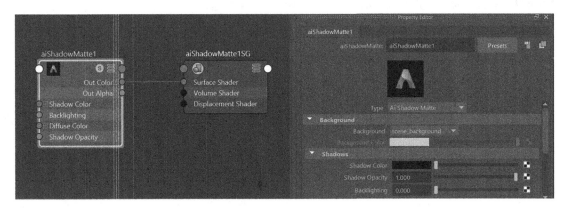

Figure 13-9. *Arnold AI shadow matte node*

After selecting the material, assign aiShadowmatte to the polybase plane, as shown in Figure 13-10.

Figure 13-10.   *The plane is assigned the aishadowmatte material from the Arnold render engine*

If the light appears all over the scene, you have to select the Skydome Light and, in the Attribute Editor, set the Camera value to 0 from the Visibility section, as shown in Figure 13-11.

Figure 13-11.   *The Camera visibility set to 0*

Once you are set and happy with the lighting, you can add some effects to the scene. To do this, choose Meteor FX and add it to your scene, as shown in Figure 13-12.

Figure 13-12. *The Meteor FX*

Since the render would take a lot of time, you can use the NCache to create a new cache. Then select Maya Fluid, as shown in Figure 13-13, and click Replace. This will substantiate your render and the cache of the Maya Fluid will be saved in the Maya Project folder.

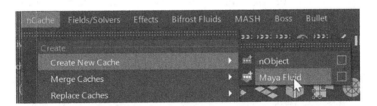

Figure 13-13. *Caching the simulation*

If you want the Meteor Fluid simulation to collide with the CG car, you have to select the car and, from the nCloth menu, select Create Passive Collider, as explained in the earlier chapters. See Figure 13-14.

Figure 13-14. *CG car integration in a real-world background environment*

Creating 3D Visual Effects with MASH

In this section, you explore the MASH procedural tools, which comes as a plugin in Maya that allows you to build motion graphics and visual effects procedural systems, all within Maya without having to do that in external applications. It's easy to use, with a bunch of nodes that can help create complicated-looking motion graphics without much effort.

Proceduralism is the art of building systems to control things rather than doing everything manually. Instead of manually animating every keyframe for every parameter change you want to make, you can build systems that change a multitude of parameters with a single node.

Let's explore the MASH network. To access MASH, you need to switch to the FX panel, as shown in Figure 13-15.

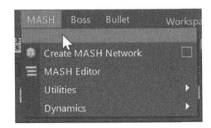

Figure 13-15. *MASH menu*

To check out the various options of the MASH network, first create a geometry using a primitive, such as a Platonic, as shown in Figure 13-16.

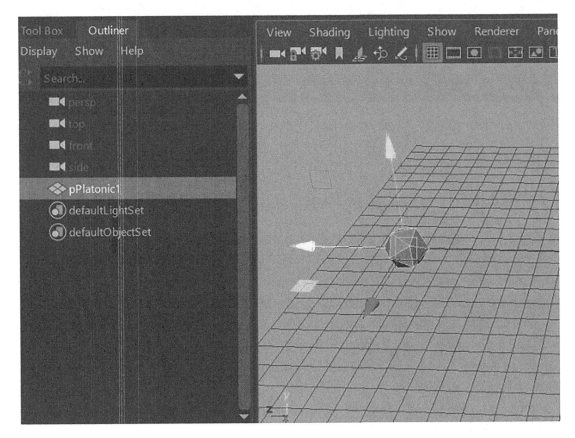

Figure 13-16. *Model of the platonic*

You can click the Create MASH Network option, which will immediately include many copies of the Platonic, as shown in Figure 13-17.

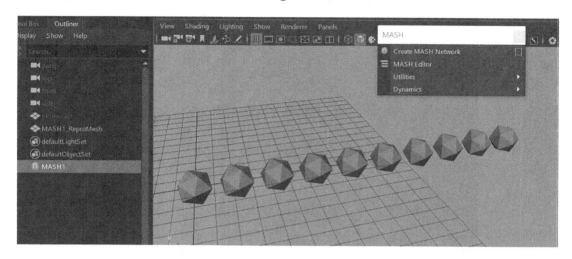

Figure 13-17. *MASH applied to the Platonic model*

As you can see, it has created 10 copies, since the Waiter value is set to 10 by default, as shown in Figure 13-18. If you want a different number of copies, alter this value as desired.

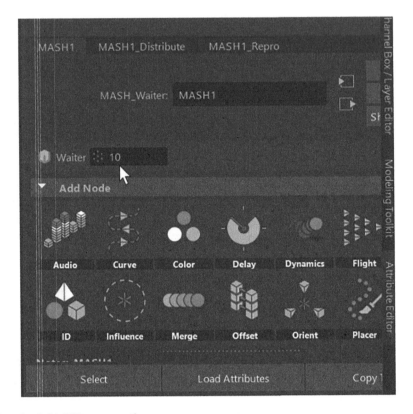

Figure 13-18. *MASH properties*

Now let's get into the details of the MASH properties. To do this, you need to select MASH from the Outliner. From the Attribute Editor, switch to the MASH Distribute tab, as shown in Figure 13-19.

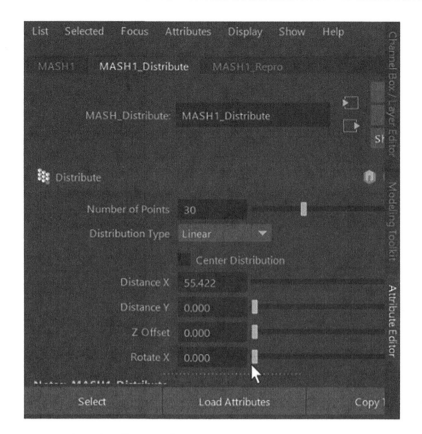

Figure 13-19. *MASH Distribute tab*

You can increase or decrease the number of points, which works like the Waiter. You can also play around with the distance in the x- and y-axes while adjusting the z-offset values based on your requirements. The Rotation and Scale options in the x-, y-, and z-axes will also give you varied interesting effects. A point to remember in this context is that each of these parameters can be modified and animated. The Distribution Type is set to Linear by default. This can be changed to Radial, Spherical, and so on, as shown in Figure 13-20.

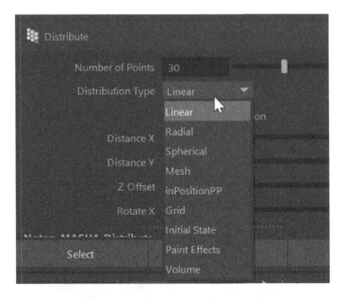

Figure 13-20. *MASH Distribution Type*

You can change this to Radial or Spherical and change the number of points to get various effects, as shown in Figure 13-21.

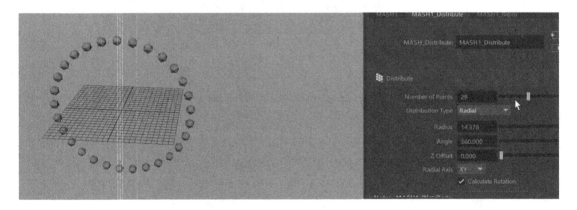

Figure 13-21. *MASH Distribution Type set to Radial*

You can also use the mesh. However, to apply the mesh, you first need to create a mesh, which provides a geometrical surface on which the MASH will distribute itself, as shown in Figure 13-22.

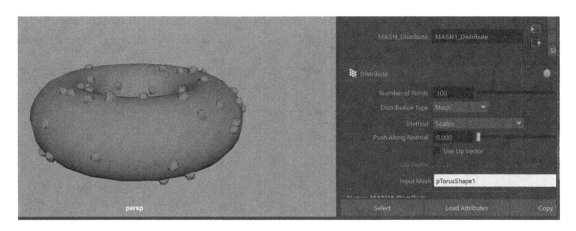

Figure 13-22. *MASH Distribution Type set to Mesh*

With the mesh you can use various methods that will make the pantroid appear, as per the requirements shown in Figure 13-23.

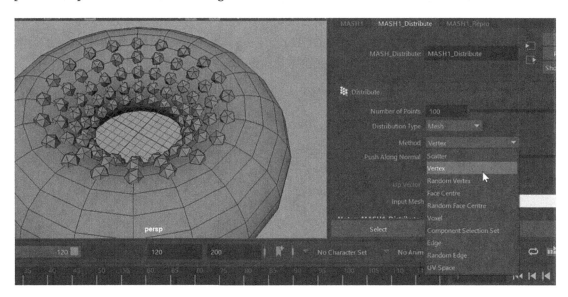

Figure 13-23. *MASH Distribution Type set to Mesh with various methods*

With the distribution type set to Grid, you can use a combination of distance and number of grids, as shown in Figure 13-24.

Figure 13-24. *MASH Distribution Type set to Grid*

With these various distribution types, you can create random effects using MASH and each of these properties can be animated. This will make motion graphics related animations easier and much more fun to create.

In continuation with this example, let's create a new model. Using the Polygon Primitive option, create a basic soccer ball, as shown in Figure 13-25.

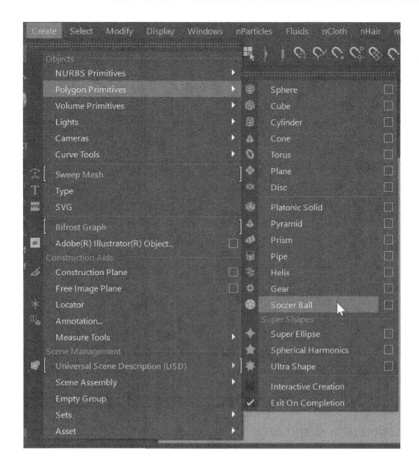

Figure 13-25. *Polygon Soccer Ball primitive*

This will pop up another window, where you will select the Each Face Separately option, as shown in Figure 13-26.

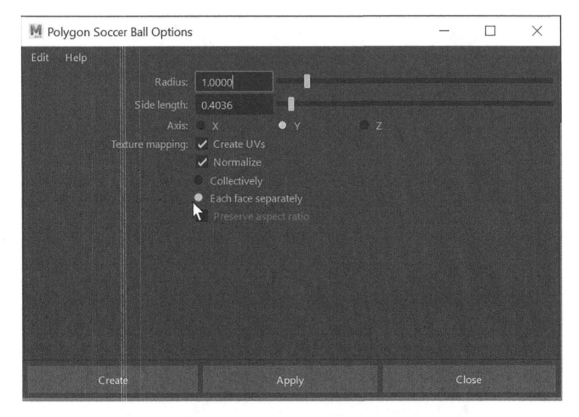

Figure 13-26. *Soccer ball options*

Using the Extrude options, you can create your model as shown in Figure 13-27.

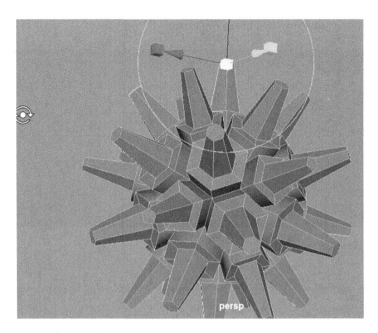

Figure 13-27. *A new model created using extrude at various faces*

Using the Create MASH Network option, set the Distribution Type to Grid and create some copies, as shown in Figure 13-28.

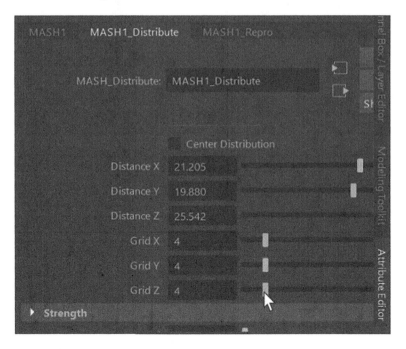

Figure 13-28. *MASH parameters*

Select the newly created MASH and click the MASH Editor, as shown in Figure 13-29.

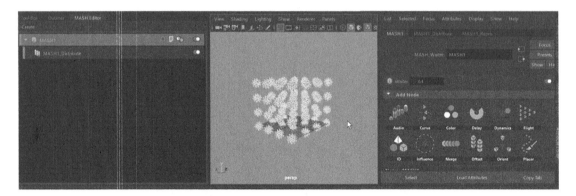

Figure 13-29. *MASH Editor*

This will help you add multiple nodes from the Add Nodes section, which include various preset animations. In order to add these to the MASH, you need to select a node and right-click it, as shown in Figure 13-30. When you play the simulation now, you can see the MASH animating randomly across the timeline.

Figure 13-30. *Adding the signal node*

To further add complicated motion, you can modify the properties and adjust them based on your requirements, as shown in Figure 13-31. There are several signal types that can be manipulated to suit your requirements.

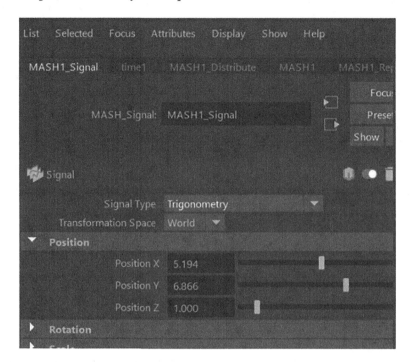

Figure 13-31.   *The Signal Node properties*

The scaling options can add to the randomization of the simulation, as shown in Figure 13-32.

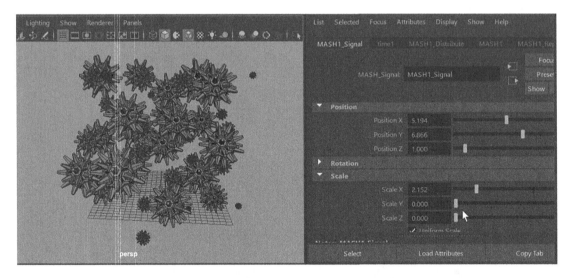

Figure 13-32. *The Signal Node Scaling properties*

Go ahead and add more nodes to the same MASH. For example, you can add Orient node and manipulate the settings to create or modify preset animations easily. The Orient node has an interesting feature called Aim at Target. Let's explore this feature a bit.

In order to use it, create a cone and, from the Outliner, drag and drop the cone into the Aim at Target options, as shown in Figure 13-33. As you rotate the cone, the MASH orient will change accordingly.

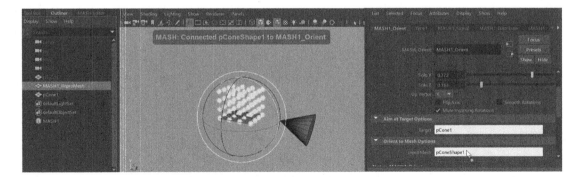

Figure 13-33. *The Aim at Target option of the signal node*

Similarly, there are several other options that are available in the Nodes section.

We will explore the Flight node, which provides a simulation of an explosion. This can be manipulated and adjusted to suit your scene's requirements, as shown in Figure 13-34.

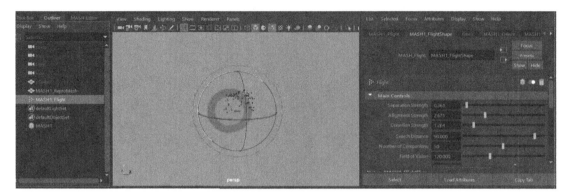

Figure 13-34. *The Flight node*

Next, you learn how to add the rendered MASH effects to compositing software and blend them with real-life footage to create a complete scene.

To do this, you will be using the Signal Node of the Cubes MASH object, which is set to Distribution Type Radial. Add the Trails node, as shown in Figure 13-35.

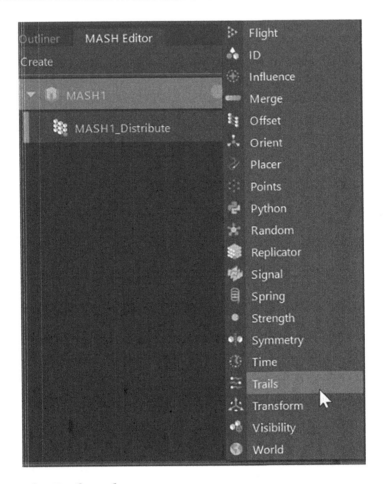

Figure 13-35. *The Trails node*

This will create a trails effect when the animation is played, as shown in Figure 13-36.

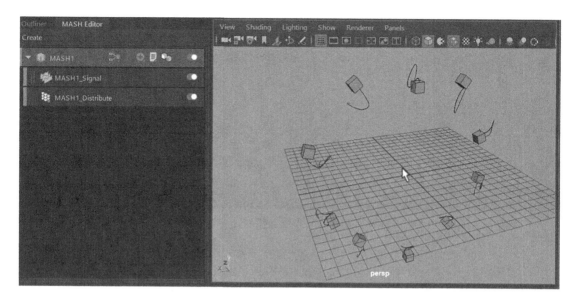

Figure 13-36. *The Trails node output*

There are several trials modes, as shown in Figure 13-37.

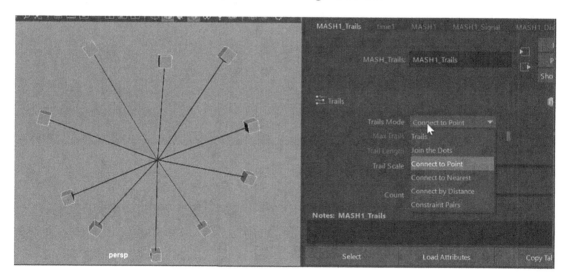

Figure 13-37. *The Trail mode options*

By combining these effects, you can create various effects like the grid effect with trails, as shown in Figure 13-38.

Figure 13-38. *A new effect*

To add more look and feel, you can add the Color node, which has the default color of white, as shown in Figure 13-39.

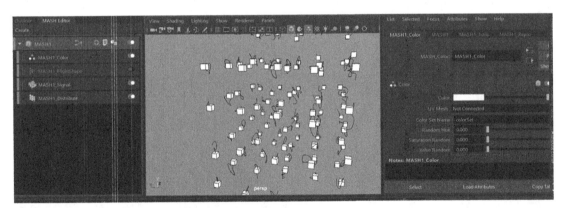

Figure 13-39. *The Color node*

You can add multiple colors by selecting the Random Hues option, as shown in Figure 13-40.

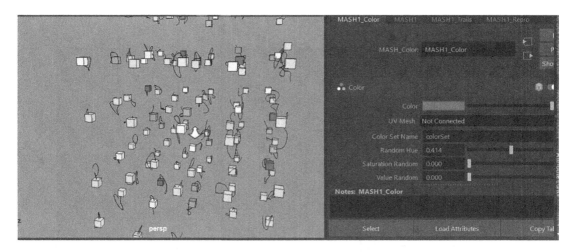

Figure 13-40. *The Random Hues option*

You can further randomize the animation by adding Rotation and Scale to it, as shown in Figure 13-41.

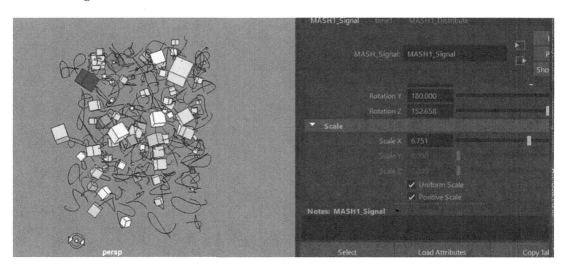

Figure 13-41. *The Rotation and Scale values*

Having achieved the desired look, you now need to render it to use it in the compositing package. For rendering, you need to use the Maya Hardware render, as shown in Figure 13-42. From the Render setting, you can render the entire frame range using the HD 1080p PNG format to maintain the transparency in the background. From the Render menu, choose a Batch Render.

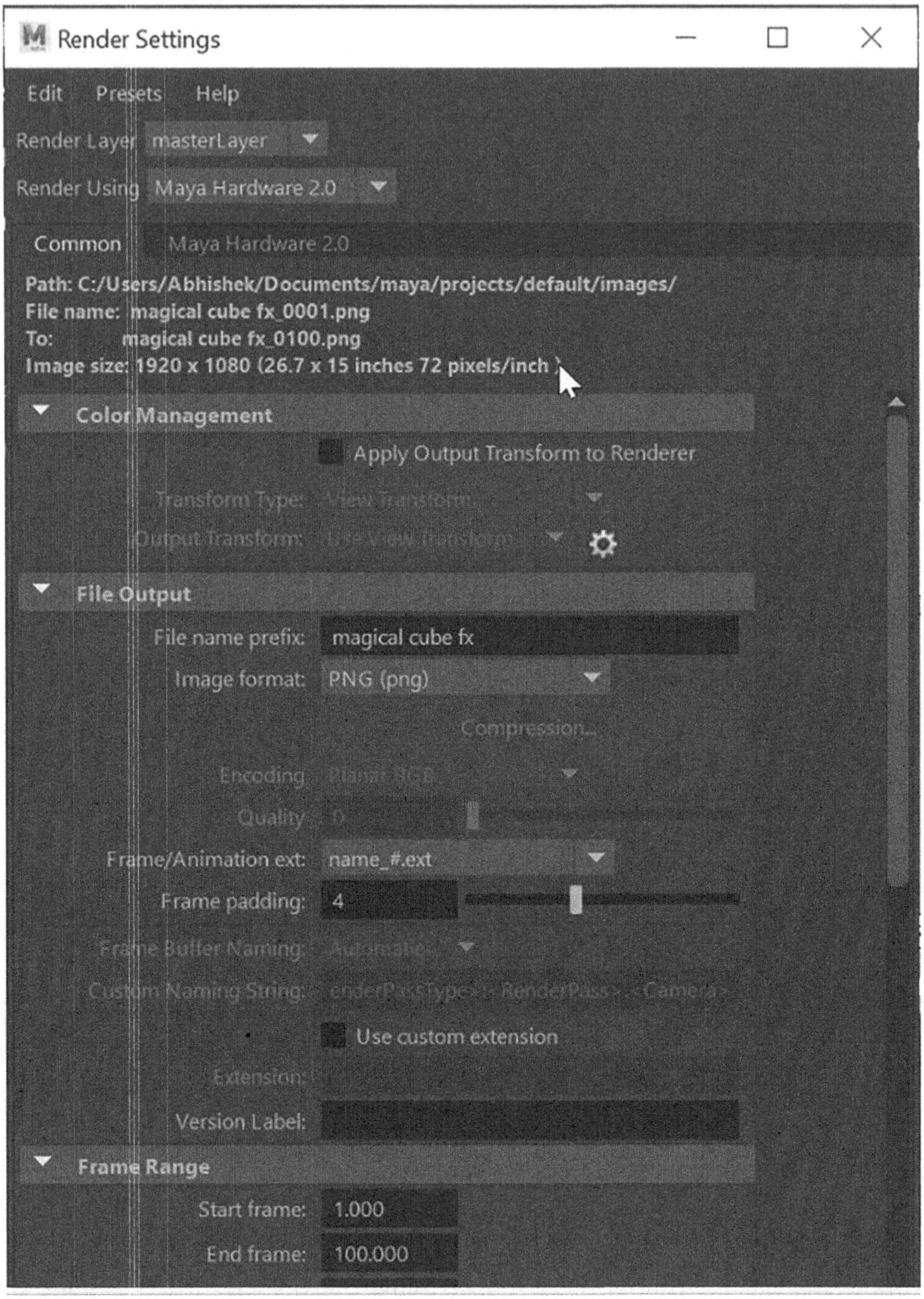

Figure 13-42. *The Render settings*

Once the render is complete, import it to any compositing software, such as After Effects, using the Import File option, as shown in Figure 13-43.

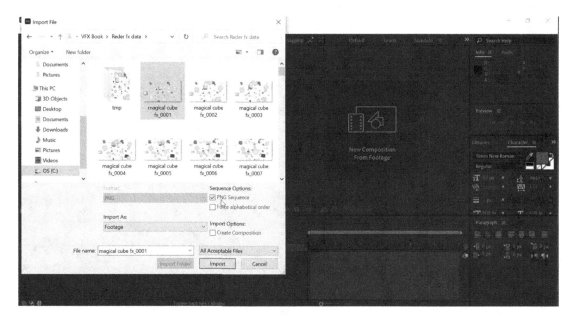

Figure 13-43. *Importing the rendered images into After Effects*

Once the sequence is imported into After Effects, you need to select the footage and create a new composition, as shown in Figure 13-44.

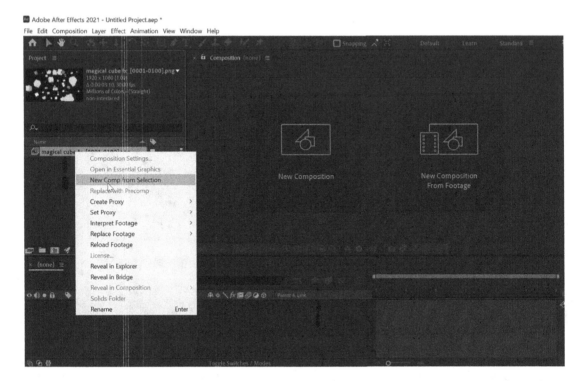

Figure 13-44. *Creating a new composition*

This will create a layer in the composition timeline, where you can see the entire animation playing. You try adding the dancing live action scene to this below the simulation layer and reducing the opacity of the simulated cubes, as shown in Figure 13-45.

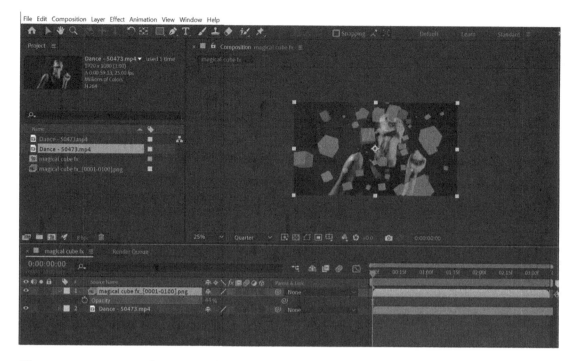

Figure 13-45. Live footage added and opacity reduced for the cubes layer

If you want to further beautify the scene, you can add the cc light rays from the Effects and Presets tab to the Simulation layer, as shown in Figure 13-46. You can add multiple light rays to the same layer and adjust the positions of each of them. You can also manipulate the intensity and color of the light ray. This will make the cubes glow as they approach the points of the light rays.

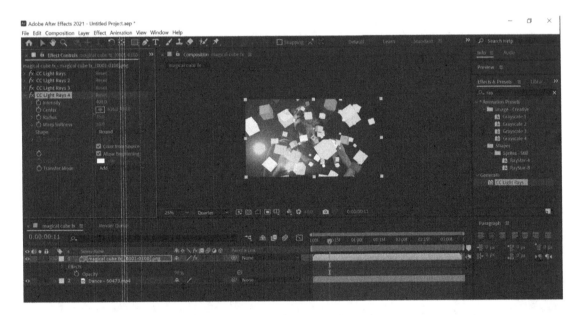

Figure 13-46. *CC LightRays*

Conclusion

Let's look back on what you have learned in this book. You started with an introduction to the visual effects industry, where FX plays a vital role, be it in film, TV series, or games. You learned about the importance of visual effects and the role of dynamics in the VFX industry. You also learned about the advent of the visual effects world. Starting from the analog medium right through to the digital era. In the digital era, you analyzed in-depth the tools and applications used to bring about the revolutionary effects that made the reel look real.

It was only after Chapter 3 that the book started delving deep into the various aspects of Maya dynamics in detail. You explored the Maya nucleus system with examples that were project based and can help make sure you can do it yourself. You took deep dives into nParticles and Fields/Solvers with live project examples that can easily be replicated. You also learned about Maya nCloth and about fluids, where you experimented with the various options of the 2D and 3D containers. You explored the rigid and soft body systems in Maya to understand how to work with the material look and feel of object simulation. You also explored the Maya effects that can be used for simple yet realistic effects, ones that are commonly used for visual effects shots. The chapter on Hair FX provided an in-depth look at how easily you can stimulate hair for your character without much hassle.

As a bonus, you learned about the Bifrost system in Maya. This system is extremely useful and comes in rather handy when you're dealing with larger masses of particle simulation.

Finally, the icing on the cake was the capstone project, where you learned about the motion graphics MASH network system and saw how it can blend into a live action shot.

Index

A, B

C, D

E

F

© Abhishek Kumar 2022
A. Kumar, *Beginning VFX with Autodesk Maya*, https://doi.org/10.1007/978-1-4842-7857-4

Printed in the United States
by Baker & Taylor Publisher Services